At the Threshold
of Liquid Geology

At the Threshold of Liquid Geology

and other automatic tales

Eric W. Bragg

Writers Advantage
San Jose New York Lincoln Shanghai

At the Threshold of Liquid Geology
and other automatic tales

Writers Advantage
an imprint of iUniverse, Inc.

For information address:
iUniverse, Inc.
5220 S. 16th St., Suite 200
Lincoln, NE 68512
www.iuniverse.com

Cover painting by the author: *Untitled*, 1999.

ISBN: 0-595-24021-6

Printed in the United States of America

The poet of the future will overcome the depressing idea of an irreparable divorce of action and dream. He will hold the magnificent fruit of the tree whose roots intertwine, and he will be able to persuade all who taste it that there is nothing bitter about it. Carried by the wave of his time, he will assume for the first time without distress the task of reception and transmission of signals pressing towards him from the depths of the ages…In the immemorial judgment of intuitive knowledge by rational knowledge, it will be the poet's task to introduce the capital evidence that will end the debate. The poet's work will henceforth be conducted in broad daylight.

André Breton
The Communicating Vessels, 1932

Contents

Neuron 1
A Solenoid of Silver Parakeets 21
Catflesh Countrycide 66
Anomie House 111
The Oxygen Bird Hive 173
At the Threshold of Liquid Geology 206

Preface

The author hopes that this collection of automatic writing is perceived not as an "art" or "fantasy" book, but instead as a chronology of poetic images to be used in the exploration of human subjectivity. Ever since it was systematically implemented by the first surrealists in the early twentieth century, automatic writing has provided a valid alternative to a busy world whose various forms of daily thinking tend to follow logical, rational and often utilitarian trends. With the efforts of contemporary surrealists all over the world, the practice of automatism has flourished in both many places and at many times into the twenty-first century.

The creation of written poetic thought, whether within this work or anyone else's, is attainable when the poetic investigator achieves a simple but disciplined state of "receptive disinterestedness" in order to capture the flow of thoughts. For example, this type of verbal reception is comparable to the mental chatter sometimes experienced during the early stages of sleep, or ultimately within a dream. The worth of automatism, verbal or otherwise, resides in its unabridged poetic content, in its ability to make a *psychologically uncensored* photograph of the mind as it triumphs over its obstacles, in an effort to tap the subconscious roots of human existence.

This method of *surreal knowledge* has its unique place among other logically elaborated varieties, creating a sublime dialogue whose content can supersede the limitations of conscious reality. With such a subconscious alphabet, it may be possible to communicate experiences and latent movements of thought that normally go undetected in the waking world. If imagination can overcome the reality principle of the moment, of today, then new possibilities for thinking are brought to light. And if we were interested in expanding the limits of our subjectivity, then wouldn't this form of poetic automatism make a great tool for discovery? The proof is in the experience.

Neuron

1

The hydraulic everglades dropped a thin, hourglass stream of sugar into the ailing eyeball of the tiger. The sugar fell in through the pupil and settled onto the retina, forming a bouquet of candied, crystallized neurons that would eventually form a lattice or fence that bordered onto the next domain of well-kept lawns and small volcanic craters that peppered the lawns from time to time.

The small volcanic craters also served as eyes for the feline hunter, and at the bottom of each crater, there was an angry ant lion, who said:

"Put me in a sanctuary or aquarium, so I won't feel so cold and alone on those frivolous x-mas evenings. And let me make a phone call to the desert beaches of Alaska, where the sand crabs are served in blocks of ice that are really the pre-cut gems of gods. You must let me visit these Alaskan gem fields, too, allowing me to leave the aquarium sanctuary from time to time. I've got the beak of a parrot, too, you know." After each of the ant lions made this insectoid declaration, they all burrowed into their volcanic sand craters and slept, focusing on the lawn and the faraway lattice fence that was really a conglomerate of candied neurons within the retina of a tiger's eyeball.

Meanwhile, the door of a shower stall slides shut like a crypt, leaving the industrial metallic plumbing painted in white. At the end of each shower head is a small red circle painted, which is unnoticeable to the wandering eye unless the red circles are being sought for their telepathic abilities which enables showerheads and faucets all over the world to talk to each other, exchanging gossip regarding the random tiltings of the electron orbits of their constitutive metallic atoms, especially those of iron. Each of the faucet's pipelines have folds of mucousy, gelatinous bands wrapped around them, suggesting that, at least in the natural world, the shower faucet pipelines are really neurons that can convey the transmissions of one pipeline to the next. In a few lively cases, the faucet pipelines also wear wristwatches that indicate the status of a full or growing moon. Of course, this type of wristwatch adornment is not as prevalent as the sticky, gelatinous neuron wrappings that contain an important type of cellular organelle.

When the sea urchin erupted a new set of spines from its shell, the surrounding starfish became terrified and inserted their liquid, collapsible stomachs in between the pages of shower head books that had unknown cryptic diagrams of plastic mannequins who had seashell adornments hanging from their elbows and kneecaps, each of which contained a miniature diagram of extremely particular and customized star charts, as if the joints of plastic mannequins had their own separate, interstellar destinations. It was odd, really, that a kneecap would be determined to go to the Orion constellation while the neighboring kneecap was destined to arrive at the Zeta-Biloxi star system, several million light years away from the former. Nevertheless, the presence of these seashell star charts and the mannequins that bore them appeared to have caught the attention of more than one author, suggesting that the longevity of these mannequins surpassed all department store estimates of the twentieth century. In the meantime, all of this mannequin star mapping was a reactionary response to the sea urchins of the oceans that had manifested a new design of body armor that was impenetrable, even to the most precisely calculated stuffed olive that fell from one of the international eye sockets of only the most loyal of Jesus' disciples. Nevertheless, Christian eye sockets tried in vain to bombard the newly improved sea urchins with Christian-conversion stuffed olives, which merely became skewered on the dreadnought spines of the urchins. Perhaps the sea urchins might have fit in nicely at the bottom of a martini party bowl, but in the end, the sea creatures preferred purely saline water.

But despite everything, the sea urchins hurled themselves into the advancing tide of sea protoplasm which contained the dismembered body parts of mannequin sailors from centuries-past—it was all a tide of warped and folded matrix that was incompletely extended, incompletely developed as it passed under the scrutiny of an unforgiving microscope that had no temporal or physical bearing to which the spiny sea urchin and mannequin body part matrix could be tied. Therefore, the telescope did a much better job realizing that this conglomerate was to be stored in a vertical skeleton canister until a later date when the mythical Noah's Ark pushed through the skies with a majestic blazing trail of smoke plumes that signified the death of this ancient vessel sparsely adorned with purple illuminating lick-snails that had allowed it to navigate even the darkest waters of time.

With the burning of the ark, the newly freed animals began to eat the mannequin body part protoplasm as well as the embedded sea urchins that had protected them from the malevolent probings of past starfish fossils that were now transformed into quaint, wooden museum pieces—now a rather harmless version of an earlier virulent terror.

The compass dial made a quarter turn, and then everything returned to normal. Or had it? The pipes remained in their respective shower stalls, with incoming beams of sunlight playing across their white-painted surfaces, every now and then revealing the red dial of plumbing telepathy, yet the pipes remained where they had been installed, with their gelatin neurological coatings, and yet coyotes had infiltrated the shower complex, investigating the creations of men that had vanished a long time ago.

Despite the presence of the coyotes, the white pipes remained unscathed and they still communicated with each other.

2

When the dog flew over the moon, the sugar vapors that sublimated from the icy satellite were finely crystallized specimens of silicon, perhaps silicon dioxide because of their transparent colorlessness. The dog had no inclination that the giant lunar chunk was really interlaced with the same sugar-coated neurons that wove through and interpenetrated even the most brisk of cat retinas, far below the earth, yet the candy-coated nerves were just the same wherever anyone happened to be.

The matted thatch on a neighbor's house began to droop because of the falling rain, causing the roof to cave in, like the teeth of a dog skull that slowly slid from fleshless gums, to fall and cut the floor—in the same way ice cuts a half-melted stick of butter that pedestrians sometimes find growing on the busy yet highly vacuous streets of many over-populated metropolitan dwellings of over-industrialized countries.

The street lamps melted in their sockets as the dog teeth fell from their own sockets. The now liquefied light-bulbs became street jellyfish that sought out the wayward teeth in order to encapsulate them in molten invertebrate swirly glass, only to make fossils of the icy, wayward molars. While the phones ring an inordinate amount of times as glass jellyfish become renucleated with dead dog teeth, the walls of a haunted house peel off their yellowed, stale wallpaper. The wallpaper is really a house napkin designed to prevent the infiltration of earthly mucous frogs that come from the pockets of young medieval maidens who perished several hundreds of years ago. Not without a lucky doorknob to worship, the handsome princes claim their skeletal maiden prizes and notice a peculiar red circular marking on the skulls of the dead girls.

A rip in the fine mesh of visual fabric causes the skulls to peel open like a can of sardines. Inside, a family of woodchucks celebrates the findings of birch bark fragments that light up the skulls' nasal red fireplaces, providing warmth to the entirety of the royal female cranial cavities. Not only does the burning birch bark provide light and warmth, but it also smells better than some of the more readily available local incenses. Within these skulls of houses, a woodchuck city is born. Within each cranial house is finely crafted miniature furniture on which the woodchucks can recline and rest when they are not busy searching for psychotropic acorns and other proteinaceous nuts. When piled upon each other, the medieval maiden skulls form a lattice of dark civilization with glowing red fire-place noses that make certain wintry and undeservingly half-sacred reindeer seem more worthy of barbecue meat than a source of nocturnal illumination.

Once the woodchucks have satisfied themselves inside of their fair-maiden skull homes, they retire for the evening, being content to knit thermal socks from the most potent of hemp fibers. Once the fibers have been placed and the thermal foundations firmly established, the cold night begins to ring out in a bloodful crescendo of metallic reverberation that scares the curious wolves away from the maiden skull metropolis.

Winter trees enshroud the city as it perishes in fields of ice that eventually advance a few decades later.

Car ignition keys are forged from the frozen bone—a fossilized silicate that outlasts even the most persistent prostate glands.

As if a kneecap couldn't answer a ringing telephone, tendrils of vocal empathy emanate from a dying flashlight lamp that was dropped by a wayward traveler with the burst of a cold sneeze. In fact, these sneezes have become more and more common over the years, as experienced people pile into their processed grape TV dinners that smack of Laurence Welk and the Smurfs. The TV dinners are said to come from Mars, but all knowledgeable woodchucks know this assertion to be a lie. In all actuality, the windows opened to reveal the weekend light of a TV dinner satellite that discharges mega-packets of TV dinners hourly. The dinners fall by way of parachute to the hungry hands of lost people who need food as well as negative entertainment similar to the process of a polarized fork that magnetically bounces on a green velvet card table where daily bets are made, where ivory skull dominoes fall and where pelvic dice are rolled in order to win stacks of red and blue discs that are worth much chameleon money—that special kind of coinage that has the faces of modern-day sexual appliances stamped on the face and reverse of mandibular medallions that mutate with every passing day.

When zigzagged, the red velvet becomes rolled up into a transportable, hairy carpet that hairless creatures implement as a standard tool in the most darkest of forest areas, so that they might walk their way through the temperate jungles of icy winter when there is no other means available after the sun goes down and the light of the fallen flashlight has died once its batteries are exhausted. The bricks and mortar are knocked away to find the abandoned, dead civilizations of woodchuck heaven, with the upper cranial velvet bedrooms and the warm, cheery, red nasal living rooms which, despite their sub-macroscopic size, can create a whole world out of a few cubic centimeters of space, that even the sexiest of forty-something year-old scientists always manage to miss in their farsighted efforts to meet deadlines instead of lifelines.

Galvanized fingerprints vibrate no lies as the spinal pathways conduct sexual electricity into the papaya munchkin vessels of amber optic glasswaves. The eyes in the walls know this, yet they cannot communicate. All they can do is absorb, as well as cook fajita meats on the weekend when cactus toes threaten to pop over ten foot high brick walls, where the morning sunlight shines through the feral cactus toes that rise in the air in order to make sense of a new day that has only gastric confusion to offer.

A solar eclipse is beamed through a piece of lightly penetrated cardboard to display a solar laser crescent on one of the more ripe cactus toes, revealing a midnight-sun moon inside of a hollowed portion of the cactus fruit, where a crystallized candy ant colony had condensed the redness of the fruit into a blue jewel that has been tucked away for later use.

When the solar eclipse passes, a hidden bicycle slips through the cracks of compressed fingers, so that the sunlight makes a beeline for a green inanimate wooden object that has fallen from a familiar thatch of a house that does not deserve to be remembered, only burned in the same way a thrilling firecracker yearns to be ignited once the minions of cactus toes have erupted chlorophyll spines from their loosely-skinned backs that monitor the progression of a loosely slipping hammer that breaks through the scrotum of a passenger ship of titanic metal which can be peeled open like a sardine can sometimes hidden within the defensive, reflexive joints of mammals.

3

A champagne flute lightly rustled in the wind. A frog burped out a platinum shiny marble. The marble rolled into a hole within the board of a pinball game, causing the metal ball to be instantaneously ejected over a replica of a wooden fence into a replica of aggregated cow shit.

An umbrella opened up to reveal a happy family sunning themselves on the shores of an island continent that was formed from green volcanic glass that was deposited several hundreds of thousands of years ago. Whenever the happy family chooses to stroll down the dusty jade beaches formed from the erosion of continental glass, the family members find that dragonfly appendages erupt from their cheeks and they become even happier than they originally were before. When the youngest cave-brat ties her hair up and pushes a polished turkey bone through the knot of hair, her blonde hands become an x-ray cross-section of gigantesque dinosaur bones that ooze pus and red serum from every opening. This filmstrip of her hands has been adequately documented in her family, and all family members regard this disposition with much pride and joy, especially when the fur of the family animals becomes striped, like the rich orange coat of a tiger that searches for empty breadfruit boxes on the shore of the island as they wash up after the sinking of passenger ships on Friday and purple Tuesday nights.

In a Monday's notice, the umbrella opens to reveal a tarantula cloud that enters through waiting distillation pipes to condense into a clear orange liquid that collects at the bottom of a hexagonally shaped crystalline vial. This container can be detached and carried as a subset of a mother tarantula's feline inventory, to be drunk whenever neon lights phase through the wall. When the orange liquid is imbibed with a glass straw, the effects cause night and day to become the same, and a feline eyeball that is affixed to the family mirror becomes detachable, unscrewable in the same way party light bulbs of parking-lot seances can.

The leopard-skin fingers grasp the eyeball and the empty hexagonal vial, placing them in a highly touchable wooden cabinet for safe keeping, for later analysis, when the urgent need arrives. Meanwhile, the distillation apparatus is collapsed and placed back into its case and into the owner's tight pocket, right next to the kneecap.

When the mountains from up above ooze their green volcanic glass, there's nothing that can be done to keep the turntable octopus from latching onto the window on the floor below, so that a sanding iron might better scratch the wrinkles from a soiled shirt. The lightning from the tiger-clouds arcs through the dry air and scorches the sand on the beach, making green melted globules of glass that solidify, mimicking the shape of the lightning bolt. The glass arcs remain there, the green gem lines that they are, the blood vessels of a beached hand that strives to grasp the discarded milk objects that float by in the ionized water.

An eyelash opens up to show a screen of silver projection that hops along until its broken leg finally collapses underneath it to create a roadblock that might even be stepped upon when the air dries out and the happy family is toasted over the coals like buttery wholesome sausages of rotten meat that deserve to be imprinted in mud and then washed away like dust on the forehead of a scavenging religious fly that lays its maggot eggs in the carcass of rotten leg meat of a fallen deer off in the wilderness of the mountain islands of giant flowers.

A happy leather cord is tied around legs. Then a knife is used to cut apart the happy human legs to create happy barbecue meat that is offered to a sponge statue that was pulled from the bottom of a dusty closet where ticks and lice dwell—a place where magma coats the walls and pustules adorn the limbs of Christmas femur decorations that wear mustaches and report to isolated shower stalls on the outskirts of a dying town that used to sell candy but now sells only cactus spines that are worn as jewelry on Sundays, of course. A nose can smell the fumes of burning flesh, but can it know the pleasures of incense that come from cut flowers that grow from a damaged ear? Could the ears be cut in any other way to release the green sand lightning? Was this the way the packaged directions indicated that the plastic ears should be cut from the green oozing glass that is caught in a perforated collection bin that can be folded into a snotty, blood-stained chef's hat? The tiger doesn't know, because its eyes are related to coconuts, and the special coconuts are peeling their hair from their brown wooden exoskeletons that are immune to the sulfurous fumes of a volcanic crater that bubbles hot magma bile—the formic acid of ant vomit—the appendaged favorites of family skulls that slowly but surely grow from the crevices of the various distinguished skull plates that once grew from a silicon seed but are now wildly out of control in their original element—between the beds of hot silicate rock.

It was then, amidst the skulls' decay in boiling water that an observing caterpillar decided to speak up:

"You must not worry about those stupid 'windows of opportunity' because that's all just a funky illusion meant to annoy you and distract you from eyebrows that are worth knowing in great detail. As sure as these are multiplicative spines on my back, you can be certain that the rings around each spine are of a happy, candy sugar color that has absolutely nothing to do with the colored fields of corn that are baptized by mouthless zealots, that crawl out from rocks around central tax time, and who hide destructive brain grenades inside of their antique wooden beach guitars that they place above their fireplaces when their grandparents arrive from out of town—whenever the need arises. My caterpillar spines each have the colored magic to surpass the false limitations that have been provided to us by our happy ancestors. You can even take a spine or two with you in your buttocks if you choose to be unwary when you blindly sit down on autumn picnic benches of festive abandonment. When a muddy levy breaks open to reveal angry blue crabs, you know I'll be there! But for now you must ignore what you don't feel like seeing, just so you can take your familial guitars and burn them like turpentine-laced cigarettes."

And with that, the caterpillar left the scene and crawled underneath a ripe fig that grew from a healthy tree in need of mandibular stimulation.

Razor sunbursts release the cold, and the headlights show the dark road ahead. The eyes see a line on the pavement that runs off into a depressed street where sunken concrete exacerbates the nightfall so that fig trees drop their fruit and head for the hills.

A motor failure isn't as bad for the car as it is for the passengers who need to go home where the happy pancakes are waiting to be eaten and played with as the archaic television drones on with nightingale promises of unknown colloids that spell the upcoming future lobotomy, in the same way spilled dice spell trouble for the gambler that wastes time on a casino boat that deserves to be ruptured by a wayward cargo vessel bearing sexy pancake mix. The boat was once used in the same way chameleons use pigments to disguise their formal physicality when they stalk vegetable insectoids that march up and down the branches of forgotten trees bearing resemblance to that flammable seafood that also used to cling to the branches when more reputable classmates remembered their true lives and selves, all before the great vomitous tornado took away the bookshelves that carried the old books of memory.

4

In a makeshift cabaret, a cute bonnet was removed from the mouth of an olympic horse. Once the bonnet was filled with eucalyptus leaves and steeped in hot water, the horse began to echo the vibrations of earthquakes that barely reached its fertile ears. Once amplified, the horse-emitted echoes were lightning fingers that caressed the black and white keys of a piano that had been dismantled such that the metal strings had been removed, leaving the ivory keys disconnected. The horse detached one of its horseshoes and pressed it into a crescent-shaped relief on the side of the piano's upright body, causing a super-secret panel on the other side to slide open to reveal a brand-new hot-red monkey-face lipstick that some girls from the south like to wear when they are shopping for packets of instant salad dressing in the more mundane supermarkets. The horse extracted the silver tube of greasy monkey-face lipstick and drew the image of elephant shoes on the walls of the cabaret. A 1970's disco ball was suspended from the ceiling, giving a sparkling shimmer to the image of the elephant shoes which started to look more and more like a half-crushed automobile that children sometimes eat for breakfast when their meddling grandparents are out of town.

Suddenly a bloodshot eyeball peered through a small and almost unnoticeable aperture in a long mural painting of fornicating alligators. The horse dropped its newly found lipstick and galloped over to the painting and peered at the bloodshot eyeball. Suddenly the mural painting fell off the wall to reveal a group of witches who were assembled around a poker card table. One of them had been spying on the horse who had exchanged one of its shoes for a greasy red monkey-face lipstick. The witches were surprised, and all of them folded their cards and started to push their metallic poker chips to the edge of the table, where the horse was now standing. The lead witch widened her left bloodshot eye and spoke to the horse: "it appears that you have forgotten the original reason why you came to this town. You pursued fugitive mannequins that did not have hearts but instead lead aprons. Obviously you did not meet your objectives and so you are here in this gala 70's cabaret playing with horseshoes and lipstick. Please try to remember why you are really here and what you must eventually do. A can of sardines cannot be packaged without a key on the outside and the occasional chili pepper on the inside. You must abandon that old decrepit piano in the corner and plug your remaining shoes into the holes found at the bottom of a boiler room, where hot liquid water is paradoxically frozen ice, where the vast blocks of frozen liquid can be subjectively reduced to a small, pocket-sized fishing lure that you can sometimes order from the back of a cereal box. Now go, and implant your remaining horse shoes as I have said, so that you can reclaim the frozen fishing lure that is hidden somewhere within the icy pipes of the infernal boiler room. Make sure you bring a cold drink with you, because you might get dehydrated." The red-eyed woman took a swig from her glass of bourbon and resumed her game with the other witches. The horse's eyes blinked as it took a step back and the mural painting of the fornicating alligators was replaced on the wall by a bartender that wore a silver ring vaguely resembling the knobby sphere of a sea urchin exoskeleton. The three-shod horse paid its tab and left the cabaret forever, but not without greeting a sullen pirate who had just entered.

Eventually the boiler room was found, and the horse felt its body turn to bronze metal as it greedily absorbed the red metallic fishing lure that threatened to burst like a pregnant rain cloud. The walls of the boiler room were of a brown sandstone construction and the whiskers of a cat protruded here and there from holes left behind by a swing music advocate who used cloves of garlic as earplugs to filter out the clacking of old fashioned typewriter keys that maintained a mechanistic timber. The cat whiskers became swords as they punctured the hot water heaters to release metallic hydrogen ice cubes that emanated a mist of silver diamonds. These special ice cubes were also sometimes used by taxidermists to stuff the corpses of maggots that occasionally arrived in the mail to the address of the house that stood above the wealthy boiler room. The cats stood vigilant as their observant eyes scanned the frozen metallic cubes that had burst forth from ruptured water vessels to lie scattered across the dirty well-trod floors. It was truly a dungeon of ice.

When the hydrogen ice melted, all that remained were white, pungent mothballs that gave the odor of stale wooden death. Knots in the wood, ripples in the eyes. The trees shot green branches into bottles, while tigers slept but kept their annoyed tails in motion, periodically slapping the concrete floor as a butterfly of liberated hydrogen fluttered around the feline ears of insistence. A bomb detonated upstairs, causing old paint to fall from the ceiling. The butterfly continued with its wavering arc around feline ears. The feline ears became annoyed and began to slap some limp zucchinis that were growing on a stale vine that slowly and agelessly crumbled in the corner of the basement boiler room. The tigers could not stand it any longer as a pink flambeau cannon shot through the wall and sent brownstone bricks flying everywhere.

The horse with only three shoes left as fast as it could, vowing never to listen ever again to the rantings of bloodshot-eyed nun witches who played poker in cabarets within secret bar chambers. Of course, the decision might have been rather hasty, but in the end, the horse realized that (on the subject of those three remaining horseshoes) there were no real shoe outlets for their supposed use, so the equine creature wrote a note to the upcoming tomorrow, acknowledging the presence of a new moon to stomp upon and to float chameleon wrist badges upon when the high tide rolled in to wash around the gas bladders of chlorophyll-producing seaweed that smelled of fresh vinyl in a new car that rolled underneath a shower sea stone that was supposed to massage the feet of whoever stepped upon the stone.

When the new moon note had been folded and placed in a cabbage envelope, the brass horse clicked a branch that grew next to its rear hoof and initiated a sequence of explosive exclamations from leprechaun tufts that had insidiously disguised themselves as mayonnaise packets— the very same packets that begged to be stepped upon by crummy office flowers that controlled an entire office of radioactive coat badges that were made of an archaic plastic film. Out of the mayonnaise explosion, a tuft of leprechaun broke loose and collided with a steel girder that was part of the support structure of a metallic flower. The girder buckled and the metal flower collapsed, allowing the moon in the sky to be the only lifted object. All else fell to the ground as the loose teeth fall from a bronze-dipped dog skull.

5

On its voyage throughout the industrial harbor, the jazzboat made many stops for unknown purposes. At some docks, crewmembers left to be replaced by others, while at other stops, ancient stone artifacts were unloaded for pineapples and red-diamond flying fish. The red-diamond flying fish generally chose to fling themselves from puddle to puddle in the most diagonally random trajectories. Sometimes they accidentally landed in garbage cans, while other times they became a silver-plated rhombus that sank into the pockets of faceless, obscene businessmen who strayed near the edge of a regal swimming pool. Upon dropping several marbles into the vast, blue swimming pool, they were rewarded with silver-plated rhombuses that used to be red-diamond flying fish.

At one of its stops, the jazzboat docked at a music missionary of very important musicians who binged on rum and pineapple juice when they weren't saving the world with their music. Upon docking the boat, the crew discovered that all of the musicians had gone, leaving behind their unfinished cocktail glasses. Behind some of the wooden doors in the log-cabin music missionary, the low buzzing voices of concerned parents could be heard. The voices repeatedly grew louder and then fainter, as if the speaking parents were having their conversation while sitting on a large swing for the elderly.

Meanwhile, the red-diamond flying fish performed telemetric activities, exploring the furthest reaches of the log-cabin music missionary, searching for name plates or imprints of ancient stone artifacts left behind on the soft dirt floor. But none were to be found. Instead, after the red-diamond flying fish deposited themselves in a red-diamond semi-circle around a locked mahogany cabinet, one of the faceless crewmembers unlocked it to reveal several cans of carefully hidden ancient bamboo jewel meat—that special kind of meat harvested from the ancient bamboo jewel meat plant that grows in secret places in the tropics, and whose meat is regularly fought over by humans who aren't happy with their post-industrial BBQ lives. Once these tins of precious meat were discovered, the crew of the disreputable jazzboat opened them and planted the ancient bamboo jewel meat in the floor of the log-cabin music missionary. Within days, a new kind of plant would have grown and burst open the flimsy log walls of the missionary, but the crew and their accompanying red-diamond flying fish would be long gone and hence not have the opportunity to view such a splendid variety of meat plant.

The jazzboat then departed and came to a rather seedy port further downstream. On the shore was a weeping horse who had lost all of his shoes over a bet with some alien, religious impostors. A crewmember said to the horse: "Take these red-diamond flying fish and place them under your feet. Never again will you feel such horrid desperation. Instead, these shoes will allow you to visit a green citrus paradise where throughout the groves of bountiful citrus trees, you will find plump, moist lemons that closely resemble the receiver of a telephone and whose pulp is sweeter than even the sweetest of Louisiana satsumas. Sometimes, through wearing these red-diamond flying fish, you will be able to locate hot chili bushes that grow long red peppers over two feet in length. These special peppers can be used as swords to sting the eyes of those that persecute you. Now go, and make sure you reach the infinite citrus groves by nightfall. I hear subsonic rumbles that tell of a coming storm."

And so the horse thanked the crew of the decrepit jazzboat and fled the city that was in the process of rapid decay. All over the city, the perfectly tiled swimming pools were cracking and leaking. In these same swimming pools, obscene, disreputable children were dropping glass marbles into the water, while fighting off flying hordes of red-diamond flying fish. Their red-scaled bodies also made great boomerangs when used to break out city windows on the highest floors.

The entire, unknown city was demolished by glass marbles, red-diamond flying fish, and the passage of time. After which, the nameless crew of the decrepit jazzboat set fire to the vessel, and the ship sank, leaving no other traceable evidence of its passage other than the ruptured cans of bamboo jewel meat. Over the next year, an underground cactus plant sent burrowing flowers that tunneled up to the surface of the soil that was located on the outskirts of the dead city. As soon as the bones of several flying fish were located in a flying fish cemetery, the tubular cactus flowers burrowed throughout the bone-rich graveyard. The interlacing, interweaving, snaking underground flower tubules became choked in the soil as they absorbed the remnants of the bones to grow until they burst through the surface to display an entire field of beautifully vibrant reddish flowers that would never bear fruit. Suddenly a school bus full of plump and reproductively viable children appeared and crashed into the middle of the overgrown red-diamond flying fish graveyard. The tubular cactus flowers immediately consumed the plump, reproductively viable children and used the digested mammalian protein to grow a new plantlike architecture—a scaffolding of green appeared on top of the graveyard in the form of a plantlike megalithic monument to the sun. As the leaves on this new monument withered and were abscised by the wind, the knotted and interweaving branches were left behind.

Within this lattice of plant tubules, new red-diamond flying fish appeared and tucked themselves within the interstices formed by the conglomerated branches. A balance may have been reached, because the flying fish then closed their eyes and slept, while the branches of the plant megalith sent out new flowerbuds that passively and gently opened and closed with every new moon that occurred henceforth. Underneath the complex megalith, jeweled locusts burrowed a new home and created a central hive that could glow in the dark; hence no artificial lighting was needed. The jeweled locusts found a way to instruct the tubular cactus roots to absorb the soil and rocks and then secrete them again in the form of a smooth and shimmery silicate. From this process, the jeweled locusts obtained an underground city of geometrically precise proportions, with dazzling rooms and corridors, all of which shimmered in the most sublime of royal green iridescences.

6

In their hotel, the Dandy Grandpa and the Dainty Grandma discovered quickly that their activities were to be curtailed. They had finished their evening meal in the lobby restaurant and were heading to the elevator when the old floorboards cracked in certain places, making their path to the elevator too dangerous to traverse. The Dandy Grandpa, whose tall stature was given to periods of obnoxious senile patriotism and grand-standing, pulled his sword from the sheath on his belt and waved the sharp, gleaming metal at some young men and women who were servants of various occupations at the hotel.

The Dainty Grandma, who was given to occasional periods of vicious nastiness, drained the vanilla smile from her face as she told the young servants to "Shut up!" The young servants, who shed no tears for the decomposing hotel, fired back with their own "Shut up," and sat down at an exquisite table to admire photographs of various four-legged animals. The Dandy Grandpa and the Dainty Grandma also sat down and the increased weight of the table caused the entire party to fall through the weakened floorboards onto an old subterranean highway below that had fallen into disuse. Everyone looked at their arms as sunburst patterns of redness began to appear.

The underground highway was nearly dark except for the occasional streetlight, revealing the dead country houses of people who no longer lived in them, who had disappeared into the mountains. The dead houses were choked with overgrown weeds, making the doors and windows sometimes impossible to open. The wood of these houses had revealing age rings or annuli, from the original trees that were cut to make the lumber. Even in the insufficient gleam of pocket lights, the rings in the wood closely resembled the markings of feline predators. In one house there was a living room with a round rug and a table set for a dinner party. Decayed glasses of lemonade littered the table, with only the brown, dehydrated tell-tale citrus rinds at the bottom of each glass. On the table were the scattered bones of an unidentifiable cooked animal, but the skull was nowhere to be found. The drapes on the walls were free to pulsate in the wind, since the windows had been broken out by plant growth long ago.

When the strange party descended the rickety stairs down to the cellar, they were horrified to see the family catacombs illuminated by a sickly green light that emanated from a small copper flame that plumed from the mouth of a carved bas-relief of a person. The back wall was entirely dedicated to the stone carving of a human form, with a copper fixture in the mouth where a torch could issue forth, illuminating the crypt in green light, even in times of utmost darkness.

The catacombs were indeed small, only holding at most a dozen ancestors. The original occupants, who were plastic mannequins, had been removed by a tiger, whose rotted skeletal form lay in a heap in the most extreme part of the burial chamber. These mannequins were pulled from their vertical alcoves and then mutilated by the once-violent tiger animal. The mannequins had been apparently replaced with mannequin replicas who had transparent plastic for an outer skin, and who were completely stuffed with transparent colored noodles. Since the plastic skin of these mannequin replicas had not been breached, the colored noodle-like filaments that occupied the body cavity had not dried out, and so upon being pressed with a finger or any other extremity, the depressed fake mannequin flesh would rebound with elastic plasticality and resume its previous, permanent shape.

Suddenly a part of a crypt wall gave way, crushing the Dainty Grandma beneath several hundred pounds of slimy brick and mortar. The Dandy Grandpa unsheathed his broadsword and threw a temper tantrum, saying: "Of all that I've ever seen! Today I lost my home and now I've lost my wife! Must I constantly go through life being forced to shed my skin as a growing crab periodically drops his shell at molting time? Why can I never speak through a clear telephone-line to destiny at the other end?" And the Dandy Grandpa used his remaining strength to swipe at the new hole in the wall with his sword.

After cutting through more congealed weeds, several unopened cans of ancient bamboo jewel meat were brought to light. Impulsively, the Dandy Grandpa opened one of the cans with the can opener on the side of the broad-sword and began to eat from the preserved hairy, jeweled bamboo meat. Immediately the Dandy Grandpa was rejuvenated, and his body went through a reversal of the aging process, so that he now looked as he originally did when he was eleven. The Dandy Grandpa now-a-boy stripped from his useless, baggy clothes and smeared dark carbon mud all over his body. The young, newly transformed boy said: "Now that they've taken my woman and the life that I used to have, I must start life all over again. I must now be camouflaged and run through this wicked village to cause mayhem and trouble." And so the mutated bamboo jewel meat boy disappeared from the cellar rubble and was never seen again. The remaining youngsters in the crypt then felt their flesh dissolve as the mass of their bodies transformed into hordes of yellow moths that flew away and began to eat from the cellar weed-encrusted rocks.

Throughout this process, all fibrous weeds were eaten and then cleared from windows and doorways, so that the yellow moths grew to large sizes and then departed from the underground town of death.

Primitive agricultural humans broke through their city streets to find the fossilized town below. In many of the houses that had been choked with fibrous weeds, the doors and windows now freely opened, allowing the primitive agricultural humans to enter. These apes began to discard the dusty glasses of dehydrated lemonade and replace them with fresh glasses of blood-orange juice with fresh sprigs of celery for garnish. In the newly-cleared backyards, children played with tiger skulls that had been thoroughly cleaned of rotten flesh by the worms and fat, yellow moths. The children placed green light bulbs in the tiger skulls and put them at the sides of roads and houses, so as to provide systematic lighting for the newly occupied ghost town that had once been stagnant and choked, but now was green and glowing.

Inside of the rotten but now appreciated country houses, the grand pianos were cleared of cobwebs and weeds, and were used as tables where wholesome family members could congregate for appetizers as well as pubic pincushion advances. This subterranean world learned how to cultivate the ancient bamboo jewel plants in the nocturnal wormy soils, and as long as this unstable equilibrium was maintained, the bamboo jewel plants were harvested and canned in the dark regions of the earth where no sunlight would ever reach.

A Solenoid of Silver Parakeets

1

Once the mechanical cowardice had been installed into every brick and cement home, the people crept out of their lairs to observe the reprehensible changes they had made. Chairs were pulled from fiber sockets and tendons of meat were tied into festive knots for the police to admire. A lonely scaffolding of paper was whisked into a dirty, dusty corner where it was ignored—a solid piece of evidence to be collected later once the clean-up crews began their work. But the arrival of the clean-up crews was not to happen until much later, once the magnificent goldfish bowl had sprung a few leaks at first.

A masked raven wept for the concrete countryside where pretty blue worms were encased in dirty concrete alcoves. The metallic cowardice would find them there, too, despite its ephemeral nature, in its shrouded epileptic glory. A mist obscured the wall from the raven so that all it could see were the burning corn-pickings writhing on the brick floor beneath its nest. The raven had quite the marathon life, flying from factory to factory in search of food for its family. In the end, the creature honestly knew that it was boxed in on all sides by oily, grimy death, a rusty hell of battery coils that tempted it with circular perfection which could only be touched upon eidetically in a restless world of troubled sleep.

Corn husks were pulled away from a sleeping rake that served no other purpose than to hold up a derelict wall of stolen street signs that modern baboons collected in their after-school twilight desperation.

The street signs were now rusted after years of exposure to sticky humidity, similar to hot cellar gases which slowly cooked the wooden floors through which they insidiously seeped. The cosmos seemed to flow unevenly through each wooden beam, centering upon the almost concentric wooden knots and tantalizing them with obscene fungal radiance. Meanwhile, sleeping eyes twitched in the throes of excited REM sleep, suggesting troubled dreams of collective cowardice and plagiarized debauchery that completely flew over their balding heads. Chicken bones were pulled from pockets in the attempt to seal the leaking cracks in the floor, to keep the blinding heat of the boiling cellar at bay. Nevertheless, the hot mists blew on through their hair, through the chicken bones, through the twitching eyes and through the gnarled concentric wood rings that encased embryonic wooden knots.

The endless maze was not so endless, when the sleeping collectivity would someday awaken to pull cowardly nails from burnt wood. In the meantime, every kitchen utensil became suspect, possibly thought to take place in the slave theater covertly operated while papers were signed everyday by cowardly hands of the surface world—those hands that wore both lace and sandpaper at extremely odd hours. The marathon race was not over yet, a kitchen stove told itself one fine day after a poker conversation within the insidious church of peeling malaise.

What could blind eyes do then but search for other twitching coils of amber rust that were hidden in the darkness of slumber? What a simple equation it was to reckon the wretched universe of mortality in its lopsided turnings, leanings and false oscillations. A universe that wrapped each shadow in a wrapper of light for human consumption. A pantry that stored these wrapped shadows for opportune moments when sleep yielded another sensuous solenoid pleasure for coiled brains to latch onto. A rusty architecture of the spiral from beyond the dismal barrier of deep consciousness, where no sane person of the rational world would fear to tread. Nevertheless, genomes continued to be fused and emotions were shared within trial-sized relationship bottles of weak intoxicants. Only vultures knew where to deposit the empties.

The eyes of reptiles forged ahead despite the warning of the foaming picturesque sea that threatened to turn fifty years into minutia. While tinder boxes slept in the tide pools, wayward humans searched among the rocks for signs of the unearthed Atlantis—the unearthed city of dreams that had fused together somehow over the years into forgotten faces of anthills and termite lairs housing those untrustworthy kitchen utensils that children used to so fondly bring home, when the utensils inadvertently washed up on the beach. The rusted axe was among them, and had lost its warlike sharpness after it was marauded by a pack of sightless fruit bats who desired nothing more than a metallic implement to worship in their eventless off-hours.

The sea yielded stone steps of algae after the desires of the sightless fruit bats had been actualized by the finding of the rusted axe. A spotted leopard crouched in the shadows, waiting for the right moment to seize the axe in its jaws, which would enable it to surpass the waves of sluggishness that kept it down for so long.

And so the pull of the ocean created a mirror-effect in which each object, each being, became multiplied by two, in each of their own reflections. Each reality became an icon with its twin—a secret package to be deposited at the depths of each archaic library, thus confirming the naughty conspiracy theory that had been in various stages of circulation for hundreds of years. A disturbing truth about the binary nature of identity, all released with the help of a handful of rusty nails and a few gallons of highly saline water, which all pointed the way to a secret hide-out of paranoid fruit bats who hid in darkened caves and ate dried fruits such as cherries, prunes and olives.

In the third-person perspective, the fruit bat deposited the salty, miniature icon of itself into an artificial slot cleverly carved into the dark rock face of the basalt sea caves. In one of the caves were several scattered cases of stainless steel tweezers. Apparently, the containers in which the tweezers were housed had long since rotted and dispersed, leaving the mountain of shiny implements to become the playground of sharks and sea urchins. The marine fruit bat changed its mind and used one of the tweezers to extract the two-dimensional icon of itself from the artificial rock crevice. Perhaps that slot wasn't the best place for it to deposit itself. Perhaps the undersea library would be a better place. Since the library was discovered to be inaccessible, the fruit bat plunged into despair and temporarily began to munch on the sad remains of vinyl record albums, but the albums proved to be a poor substitute for the fruit that it had grown accustomed to consuming over the course of its long and pregnant life of weathered hypnosis—a texture of silicon-based joy encrusted around bony hands in the dark, dead-ends of soft beds hidden from the light for years. This voyage through the darkened soft beds was better than two-dimensional concrete, so the floating current slowly maneuvered the boat hallucination of death into its lonely port. Somewhere the whistling of off-key notes was about as distracting as the knife that got thrown overboard after the last unauthorized police raid, as the hypnotic ship of death slowly but greedily drank the waves of dual-intensity seawater which was an alienated representation of itself from a vision of its uncertain future. With every new aquatic terrain available, with every restructuring of the fluid sandy bottom, the rusty blade of the knife became bent upon itself, fluctuating into a tightly wound coil to be found some day as a worthy artifact for some old sea captain's fossilized, pompous museum. A travesty of geoactivity, a mockery of the salty elements. And so the current forced the water through the locks.

"I don't know how to do this; I just don't know how," complained the sea as it drained the noxious color from sterile cinder block places of learning that had been coated with a putrid orange paint of desolation and abandonment, all the while, fat, middle-aged hippies reveled in dream showers within dark, industrial places. The ammonia flashback of hypnotic sweetness became a cute, pink bunny-rabbit that was shot on sight by the happy reveling, fat, middle-aged hippies. These fat hippies pushed aside emaciated wretches who fought over the limited shower stalls clearly marked for use only by insane Midwestern imposters that visited the sex-toy museums on Sundays after a stroll through the opera-like meadows of oak-tree decay.

The feverish dreams evade the perceptions of eyes that can't hear and ears that can't see. A stumbling corpse shivers amid the cold cinders that bleach skin and powderize bone. A world continues to turn its indifference while the fevered head bobs with shivering visions of houses with fire-places in every room, with rings on every finger and kitchen utensils that undergo various states of nausea with every turn of the steering wheel, with every blue crab that gets pulled up on the levee in broad daylight, while intelligent minds work in seclusion in private rooms of artificial lighting. Tweezers are used to reconstruct the limbs and feelers of verminous insects that contaminate the shoes of whole-wheat goodness. Bleach water is used to wash off a plaque showing the materials and methods of torture, where the only results available are those that point towards a distant star that can be reached by way of a platinum kite, or maybe the lost colony of the silver parakeets.

The silver parakeets, iconic representations or doubles of their lost selves, can be readily obtained when the rusty lids of coiled iron boxes are opened. Of course, the boxes were extracted from rusted honeycombs that were never tasted for their intrinsic honey, only collected after the dust in the road had been allowed to settle. It was as if the sleeping bodies had kept on sleeping without being disturbed. It was also as if fluid pumped through plant veins in the same way a broken record agonizes over the repetition of a feverish opera verse, over and over again, oblivious to oblivion while hot eyes secrete tears of sublime sweat. Home is not so far away now, even though the sentient walls have become deaf. Despite the opacity of the deaf walls, the silver parakeets slumber in their rusted coiled cocoons, being told by their doubles that they can have as much rusted solenoid casing as they desire, since they have indeed once been to Mars in the effort to escape the dizzying terrestrial heat of animal fermentation, which now only relinquishes a laboratory of dried plants and broken female artifacts, including famished and impoverished photographs from the depths of the rusted salt-water well where tears are sold for very low prices.

Such are the troubled dreams of the silver parakeets. With the issue unresolved, the only choice remaining is for shoe salesmen to relinquish their grasp of pretzels and to get on with their secret quest for rubber insects that would be best suited to hanging from festive, wintry pine trees. Only then could the silver parakeets thrive in each of their twisted, solenoid rust cocoons. Meanwhile, unseen hands throw a congealed watermelon into an explosive dishwasher.

2

Somehow the chameleons weren't ready to be plucked from their branches so quickly, and so they resisted. The chameleons squirmed and changed from green to brown in order to disguise themselves, but they were too late. Upon being tapped on the head twice, they projected their tongues to each reveal a solid 24-karat gold corn kernel. After the gold kernels were plucked from the sticky tongues of the lizards, unknown hands placed the corn seeds into the bleeding gums of a toothless mouth. Now the faceless disrupter of the lizards had a flashy smile of 24-karat gold, and then abandoned the lizards to their cornless fate. The lizards on the branches began to dissolve as their forms fused with the brown wood. In turn, the brown branches began to dissolve and become lost in the brown rings of wood that characterized the hungry wood paneling of the office room. In the end, after the kernels of gold were removed from this once-living system, all animated life reverted to a latent, wooden form.

After this peculiar regression, the thatch hut of wooden popsicle sticks was collapsed and inserted into the back of a religious incense truck where organic ice-cream was to be sold to hungry religious children who all had six fingers and toes due to their parents' obsessive interbreeding. After breakfast, the incense truck delivered the popsicle incense to a deranged demolition race-car track. Within this car track, another world of derangement was taking place. All of the cars carried explosives attached to their bodies which were detonated at crucial moments, as when accelerating out of a curve in the road. At each moment of explosion, time stood still for a moment as flames consumed each exploding car. Yet the parts of each car never disassociated following the explosion; they simply continued with their dangerous journey around the track, forever exploding. None of the cars was scorched, either.

In order to retain a sense of the festivities of life, the methodist race track managers took the collapsed chameleon trees from the religious incense truck and planted them on the sides of the track after their hydrated, wooden reconstitution. The chameleons were happy as they watched toothless cars burst into flames again and again. They even smiled, but had no golden teeth to show. There would be another day for golden corn teeth, but today was not that day, especially when blue clouds threatened to swallow the skulls of the chameleons.

Suddenly, a swarm of silver parakeets appeared and inserted themselves into the thick skulls of the toothless chameleons. This transformation caused open doors to slam, and the irises of the lizards' eyes conversely opened. The blue clouds were absorbed through the eyes, enabling the chameleons to break free of the feverishly repetitive explosive Methodist racecar track.

Out on the street of the neighboring countryside, the lizards grouped together to collectively witness a Mormon ice-cream truck pass. Instinctively, they avoided the sweet pulsations of the promised Mormon ice-cream, and side-stepped the hazard in order to finally pass through an unknown wall at the heart of a palm tree that was conveniently growing next to the kneecap of a sexually aroused leprechaun.

The palm tree withered upon the bewitched penetration and the leprechaun thrusted its three-year-old organ into the folds of a mutilated papaya flower.

As the bell of ice cream began to chime, the dark clouds expelled torrents of muddy rain that had the tendency to release aliens and chipmunks that had sequestered themselves behind folded curtains in dusty, plush drawing rooms. The bells rang even harder, causing nerve-wracked ears to bleed, and flight attendants who wore purple velvet pants to run away. Chaos ensued.

A wooden dradel only remained of the confusing clutter. It slept like a disease in remission, and awaited the day when a falling pine cone of pure evilness would rouse it from its restless slumber of neglectful silence. More bells began to ring as the wooden herpemorphs crawled out of latex boxes to revisit burning obstacles of endless, blind repetition, in the same way naughty children are forced to write: "I will not write, I will not write, I will not write," over and over again as the piano goes from B to B-flat. The mousetrap closes its pages to the echoing piano strings that cry out for a restful sleep. Oh, if only those piano strings could get their much-deserved sleep. Instead, moral voices from upstate Alaska hiccup and chatter within the legs of the chair sat upon by the man with the golden corn teeth. An endless repetition of these tooth clackings demonstrates that the sub-dental root systems go deeper than previously expected. The moon shows on the surface of the monocle worn by the gray man with the extracted corn teeth. Still no names are available. Let's open up the scented candles to celebrate.

We can hear you over in the next room choking on your own blood. Perhaps the noise is just the muted thumping on stilled piano strings. Perhaps your well-ironed shirt has popped a few magic buttons and is in need of repair. The owl can see your feet, even in the dark, where you sleep amid the bank notes and perforated seashells that your grandparents harvested from an unearthly beach squall not too many months ago, where the mucous caves readily yielded the fruit bats to your touch, when you called for them with the sonic dog whistle. But that was only months ago, and now the clock implements are lost upon you, wasted spirit and wasted magnets. The moths won't care when they arrive two days from now.

Your two-dimensional representation came to me from a distant dream, a blueprint of something else, perhaps even horrid. When the leaves fell from the hand, a half-sliced fruit became available for the taking, even though those unknown eyes peeked around the corner to initiate that final pursuit several years ago. And yet nothing happened after that, because the notebooks were confiscated by the fog and washed to another, less accessible location. If the window was broken at that point, we could have swept up the glass in order to slowly polish the shards into volcanic rocks for your honeycomb garden. Instead, there are no rocks here today.

Freezing temperatures keep the insects at bay, but the bugs nevertheless swarm over the farm tractor that has, instead of metallic engine parts, the transformed sticky morphologies of wooden chameleon tongues. This type of insertion has been well documented, but never before seen until today in this cold, inhospitable weather. A two-dimensional hand is now groping from the inside of the wooden reptile engine manifold, but the fog impairs the two-dimensional hand in its efforts at navigation. The timeclock still hasn't stopped.

Magnum panty-liners reveal the outline of a great vessel, a wondrous statue erected in the name of the deadly cactus trees from places where English isn't spoken with pleasure. The bronze panty-liner is actually a medieval and extremely primitive chastity belt that was recovered from a sunken ship that went down off the coast of Spain. What a priceless recovered treasure, a gem to set next to one's fine pumice bathtub in the full heat of summer when the alien garden is no longer kept at bay and the weeds are choking out the fine, fragrant roses of pinkness that are regularly pruned and maintained by vigilant, reptile people, each with two heads and two hands. Without this maintenance, the morning coffee could not be successfully brewed.

Sycophant playthings break the reeds when they trim the bushes to reveal sleeping anthills below the lowest branches. The fragments of leaves are falling to the ground, disturbing the anthills. After chicken bones have had a chance to rest on the zenith of the anthills, they are completely clean and ivory in color, sucked dry of all blood. Surely the picnic of boy scouts has passed this way!

3

The cowardly slowness of life, with its crawling gait, like a piano box with metal holes in it.

Through the holes grow the cured flowers that are sterile and devoid of pollen. After the lamps with the glowing faces have taken the pollen to another staircase, the light continues, throwing sideways glances of unnerving blond moments into the cups of the flowers, causing them to glow also. Repeated fragments cascade through the iron cages of pollen-dwellers, with uncertain breaths echoing like footsteps at curious intervals. The creaking staircase of fuel turns the shapely locks into caresses, which are but a mirage under the appropriate form of lighting. A mysterious keyhole blocks the way to umbrella understandings in highly motivated parasol afternoons when dainty satin slippers drop from trees like leaves. The paper leaves peel from the trunks, and the skin is woven into a premature pretzel of unnamable calamity for tidal waves that spell time backwards, when in the process of jettisoning false promises of spectacular rose bushes hiding the tunnels to rat lairs. These are the domains where glowing eyes grope their way to the staircases of violin uncertainty. This is where time is once again held prisoner in the shaky, swaying tower when breathful fireflies burn up the paper and the carpets of dust-covered mediocrity—a flimsy paper guitar buckling under the slightest effort to tighten loose tendons of connective advances towards harmony. The swaying loosens the scripted rocks and the figures of shadows shiver with deformities of firmness.

An eternal agony of lighthouses where women refuse to visit, where the clocks stopped and the phone lines have been cut, conveniently, of course. If there was ever an appropriate occasion to import bronze chicken heads, now would be the time, before it is too late. The sun had already set hours ago, sending in the darkness like a plague of paralyzing tendonitis. The beetles refuse to relinquish their saprophytic mulching and eventually the wooden chips are splintered into fertilizer. The flowers have vanished through the chain-link fence. Already the pink cloud has wafted through the metal coils and frozen the pink waterfalls into a state of timeless vertigo.

You walked through that frozen pink waterfall with your magnificent tennis elbow, while the rest of the world degraded into degenerate gibberish. A branch of your inadequacies drove your madness through the roof as the world spontaneously aborted its own deliverance. Poolside statuettes began to abandon their own digits and extremities, eyes and ears were given to reckless abscission, and the notes of bird-song became clipped residues of half-consumed liquid trails forging ahead into the icy pillow of restful sleep. Organic fingers took the brass, chicken-head keys and inserted them, one by one, into reliefs found underneath mailboxes on every lonely, desolate corner. Every snake thereafter became a smoky quintuplet of amber arrogance; every leaf became a strange song that affected one's sense of smell, at least for the moment.

The icy telephone shadowed the night-clock that was fitted with insane, epileptic exclamations of repetitive madness—the virgin pumpkin that would not die, the log cascade that would not reintegrate. A perfect moment of perfect motionlessness cramped up within the packed coil of a young, unextended fern. How far would this road follow? How long until the end of the mysterious road that was paved with dank stones which crushed the gravel of footsteps into the legs of the medieval followers—followers that could be seen with the aid of the candle from the bedroom window aboard the wooden ship mired within the oak tree on the barren hill? When would the cramped tension be released in order to finally be wound up again? How could the dimensionless and ghostly formless clock still exert its tyranny over the present moment? The star-nosed mole was unable to tell. All that could be burrowed had already been done so by the bread ambulance of the rats, but even still, these efforts of meager aptitude were not satisfactory, and so the candle continued to weakly burn under the blinding moon of uncertainty.

4

After the marching alligators collided with the burnt remnants of a wooden vision, the vision became a celebrated memory. Burnt embers trickled down the sandstone to create a menagerie of bootless priests who drank the essence of pine-needles from a contemptuous flask, which each of them carried at their hips, as they enjoyed a fleshless stroll down treeless hills where mongoose primates dwelled in the macabre shadows. The fleshless priests did not have time to shed their wind-burned skin before it was necessary to resume their studies in the arts of fish hysterectomy activities that fertile nuns used to teach when they were bored in their horse stalls under the guise of a confused lantern advocate. The dumb pineapples were confused in their bourbon shoelaces, as they stumbled amid cobblestones of impatient stupidity that rolled free from the wooden alcoves in the tree walls. As if there weren't more pressing matters to be momentarily dealt with.

Immediately the rain began to fall on the wooden priests who littered the barren trail like despicable clothespins. Eventually a biblical flood eroded the loose soil so that the religious clothespins were carried away from the sight of those who stood underneath the invisible trees, waiting in vain for a promised shadow that would never quite fall on their shoulders. The erosion of the loose soil also revealed fossilized tree roots which, when turned upside-down, could be used as very comforting furniture in times of great stress and sweat excretion.

Immediately the fossilized root furniture cried out to be consumed as rigid crows' feet, and so the transformation took place willingly, as invisible forest elves looked on while fiddling with random pieces of metallic hardware that were salvaged from an eighteen wheel truck that had jack-knifed on a dangerously wet highway. The faces of the concerned onlookers clicked into place as they evoked the disturbing mirage of red, vicious cocktail fruits which most informed citizens would habitually avoid at unplanned social events where alcoholics and independent nursemaids walked hand-in-hand into the rolling sheets of metal that were spun off at a sardine can factory, minus the sardine-can keys, of course.

The padding footsteps of a prowling cat added to the unsupressable hysteria of the moment, and the leaves began to deny their own flat identities, writhing in their vain efforts at photosynthetic wholeness. The work-boots jumped out of the domestic chair and kicked the sullen, flat leaves.

A well-manicured gorilla longingly twisted the dial of its portable radio, blindly searching for a straight, procurable thread of ancestral music, but the task was almost an overwhelming challenge. After the radio was pushed and prodded like a dead cow, it expired with a well-placed belch and gave up its transistor ghost. Shapes of wooden, dishonest letters began to form from the rotten timber of the forest, and mossy logs began to moan and exhale a sigh of complacency that could put any cowardly insect to shame. It was as if the walls became a soft loaf of hysterical bread, foaming with yeast and saliva, like a legless dragon that hunted local bathhouses of antiquity, deep within the metropolitan parks and other recreational sectors.

It was a shame that the naked table could not be set for more than one person, and yet the bare furniture reeked of a sickening starvation, an unbecoming famine of courage and cowardice, where all things and ideas decomposed into false opposites, where eyes no longer could look up at the surface of oceans, as meandering strands of digital algae kissed the foreheads of lost souls. The hearth of the fireplace was bare and had no special birch bark that could be burned as a cleansing incense. Only the marauding spider webs remained as veils of secrecy and non-communication. Watch how the tepid flower begins to decay into flashing crystals no bigger in size than orange kernels of corn. See how the strands of dried tissue become dusty hands of necrotic silver which could someday be the hands of a finely-crafted pocket watch used to time the arrival of thirsty, confused rain droplets falling on the confined primacy of a bulging-eyed goldfish bowl. The double hands of paper reach the threshold of a tempting ignition, the burned face stands sideways.

Once the paper humans are torn to pieces, the sclerotic diaphragm inverts and turns an entire goldfish inside out, so its hot, feverish belly becomes a nightmare capsule of adhering organs of a cosmic stickiness. The adherence of the guts to the body cavity could put any group of dizzy sleep-deprived children to bed for an entire weekend. Even though the eye-catching fishhook might be pulled away like a cocktease, the bait always remains within one's fervid reach. Likewise, the floor never remains stable as the slats move back and forth in opposing directions, alternating movements so that even the largest of the gold pieces gets lost in the cracks of the floor. Will the wood turn to stone or will it become ice? Will the floor be friendly or will it release its concentric patterns of eyebrow hostility that seep among the body mass of the harvested trees? Could the most expensive diamonds buy the silence of the wood? Only the squirrels know, when they trot down the walls, two by two, in pairs and mysterious couples that set off their brown, rich fur with their curious ruby eyes.

The vertigo never leaves the open, outstretched hand with its clean-shaven palms. The raindrops drive insanity into parched scalps in the same way fine leather is cut for shoes with steel toes and with festive bows used instead of laces. The finery of footwear is no alternative to a parched skull that is half-buried in a pool of mud, invited to reside next to the cleaned porcelain swimming pool of an eager family of beavers waiting to get their paws on mountains of wooden bones excavated from the reeking carcass of a maple-leafed organism or yet one more ephemeral plant thing. Even though deja-vu might be the cause of the self-identifying disorientation that ends up making crabs think they are orchids, making orchids think they are rotten olives, making rotten olives think they are pregnant goldfish of indifferent eye lobes, the black armor of fish scales pervades the sacred forest and the pumpkin nymphs wash their faces of identity confusion, preferring to suckle the musical instruments that grow from the soil at their feet. Could this fairytale get any worse? Could the bones of tender, flightless ornamental sparrows get crushed like frozen rain? Could the elements still vehemently tear apart the so-called natural relations of the world of living reality? Where did this eye-drying rainstorm come from? Which mountain did it pass over in order to arrive at our small, humble dwelling?

The storm immediately became a chorus-line of female spiders who generously passed breath mints and checkered collars out to all of the fraternal well-wishers who secretly lusted after the priceless alloys of purple metal. The purple metal was really just a stone in the bucket, an ashtray that deserved to be dumped without the least evidence of air-circulation disturbances. It was true that the alloys of purple sacred metal were mined from mysterious places, but what was important was not so much the origin of the metal, but where the purple alloys would eventually reside after they had made their way around the breasts of the arachnid chorus-line girls who wished to welcome the world with mints and after-dinner collars.

It was said that the purple metal gained its deep hue through prolonged exposure to oxidation, courtesy of the atmosphere, and that the special alloys were being used in the construction of a dreadnought submarine which traveled deeper than most fishes and would rise for air during only the most desperate of occasions. Even the clean-up corporations could not fathom this alien family member who used oil like it was water. Once the purple metallic submarine was fitted with the most powerful of available engines, it soared down to places that didn't exist in the minds of the collegiate shop-keepers. Even the Sunday meal had to be put on hold due to the intricate plating of the purple metal that comprised the outermost hull of the master-submarine. The vehicle was an utter jewel to those faraway families that lived out their existences in a miniaturized state, within a homely living room that used to be the eyeball of a domesticated, flightless sparrow.

When would the highways break down upon themselves? When would the melted glass be roped into loaves of rich, silicate bread? Why were the purple metals hammered into a talisman coin that got lost in the shuffling slats of the motionless wooden floor? Once the purple coin was lost, the wood rats began to seep out of the woodwork, with their massive, oblong heads on which the world refused to look. Grimy paws indeed grappled in the dark for even the faintest glimmer of purple, a distorted reflection only viewable from the bottom of a moonlit swimming pool on the outskirts of dead cities where urban honeycombs hide meaningless valuables, and where the converted nectar no longer flows freely through the domestic pipelines. The raven feet are held at bay as blood vessels burst in over-pressurized skulls and the diaphanous wings of purple goldfish set up an unwelcome residence behind the mucous eyelids of sleepy streetlights forcefully added to a unique key ring to be hidden under bathmats, rugs and other woven articles of foot correspondence.

"We will make it to the surface someday, I promise," shouts the bald captain of the purple metallic submarine. "We just have more stalkers to flee, I tell you." The purple metallic submarine captain strokes his beard and regards his fine, inorganic vessel. He throws a twig onto the fireplace and watches it burn. Even in the depths of the purple ocean there are fireplaces and empty sardine cans that the crew uses as ashtrays.

Even at these depths the ship-dwellers know how to knit sweaters and convert honey into wax. When the raven's feet caress the eyelashes of the dark-haired girl, the cactus totems mark the trail through the watery desert. The one purple coin becomes many coins with the scattering water reflections of darkness and the metal sinks, amazingly fragmented like a kinky lemon meringue pie.

"Would you like a coughdrop, ma'am?"

"No thank you."

"Or what about a complimentary beverage?"

"No, no thank you."

The submarine bartender took the parrot-lady's declinations with dignity and humor, and began to slap pieces of amber that contained fossilized insects. The architecture of the amber prevented grave robbers from entering, and so the orange paradise remained untouched except for the obscene groping and fondling of penetrating, wayward eyes.

Immediately from the amber burst forth several sprays of archaic formic acid, followed by some of the largest giant ants only seen on mysterious lost episodes of the Twilight Zone. The ants shed their chitonous shells and their moist skin glistened with the formation of a new layer of exoskeletal body armor. The ants took their bony legs and began to use them, after all of those long, difficult centuries of fossil amber entrapment. The ants devoured their sweaty, leather wrist-watches while walking over to a radiator, which they immediately destroyed with their mandibles. The parrot-lady at the bar screamed, not regretting that she had not taken the sub's bartender up on his generous coughdrop and beverage offers. As the frightened woman backed away from the formidable ants, she noticed a faint object of glass or crystal that glimmered faintly in the dim light. The clear object was actually a shard of amber from the original fossilized conglomerate that had housed the suspended ants over many aeons. The woman kicked the amber aside as she reached for an emergency sardine can affixed to the wall, next to the escape hatch.

"Please, if anyone can hear me, I am in dire trouble. I am currently experiencing a mid-life crisis and need to understand why this uptight grand piano has been fortified with only aluminum boy-scout shovels so many oppressive miles beneath the ocean's surface. I can't hang on to this state of affairs forever, you know. Please have a crewman report to this submarine's musical drinking sanctuary as soon as possible so that I might be able to make it back to the surface world of air-breathing mammals."

The woman stopped to catch her breath and eagerly waited to hear a response from the other end of the genetically modified sardine tin. Unfortunately, there was no response, so the parrot-lady pulled her trench-coat tightly around her, put another orange feather in her cap and turned to vacate the bar, leaving the struggling bartender to his uncertain fate with the ants, possibly his last group of rowdy customers in a bar many miles below sea level.

"So what'll it be, boys," said the bartender who began to arrange some glasses before the large ants who had seated themselves at the warm and fuzzy oakwood bar.

"We desire the juice of a green lemon that has grown from a rather specifically planted tree. A fruit from a tree that was grown on top of stalagmite outcroppings, where subterranean formations exist that excite us and fondly remind us of better days, where college professors wore leopard skin briefs and where monopoly icicles grew from parrot bird cages. We desire this lemon juice for its extreme bite and acrid flavor—a pungent bite of low pH excites the tongue and lets us dream of greener anthills on the other side of town. Oh, and what's there to do now for fun around here anyway, on this here dinky submarine? We've got a busy schedule just like you do, Mr. Bartender, so let us have a prompt answer!"

"Well, my fine formic friends, there are many pleasures to be had on our humble purple submarine. If golf is your favor, you will find a magnificent driving range on Deck 5. If you enjoy meaningless pseudo-intellectual political banter, you will find many friends in the Jade Room, on Deck 3. If you enjoy sweating rituals, there's a place for you on Deck 13, the lowest deck. All the rest is just fluff. Make sure you get yourselves some visitors' passes, ok?"

The ants thanked the purple metallic submarine bartender before each downing a pitcher of salted rim lemon juice. Even though the ants spoke with a rather nitwit variety of US accent, the bartender forgave them and decided not to take their ignorance too personally. Instead, the bartender helped the ants settle their tab and then assisted in finding their cramped living quarters.

After taking the odd fingerprints of the ants off of the empty beverage glasses, a dark, speechless feline informant confronted the bartender with the evidence. "And so you say these ants identified themselves as Huey, Duey, Louie, and Steve?"

"Yes, they did," answered the bartender, who was now in the process of closing up the bar for the night. The feline informant finished collecting the fingerprint information while toying with its blue lantern collar. The odd feline informant closed its eyes momentarily for a poignant moment of darkness while its keen furry mind began to calculate its next movements, its next area of investigation. Beautiful mushroom and celery growths began to poke themselves through the feline's outgrown sports jacket, and it was at that moment that the feline informant received the premonition of the purple metallic submarine's watery destruction. Within the hour, after one last game of fungus billiards, the dark cat creature left the submarine in one of its compact escape pods and narrowly avoided a premature death in a watery grave. The ants and all of the rest of the purple metallic crew could not boast of the same fortune.

In the morning, after a glorious sunrise, the sleep-deprived feline informant regarded the ant fingerprints while awkwardly reclining in the sub's escape pod that lazily bobbed around in the salt water. In its hungry hands, it held the remnants of a glorious era, a bygone time when purple metal was in fashion and when fossilized insects were obedient when it came to remaining embedded within cities of amber thought by fools with big red noses to be of a greater value than a handful of miniaturized, transparent crystal brains shorn of all impeding skull plates and ephemeral cowboy hats. The feline informant squinted its amber eyes while stuffing an evidence bag full of fragments of purple metal and orange matrix fossils.

5

The magic shop-display mannequins materialize in the corners of a run-down, flaccid wooden church, while bloody corpses cowardly kneel, almost prostrate. The happy organ flares its music up through the aquatic chimney that houses many purple metallic, industrial-strength goldfish. But there's nothing to eat in the pantry and all of the shelves are bare. Dysfunctional jars of non-dairy creamer sulk amid played lotto tickets and melted poker chips. The shop-display mannequins shed their purple velvet attire and wear new grass skirts made from the bleached hairs of coconuts. The polka-dotted walls are the same as they were yesterday.

Once these mannequin conclusions are reached, there's nothing left for gloved hands to do but begin the refinishing of the wood so that the old stains might be hidden from detecting eyes and flapping snores. The old dishwasher is still functional, however, and inside it are several luminescent coats sometimes worn by wayward silver parakeets after they have tasted the sumptuous kiss of hot plasma. When silver parakeets get dressed in the morning, they wear their glassy, luminous coats and perch on the shoulders of faceless, purple velvet mannequins that have no hair or sensory organs. All they have are their colored light bulbs and purple velvet.

Jeeper, one of the special silver parakeets, suddenly decides to transform its brittle little bones into wooden matches. When this special silver parakeet comes into contact with the hard concrete down below, the magic bird spontaneously ignites into gracious plumes of green flame. The copper bones of this bird are the pipes of recent plumbing. With a happy lampshade as a cigarette lighter, the cordon bleu of the whistle is blown, and electric puppy-dog eyes are sardine cans pregnant with lipstick enclosures that really scratch the backs of cordless telephones that ejaculate replayed messages into ears of businessmen who have large hearts and giant, watery blue eyes, especially when they become emotional over such mundane issues like the electric bill or a leaking toilet. Jeeper is now a burning geometry of high tide, with succulent starfish gliding over his now scorched skull. The hot body heat from the copper pipes is breathless now, as colored ribbons decorate the walls of hospitals and serve as guidelines for hospital visitors. At last the chlorine vapors permeate through the spider webs that serve as dividers between the various wardrooms of the hospital. No one can pass from room to room without first dissolving an entranceway through the thick webbing and then reestablishing the seal upon safe passage through. In this way, sick senators can get the quality health care they need without suffering devastating viral infections, which most other less special and less important people must endure everyday.

After water cups are passed to the sick and the dying, the bricks in the walls are removed for their daily polishing and kissing. A lot can be done with those bricks. Sometimes, when parchment dragonflies land on the edge of a lucite drinking cup, the dragonfly enlarges its wings so that the insect can surround any object of reasonable size that it encounters, such as those marvelously large pimento-stuffed olives. The wings of the dragonfly are also the family herald and symbol of exotic, emotional extravagance, where the teeth of a crocodile are used in tandem with a ruler to measure the overall flavor of fish liver when involved in nationwide taste tests. The smell of the insect's wings evokes the electric crack of ozone, after a ball of lightning has dropped into one's tea during a cold, rainy night of solitude and matchbox infinity. The solitude of the wet night begins to saturate the matches with a flammable copper compound, causing a green flame to echo the brilliance of the emerald dragonfly of living parchment. The pretty dragonfly appreciates the intrinsic movements of the black clouds that give rise to the opalescent arcs that create its ozone analogue. Imagine a dragonfly of ozone that could peel the face off of any creature who happened by, and recreate that face with a bolt of lightning. It's enough to bend a troubled starfish backwards.

Once the invertebrate disks are replaced in their very own pot of soil, the magnetism of the earth causes a slight change in the tidal patterns, which in turn causes the troubled foliage of winter to hibernate even more securely than before. The wolves will not leave the countryside in peace tonight! Hear them chewing and pacing, while they check their paws for those tiny print-set letters that get dropped all the time by timid postal agents. See how they turn the dials up on their machines as their canine jaws seek something pliable and organic to grasp tightly. Also noticeable is the way their skin is as clear as that of an old-fashioned telephone booth that some people avoid visiting because they have such small bladders. The skin might peel if they are boiled, but as long as they have wreathes of rosemary in their pockets (along with a tooth-sized transistor radio), they will have gifts of complacency to present to the rodent mammals with the lucky spotted shoes and the regal swimwear that certain beach-going females sometimes like to display when their uptight husbands aren't around. Only the lens of highest quality can make a laser, and so only a great arse can provoke an equally great emotion.

Based on these magnificent skin observations, the furry wolves gather their lucky horseshoes and satellite plants, and externalize their one and only internal matrix of sensuality. Their thoughts become a giant sun umbrella that is kept at each of their sides during the cold and wet weather, facilitated by the mastication of the emerald ozone dragonflies that use their wings of plasticality to encase choice specimens for further dissection and coffee-break discussions. Once the footprints of the dogs have been immortalized by way of poured concrete, the box is then closed and drawn together tightly. The sweat of the process must not be seen as intimidating. In the sky, the green moon begs to be colonized by silver parakeets and emerald ozone dragonflies. This desire can be fulfilled if freshly cut wood is transported to that amorous satellite. The wood can be boiled and then molded into a Swiss cheese-like structure. The birds and insects become embedded in the wooden propionibacterian bubbles, with exactly one dragonfly and one magic parakeet each assigned to a cheese bubble. This is the secret desire of the wolves, for which they will not rest until the dream has been actualized.

Meanwhile, unknown passengers sail on fragrant ships, the feet of raven tumble to the bottoms of cherry trees in the same way that a blizzard can drop metallic stones to the bottom of a water well. The frigid people check watches and wallets, and wait for their paper salvation to bless them and set them free of all conscience and regret. The pocket monkeys are arranged in chains and can spell the names of famous felines in a backward configuration—almost identical to the backwardness of dead bodies. In the same breath, a woman reveals her thermometer legs for the enjoyment of her mate, and the magnolia soaps are thrown into the river. An old man weeps for his fruit cocktail after losing a bet to an economical tyrant of the defrocked nobility, so that he, in his old-age wisdom, must now remember once again the playful memories of octagonal snails. If only silver fish could mate with mercury.

Fruit cocktail mannequins spell relief for the fat, sluggish goldfish who have protruding eyes and graceful fan tails. The fruit cocktail forms a melodic keychain that can be used as a wrench to pry open reticent oyster shells to reveal the silky pink gills of the most cherished mollusc. After the shell of the popped oyster has been shucked, the plastic mannequin shrinks in size from six feet to six inches and then becomes an inanimate chess piece—perhaps a throwaway pawn on the uptight battlefield of miserly and highly consciously elaborated forms of degenerate human entertainment. As a rush of hot water cleans blocked pores, the mannequin of miniature purple velvet is pocketed and then sold on the black market as an adornment for a smoky, ashtray-adorned Cadillac.

Yes, Cadillacs also become vacuumed by the vortex, creating feline flashbacks of endearing catcalls, the cats that can't hear the beauty of their own voices. So much untapped strength to be accounted for when a lopsided, fat-bellied, totem pole big-mouthed idiot falls over with a thud after receiving numerous deep lacerations that cause his barely contained entrails to fall forth from the ugly, despicable body cavity. If only more of these totems could be razed in a similar manner. But suddenly the razed totem, very much dead, sprouts several graceful molecular cat whiskers from the top of the wooden execution, and the feline characteristics, kept dormant for so long, assert themselves out of the dead, loudmouthed driftwood. And some people thought thanksgiving day was all about being grateful for one's sardines and crackers! Out of the death of the loud-mouthed totem, there arises the beginning of a new feline forest, full of protruding goldfish eyes of purple submarine metal and raised tails of feathery tickliness that grace the barbaric ecosystems with freshwater— the freshwater that should have been a gemstone of collectible and cherishable brilliance. All of the hands within the wooden feline forest transform into opening frilly oysters that are one with the wooden aquarium. All of the snakes in Australia couldn't measure up to the splendor of the wooden feline forest! And look within each of the hollow knots of the rejuvenated wood: within each wooden chamber sleeps a graceful silver parakeet embryo in full shimmering radiance, with a metallic green umbilical cord that could only form the tail of a luscious emerald dragonfly whose head and surrounding folded wings are really a dormant rosebud to be opened tomorrow, because there will always be a tomorrow. The embryonic birds do their best to sleep through the bad but inspiring weather. And as they sleep within the warm safety of their wooden pajamas, they dream of the plastic popsicle sticks that can be used to construct ephemeral houses. As the dreamlike houses are erected on barren soils, false hopes arise that are quickly dashed by a special sort of vaginal comet that collides with the azure skies of the Earth, forcing people to breathe strange atmospheres that were never meant for normal earthers.

Maybe the popsicle plastic stick houses weren't meant to last for more than one dream, but the skies collide with the dreaming foreheads of the silver parakeet children-embryos in their hexagonal sleep chambers found within lacerated, loud-mouthed trees. The touch of the breeze chills their young, newly formed spines and the dreams shift from land to air, and then to water. The water dreams shift to land dreams, and so the cycle is complete. When such parakeet dreams form a cyclical pattern like those of the circular mannequin chastity belts of Mars, the terror of the universe becomes apparent, but in roughly tolerable doses. The terror of the Earth's magma is also evident, yet these sleeping birds in their wooden pajama chambers somehow know what to do with this strange reality in a rather constructive way, at least to the extent to where they can keep track of the passage of time by noting the thickness of the wooden annuli ringage in their hibernaculum bed-chambers.

6

When the North wind blew over the guarded fence, the iron railing began to freeze. A thistle plant opened arctic blooms and radio was very successful, singing great success songs. A mirror bled dry ice over the fence and it was at that moment that a candy-cane tusked woolly mammoth sauntered onto the front yard. With its knowing eyes, the pachyderm identified all of the electrical relays that were camouflaged by the intricate ironwork of the frozen fence. The woolly mammoth with the candy-striped tusks used its trunk to lift the hat from its head and then said:

"Hello, my name is Shlishka, and I'm one of the last remaining woolly mammoths on the whole face of this unhappy, troubled Earth. If my hair doesn't offend you then perhaps you'd allow me to show you my entire line of dry-rotted rubber shoes." In truth, the mammoth had unpacked several pairs of black rubber shoes that had suffered long-term exposure to heat and thus were in a horridly deformed state of dry rot.

The sentinel paper green dragonfly of emerald thoracity cocked its head and used its large compound eyes to firmly regard the well-dressed woolly mammoth with multi-striped candy-canes for tusks. In the end, just to be civil, the paper emerald dragonfly sentinel agreed to purchase two pairs of decrepitly dry-rotted black rubber shoes. After Shlishka, one of the last remaining woolly mammoths with candy-cane tusks, had departed back out into the freezing weather, the emerald dragonfly began to accost various street lamps, attempting to sell the worthless dry-rotted shoes to them in order to rid itself of those troublesome artifacts.

The straw hairs of a scarecrow are traded for the awful shoes, finally. The straw hairs are golden, and are pressed into the mud so as to fortify the streets and thus make them pleasant places to walk, including the cleaning of feline litter boxes. Once the deal is closed and both parties go their separate ways, the streets come alive with amber music that stain the walls and any molecular surfaces that get in the way of the artificial music.

At that juncture, the walls of the cave become the woody skin of coconuts, and so fish that had been sacrificed to the magic amber begin to enjoy their magnetic swim through the special glassy waves of fossilized tree resin that became elevated to almost the magical status of an ambrosiacal food. The amber became an insect and fish marmalade that fancy princess guests offered to some of the sidereal feline residents who plagued the halls like blistering sunspots. This action spelled out the only name of the black and red tabby that is rumored to grace the halls of only the most disturbed of moldy sandstone castles in magnificent underground caverns beneath the frozen arctic ice grounds, all cared for by a caring arctic groundskeeper.

The woolly mammoth fossils that have left their shoes at home will most certainly be scolded by their mothers when they return home late, and without change from the milk money. A guppy darts across a sunken television screen but it doesn't distract the reclining mammoth family the least bit, and so the overweight clan opens the nightly continental TV dinners and joins the ranks of well-behaved, law-abiding consumers whose trunks and legs bear beautiful bracelets of crocodiles' teeth. Deja-vu? Perhaps not, since a starfish shadow that was creeping up on the legs of the mammoth family is immediately peeled off and ironed onto the back of a new, colorful T-shirt.

Unresponsive shadows of starfish are harvested from other places in a likewise fashion and the two-dimensional doubles pile up like drink coasters. Once a myopic eyeball submarine gathers its underwater belongings and resides at the bottom of a stream with perfectly smooth water-worn pebbles and cobbles, it becomes a fat, rarefied goldfish with transparent fins. These clear appendages are periodically nipped by the more violent piscine neighbors of the world, whose lockjaw cynicism propels them to vicious acts of spite and jealous dementia. After these activities, the bullies wear silk smoking jackets and put their feet up on footrests, leisurely reading the paper, spreading sea urchin preserves on toast, and admiring each other's fancy and extremely rare wallpaper collectibles. Of course, these wallpaper collectibles were actually bought from tacky television ads that were broadcasted from inverted elephant tusk cornucopias, inside of which hide the sneaky, black-and-white monitors that showed images of consumer destruction.

Once the man stops to tie his shoes, that's when the herd of woolly mammoths with the candy-cane tusks decides to stampede. All that is left of the shoelace-tying man now is a mangled felt hat and a pool of blood, mingled with sullen strawberry preserves, seedless of course. The lightning rod projecting from the side of the sandstone building casts an eerie shadow over the body, or rather, the puddle of liquid sweetness. The rod's shadow is the terrestrial restraining bar that is the result of the mammoth stampede.

What was it about the lightning rod shadow that caused the liquid sorrow to evaporate right out of its tracks? The arsenal of woolly mammoth tusks that contained secret video monitors remained hidden behind the cozy brick wall. Once the wall had been playfully patted by the alexandrine saber-toothed tiger, the skin of the bricks became that of a shiny goldfish, and all feline madcaps became joyous and jubilant because of the transformation. What a day to be selling wallpaper to coffee shops. A brass band appeared and a distinguished flute player wooed the public with sullen flute songs of azure glue. The glue stuck to the fingers of woodworkers who created giant balsa escape planes that would eventually be captured and stranded within the domain of fancy garden necklaces, which were limited to the seedy outskirts of a dismal but highly worshipped metropolis. It was uncertain why money was so important to the metropolitan inhabitants, but it was thought important nevertheless, and thus they sold their souls just for a few dust particles of fossilized ivory.

When the ivory dust particles of fossilized monetary emptiness settled to the bottom of the stream for good, the time was right for goldfish to eject their x-ray guitars that they had hidden within their orange bellies. Once the fish became transparent, their roving eyes became more salient, and so did the guitars that they had hidden inside them. With the penmanship of distracted doctors, the fish scribbled out libidinous prescriptions for tastefully handcrafted teapots of cast iron, more symbolic for use than for practicality. The teapots could be acquired from the amethyst caves that were located several quarries below, further down into the depths of the brackish water. Once the hidden guitars were ejected from the x-ray fish, they were encrusted on the rocks with an organic glue made of silicates. The bones of the fish glowed through their transparent flesh with uncharacteristic warmth as they gracefully departed the scene with their heavy, surly tails slowly propelling the massive creatures down into the inky darkness of the water. The x-ray goldfish were never seen again, but for those tourists who managed to find the low-dwelling guitar-encrusted rocks, the memory of the event was preserved forever.

The wooden rings on a table do not lie. They are discus in shape and are the end result of a long progression of guitar ejections and encrustations. When a table is set for dinner, the candles become important because carbon resin is available for the taking. A parakeet can sit on the edge of the wood and nit-pick about the walrus teeth that are embedded in the wood, inexplicably. The feathers of the parakeet grow like clay and show a silver brilliance when looked at in the right angle.

Apathetic and/or busy girls carry on with their tasks, heedless of the birds perched on their Sunday tables. The setting sun is a gasp for dying, waning light as the atmosphere refracts it into the oranges and pinks of sunset. An alternate light source is usually required, but not always. The silver parakeets open their irises to the monolithic memories of camouflaged, jeweled crescent moths that used to pulsate on Martian walls on better days when the craters of the moon were still untouched by human hands, long before the primate mannequin parts invaded the pristine dusty territory.

But those days are now gone, and the moon and Mars are now inhabited by purple velvet mannequins of varying degrees of utterly vicious plasticality. Nevertheless, the pulsating gray camouflaged moths still reside in the more untouched regions of those not-so-faraway places and avoid all contact with humanity, with a genuine passion. No more stupid phone calls, no silly letters, no ridiculous television documentaries for these moths (and also for their distant relatives, the silver parakeets) as they now spend their astral Saturdays plucking gems from wooden terrestrial tree knots of xylem freshness of pure water, covered by the curious whiskers of catfish.

When fresh brains are wrapped in tinfoil, they are placed on the shelf for knowledge consumption, when the young political party-goers prance into marble buildings to determine national policies, like, who gets to buy which kinds of fruit and at just which times. Hence, this policy-making necessitates the presence of the fruit police. With the fruit police, all fruit sales become legal and are carried out peacefully in neutral territory. Under these circumstances, "equality" is thought to be achieved by these great ruling minds when all they have done is imposed an artificial constraint on the natural transfer of fruit molecules throughout the circulatory system of the globe. Eventually the rain will wash away even the strongest wall of salt, and only the pepper will remain, after all has settled.

The catfish whiskers poke through the bricks in the coffeehouse wall. The building is destroyed as a fire hydrant makes an unprecedented fly-by into the window, sending showers of glass shards into the vulnerable watermelon rinds that litter the oily streets of the conventionally balanced alleyway, which harbours pepper trees, among other sanguine representatives of guitar life. The catfish whiskers know where to travel; they also know on what frequency they might grow from other budding geriatric opera champions that use tubas as football helmets and espresso machines for electric toothbrushes. The catfish feelers are the instruments of exploration, as they erupt from forest reeds and other organic objects that never know the pleasures of foraging for dead things on the bottom of a murky pond. A radio signal that cannot reach the antenna of a radio is useless, as is a catfish whisker that has no earth tree from which to grow.

The now-or-never ultimatum is barely dodged in the way some kindergarten classes dodge those nefarious sugar-coated Walt Disney sing-alongs, where happy paper cutouts are created with safety scissors so that corpulent, naive hands won't get cut because of reckless horse-play and Halloween whisper dress-ups. The broomsticks are put there for one's morning chores to clear the green and black checkered religious halls of all subsequent saliva outbursts, in the same way nurse shark guitars become the mermaid's purse. This purse contains the embryos of cartilaginous happy hats—those special shark skates that run on crude oil instead of tea tree extracts, like all of those unholy Wednesday outbursts that the mermaids used to wrap around their sore kneecaps when the sun set for them at a lopsided angle. The mermaids take their nurse shark purses and go to town, and all of the lincoln logs on the sidewalk get caught up in the current and go down along with mermaids, like a glorious shipwreck that helps remove a few extra boisterous larynxes from the over-inflated human population. Could the now-or-never of infinity really apply here as anything more substantial than just a plume of dust, or an inconsistent illusion that has no firm notochord running through the flesh of reality, with which to control the captive elements? Nothing demonstrated thus far reveals any track record of consistency or thoroughness, and so the nursery hymns remain in the nursery, next to mermaids' purse pillows and several notochords that litter the tiled floors like the organic shrapnel from a primitive rubber-band war. After the rubber-bands, there might be sonic rubber fishes, but until that kind of artifact begins to be seen, the presence of the sonic rubber fishes and the accompanying shrapnel will just be limited to frozen, simmering pages of icy conjecture. In the meantime, we still have these rumors and chants to deal with. Several spinal chords or not, the encrusted guitars on the underwater rocks will someday beg to be taken to the surface so that they might be touched by anything other than piscine digits.

When the holiday wafers are finally released, they sink to the bottom and drift past the deeply encrusted fish embryo guitars. When the guitars start to develop fully functional eyes, the expatriated mermaids clasp their nurse shark purses and begin to grasp the candy-cane tusks of the ancient woolly mammoths who have come to visit them in the lonely, early-morning hours. Upon having their colorful, candy-cane tusks grasped in such a loving manner, the ancient woolly mammoths momentarily shut their eyes and then resume their very heated dialogue with the expatriated mermaids, with their soft nurse shark purses which contained walnuts, of all things.

The mammoths questioned the lost mermaids regarding their uncertain origins, but the underwater women could recall no pertinent details of their distant past, and instead repeatedly insisted that their own fishy legs did not taste like tuna but more like chicken. The last of the woolly mammoths each momentarily withdrew by closing each eyelid halfway and contemplating the mystery of the mermaids who were currently wearing gloves made of a kelp-derived organo-technology. These artificial kelp gloves protected the mysterious mermaidens from handling items of high radioactivity as well as over-all sassiness, and this form of protection proved effective and invaluable at an extremely early hour. After the gloves were used to move the radioactive vials into the lead briefcases of the last of the woolly mammoths with the striped candy-cane tusks, the mammoths accepted this form of payment from the mermaids (in return for their freedom, of course) and suggested that the two groups go to a cozy, arctic observatory, in order to celebrate.

"In the observatory, we can watch the frozen planets cross through our hair; we can celebrate the passage of the moon which affects our most intimate hours," said the mermaids, as they let their nurse shark purses dangle from their fingertips. The candy-tusked mammoths agreed and built fires in the arctic wastelands. The fires melted the surrounding snow and fields of ice into exquisite specimens of winter furniture, so that the loving mermaids and woolly mammoths would have places to sit while they warmed themselves in front of the fire. After the cooled liquid furniture had a chance to crystallize, mammoths and mermaids were comfortably seated, and then the two groups exchanged butterfly stories and daytime phone numbers, so that the distance between them would never be more than the width of a butterfly's wing. They rejoiced and began to harvest crate after crate of miniature pumpkins that were to be used to make a most nutritious fish food with lots of beta-carotene as well as marshmallows with the anchovy filling. These magic pumpkins grew from the vines that had attentively wrapped themselves around the ice furniture in order to get close to the fire. This rare breed of ice pumpkin was oblivious to the thumping of the bass on the thin walls, and manifested the flame-colored pigments that mimicked the heat of the ice blaze. With the pumpkins safely packaged in cherry wood crates, the expatriated mermaids greeted an arriving entourage of gray feline observers who promised to deliver the highly cherished pumpkins to young boys and girls of feline descent all over the globe in a timely fashion. The mermaidens gave their feline friends a knowing wink and an almost sultry sneer, and watched them depart through fields of dark, gray ice.

After the mammoths and mermaidens threw more wood on the arctic blaze, they resumed their seated festivities on the frozen liquid furniture. A wind-up music box was gently placed on a conveniently frozen table next to the ice couch. This music box produced an icy song of feverish notes made from the percussive actions of frozen crystals on a smooth sheet of perfect metal. The icy song was rudely interrupted by the telephone, which seemed to ring many times a day, sometimes for no apparent reason. One of the last of the woolly mammoths with the candy-cane-striped tusks rose from an ice recliner and picked up the receiver.

"Hello? Yes, I had called earlier about some sonic candles with which I had great difficulty lighting. No, I do not have them out right now. Well, I suppose then that you'll just have to come out here and examine them for yourself. No, I'm busy at the moment with my friends, discussing very important things like the gold corn kernels of the future, and our lives when lived outside of an eyeball. You will just have to swim out here and make your own assessment."

The woolly mammoth replaced the phone's receiver and resumed his conversation with one of the repatriated mermaids. As the mermaids and mammoths talked long into the night, the investigative leopards allowed pulsating moths with gray, crescent-shaped wings to land on their foreheads and send telepathic signals of light to their brains, while they slept on the great sheets of ice somewhere out in the wastes of the arctic. The wings of the dark moths pulsated while the leopards scanned the cosmos with wide eyes.

As the leopard creatures stared at the stars, they began to hunger for raw fish, as their ancestors had done for all time. The leopard creatures touched the peculiar gray crescent moths on their foreheads and then the cryptic insects flew away to search for small, raw fish (perhaps shad) to bring to the hungry leopard creatures who were gazing at the stars and planets. The cats reached their paws into a quickly forming strawberry rupture in the fabric of reality. As they grasped into the strawberry-flavored rupture, the cats growled low notes that sounded almost like game-show music. The strawberry reality rupture was indeed growing and had almost enveloped one of the felines. The particular leopard creature caught in the rift quickened the pace of the game-show song as it started to tap-dance in a very flamboyant manner. Faster than a ladybug can suck out the liquid viscera of an aphid, the tap-dancing leopard creature was approached by a gray crescent moth bearing a twitching, silvery fish. The cats could barely keep from drooling, upon imagining the succulent raw flesh beneath the skin. After making contact with the strawberry flavored breach in reality, the small shad had qualitatively fused with the enveloped feline creature. The leopard cat took on the coloration and textures of the fish, so that now, instead of hair, the feline had silver and transparent membranous fin-like appendages. Its skin now looked very shiny and rubbery. Now the eyes were bleached to a sparkling platinum hue, and they followed every movement the moth made. The transformed cat sort of looked like a fish with two legs. Instead of being called a "catfish," this creature would be aptly named the "fishcat." The silver fishcat addressed his comrades and began to smell of a popular men's cologne. He informed them of his plans:

"Yes, my brothers and sisters, I must leave the universe as you know it, and travel across interdimensional distances in order to bless an alien's ornamental fish pond. I shall be the exotic species and get foot massages at least three times a day. They will bathe and clothe me, and groom me with a barbecued automobile. I will please this alien with my wit as well as my charm. However, on the weekends I will open up those colorful paper cocktail umbrellas and then create polka-dotted tempests with just my gloved fingers. The tarantula cocktails will come home, and certain rainy serpents will wiggle between your toes. Once the paper colored cocktail parasols have remained open for a few hours, my flesh will develop neon veins and arteries, so that I might have the opportunity to be as sensual as a six-sided snowflake. In this manner, I shall manifest a liking for the dendritic trans-dimensional lifestyle. Also, I will be able to come visit you, at will, when you need to communicate with me. By opening up dimensionless space, I can create the means to catch only the choicest fish. Now we will never have to worry about food again."

The silver fishcat then relaxed on a silver satin reclining chair and summoned forth some amazing fishes that come from the unexplored regions of the ocean down below. The fishcat stared into the rift with his icy platinum irises and soon tuna fish were seen coming through the reality breach. The rest of the leopard felinoids oohed and ahhed upon seeing the tasty fish flesh.

The mermaidens and the last of the woolly mammoths had observed the entire spectacle and were jealous that none of their respective species had ever been able to pursue a transdimensional lifestyle. Impulsively and compulsively, the mermaids began to greedily lick the candy-cane-striped tusks of the woolly mammoths. Then, in perfect synchronicity, the frisky mermaids exclaimed to the woolly pachyderms: "Oh come to me, my darling; let us make love at the zenith of a sunflower; let us soak the earth with our sweat." And so the last of the woolly mammoths with the wet candy-cane striped tusks embraced the panting mermaidens and carried them off to moist fields of green clover. Apparently these species weren't quite ready for the transdimensional lifestyle experience yet, concluded the fishcat to itself as the two lover species eventually disappeared.

The transdimensional silver fishcat summoned the silver parakeets, who immediately burst forth into the transdimensional playground. The silver parakeets landed on the outstretched arms of the fishcat. The ones closest to the fishcat's silver-sealed ears whispered to the feline:

"It is so good to see you again. After a cup of tea, we will resume our observation activities. You know that we refuse to intervene? I hope so. We will provide you with plasma glass medium, which you can use to weave your pristine music. This new medium will put a spring in your step, and create coelacanth breeding grounds, where you can farm-raise living fossils that might do well in your bathtub. But now we have told you everything you need to hear. We will now sing silent songs of twilight."

The silver parakeets fell silent and eagerly perched on the arms and shoulders of the fishcat.

7

The rails of the dirty coal car bounced off the tips of fangs as droplets, cascading into the snowy ravines below. In the ice forest, crystal structures had been manufactured around the trunks of trees, like knowing smart-collars that knew when to bark like a dog and then to whistle like a pelican. The wooden paneling was frozen beneath the snow, and was visible in some places, jutting out a wooden arm or leg here or there. Fiery plum trees had grown up through the oppressive snow in certain places, and the red fruit of the short trees sent out several degrees of heat, at regular intervals. The magic hot plum fruit was the result of several months of careful cultivation on the part of one of the frozen tree collars. Somehow these icy collars could grow fiery red-hot plum trees just by thinking about tasty icy fruit drinks that came from the ice spigot at the local arctic teahouse.

The frozen trees with their ice collars whistled old camp tunes while waiting for a somewhat damp pile of phosphorus sticks to spontaneously ignite, which they did after several minutes of intense wishing. Once the blaze had started, the growth of newly spouted fiery plum trees slowed to a mature pace and the plants bore healthy batches of fire plums to be used as happy ammunition in the next pow-wow with the arctic clam priests. These special priests lived up in the most extremely coldest hills where clam wells could be dug down through the rocks in order to retrieve only the strongest, largest clams from the cold, deep arctic waters. And somehow these rumored clam priests lived in the high frozen hills where they maintained a strict diet of giant sea clams. But the clam priests kept to themselves and never crossed paths with the lower-dwelling plum trees and ice-collared evergreen forest. The lanterns in the forest had birds circling above, surveying the merry scene below. The lava plums, as they were called, had swelled to maturity, with a firm flesh and numerous black seeds.

A lamp momentarily converted its electrical apparatus into a solid, wondrous antique piece of cherrywood sculpture. The red wood was innervated with sensory fibers, and so the cherrywood life form was born. It rose from its lampshade and rolled into a mail tube faster than a bumblebee could swat a fly that slowly roasted on top of a hotel elevator. The false insect became a lettuce flower bouquet, and all of the wasps and bumblebees came out from under a bronze tire and formed the outline of a fantastic crystal lattice that was deceptively well-defined. A boxcar from next door rattled the frozen walls as it passed close-by, in a fragmented moment of time, in the same way a light bulb becomes a torch of ammunition used in reviving the old city wall layout that used to define a shanty-town that once stood in these frozen wastes more than a hundred years ago. But the boxcar passed on through the mannequin-populated town and soared through the icy mists of the frozen forest in the dark dead of winter.

The amazon plum fruits were also used for artificial lighting, and so they were free to populate the frozen mannequin ice-city in whatever place the hot plums chose to continue their rather hot life. The bricks of the underwater currents sent a message by way of a magnetic flower. This magnetic flower was really a green emerald dragonfly. The fuzzy side-flowers pulled out trumpets and played an appropriate song to accentuate the arrival of the dragonfly from the magnetic flower.

As fast as the trumpets appeared, they were put back into their alcove maze hiding places and allowed to breathe the cold air. At the axis of an ashtray, a red and white spinning top gyrated in a haphazard motion as it teetered on the edge of the glass. The soft glass held the top in its orbit and refreshed itself with ginkgo extracts and nonchalant candlestick holders. The candles were nowhere to be seen, but it was apparent from the state of disarray next to the fireplace that the candles had skipped town and had perhaps headed off to the cold wastes of the hills, where it was currently snowing.

Galactic fleets of icefish only waited at the depths of the mines, next to the reposing giant clams. The fish were new arrivals, their purpose unknown in the deep ice-fishing wells. Once a spangled doorknob was turned, the fish dropped their scales in order to show off their under-colors. Even in the near-total darkness, some striped patterns emerged from the exposed skin of the ice-fish, and the large clams studied the arrangements with a keen persistence. When orange crystals began to protrude from between the cobbles that lined the interior surface of the deep well, the clams grew restless, beginning to sing half-hearted songs about canned cherries, flour and vegetable shortening. These cooking songs continued for at most a half-hour, until the clams decided to meditate for another half-hour and then climb up the sides of the wells, via the orange sea crystals. At the surface of the arctic world, the clams would be picked up by snow clouds and ferried to the nearest gas station, where they could purchase an oil filter that would be given to an old gray ford jalopy that was permanently parked in the ice forest. Then, the deep-sea clams would have mobility in the surface world and could be taxied to any location of their choice. But until the giant clams had finished their meditations, they would be going nowhere, and would remain at the bottom of the well in the dark, with no one but the naked fish fleets for company, not to mention the mystery of their unprecedented arrival.

Meanwhile, the amber stirrups are thrown into a box, which then gets gently lowered into a cherrywood cabinet. One of the frozen trees is now in the shape of a horseshoe, arched over in a fixed contortion. Sometimes these trees respond in this peculiar manner, taking on new shapes whenever something is slightly amiss. But then little do the frozen trees know of the coming march of the clams to the top of the well.

More frozen trees, now looking more and more like plastic horseshoes, are taking their interchangeable language commands and using them like electrical relays or circuits. The frozen horseshoe trees understand when a light bulb is placed inside of a plastic head of lettuce that gets sold from daylight crispers, residing beneath cozy igloos. The backwards light bulb is probably of the blue variety, as blue is the sacred color of malevolent leopard fruits that become available in the spring when the arctic ice storms aren't so bad. But even still, a frozen, magnetized rock pick is an excellent tool for frozen leopard fruit excavation. Somehow these great batches of speechless and mysterious produce will someday have their places at the table. They will someday serve as historical bricks to be used in some faraway, magnificent wall that shall be erected for an unmentionable purpose, but not for ordinary mortal, protoplasmic life.

8

The dead of winter, frozen solid, stopped the snails dead in their tracks. The icicles of blood on the castle wall showed encased fragments of lichens that had attempted to force their way into the interstices of the rock, in order to chemically and physically break the stones apart into smaller pieces. If this goal could be attained, then the prison walls might be removed piece by piece. With the removal of the dungeon walls, the sun would shine again and the ice would melt. If the ice dissipated, then all captured snails could roam free, never thereafter worrying about the tortures of salty desiccation. The trees would again bloom and the paired companions of the distant, brilliant ark would disembark from their vessel holding hands and feelers, and telling stories of forest feathers with Amerindian eagle demigods who came from secret limestone caves where green, phosphorescent tigers used to dwell within the darkest reaches of subterranean earth.

The soapstone figurines left behind by the last inhabitants are the lucky charms of grave-robbers who enter the shrouded domain bearing spikes and shocksticks. When the paintings on the walls are disturbed, haunted portraits of pumpkin-eating witches are restless and their eyes rove through the waves of a tidal break where majestic, fluid bicycles are discarded by lost frog-children who run to the safety of a dark ocean, where rigid games of checkers and state income taxes are replaced by delightful numerical sponges and anemones. These latter items are the umbrellas of mermaids and other saline saviors that are hiding until the ice melts from the polar caps.

A sun-hat is tossed onto a peg, and the blinds of a window are closed to the hot sun, for as long as the dark, desert cowboy counts his crystal fragments that leak through the transformed cracks in his black, gloved hands. All doorknobs lose their bulb-like appearance and become eyes, so that all one must do to pass through any threshold is to wink at the eyes on the doors. The doors are glass, ice and stone. Unmeltable, but flimsy in initial conception, so that pine logs of skeletons form tenebrous structures teetering on the edge of geriatric easy chairs. A papaya is hurled at the mailbox and a silver parakeet forces open its matchbox coffin to exclaim: "Peekaboo, I see you." The silver parakeet then withdraws back into its matchbox and sleeps for another five years, or until the dubious wake-up frog kiss arrives—or will it?

Frozen blood and mucous fragments fly like shattered glass, as a tank rolls over a discarded hot-dog and pretzel stand. The frogs in the road barely escape being crushed by heedless taxis, and the same human body that floated down the gutters of the street ten years ago has resurfaced with unpronounceable baseball hats. The city glacier releases obscenely large maritime insects of various colors, wings and spikes. Frustrated adults wear their unconscious green and orange tribal body paints and run through various municipal buildings, screaming of half-thought, half-baked, hare-brained schemes of sexual festivities and metallic bolts of hexagonal perfection that have become loose over the years and are in need of a caring ratchet that would restore order to the leaking flower madness, which enables ceiling fans to become swinging saws. These dangerous blades slice the unfortunate gladiators that get thrown into the air by remote-control psychic bombs placed and detonated by blonde beauties who wear drawstring leather uniforms as a matter of habit and honor.

A crawfish lights a candle in the shape of an obelisk and lowers it gently into an argon fish tank. The gas is ionized by the sparks, and the tank glows, illuminating armies of sea-ants that march in pairs over rocks and fallen logs. These aqua bullet ants are toxic and can fit into a thimble when the bathtub is drained of blood and ice. The toxic voice reverberates through the water and does the loop-to-loop of a roller-coaster track in under five seconds, as the fangs tear through a camping tent erected in the argon tank of irradiating gases—greenhouse gases that spell out the magic, far-reaching music for cats.

With their hair standing on end, mammals of uncanny hairiness wield their kitchen utensils and create their newest version of the twilight chorus, in the same way piano strings are mutilated by love and rhythm. The sea plants grow from crevices under the keys, and ivory toes are observed to be tapping on rhythmic bicycle pedals where rodents fear to tread. The icebreaker drops with its fragmented candles, matchsticks and snakeskin satchels. A jazzy end for a forest beginning that hops from limb to limb as a toad will do on a calm day without mountain winds of icy mists that sometimes blow down from higher levels, where owls sleep in the hollowed-out parts of trees. The same places where fires haven't yet rampaged the earth with brilliant countrycide that usually gets hidden from the tired, red eyes that reside in cinderblock rooms. The trees grow and fall while half-eaten bourgeois salads are abandoned next to tacky trees in money-hungry parking lots, where the story of the stolen heart is told and sold over and over again. The flipping coin lands on heads, then tails, and then heads again. If only the coin could be melted and recast as a bird's foot that can be clipped onto all worthy tree branches which have never been exposed to the tacky toxins of the salad-littered bourgeois parking lots. It was the purpose of the silver parakeets to smelt that terrible parking lot into an ingot of precious metal, a recasting of abandoned ambergris into a regenerative perfume. The silver parakeets apparently still haven't succeeded, but state opinion is that the fuse has been lit and now all parties involved must wait for the inevitable facial transformation. No more parking lot salads and cinderblock programs. Where would the eagle fly if it had the metallic perching bird's foot that was once a binary coin of non-dialectical misery?

Charlene, one of the arctic oyster/clam priestesses, remarks at how often she has forgotten to bring a fresh bottle of ketchup to the temple, in the same way ex-presidents forget to bring a bottle of wine to a housewarming homecoming when an adolescent pack of female baseball champions gets stranded in dusty, collegiate laundry rooms with fried chicken carcasses. They must fend off verminous love-rodents with fine whiskers and oblong skulls. The clam priestess thanks her hosts and returns to the frozen mountains. Someday the adolescent female baseball champions will become mollusk priestesses themselves, presiding in the frozen forest hills, but until that day arrives, they are content with their batting practice and playing patty-cake with the large leather shortstop mitts.

Without the safety of the shadows, the lantern snail glides from the clutches of the city courthouse and commits itself to working as a news reporter for a rural tabloid which features the tear-jerking stories of trees that only grow in the humid darkness of a nightscape occasionally touched by bursts of red and purple plasma. Thus, all bases are covered and the bullet ants clean the bones that are pushed into their anthill home. Talk about efficiency.

Passive stance. Clipper fish break their knuckles on a starburst chain-saw, as the bow of a violin glides back and forth across curly hair. The stained glass is fit into place, to help with the harvest of the moon, sending out mercury parcels every day at noon. This action helps with the humid sweat that is a xylophone of trouble. Can we look now at our cryptic pocket books that were suddenly forgotten?

Cats will retrieve their paws from the rocks in the mountain stream. They will perform this action proudly, in the same way their plastic young are retrieved from hot-spring tide-pools on camping trips. When these felines are able to sheathe their claws in such a respectable, civilized manner, their neighbors will adhere lantern snails to their foreheads in the effort to provide light to an otherwise dark conference room where shotguns and shells are conveniently placed under a vampire's pillow. Who disturbed the octopus when it was grooming itself with these lantern snails? The cats with the withdrawn claws immediately flee when a fire breaks out on one of the trees. The fire releases more arctic insects of morbid colors and spines, and a meteorite is caught in your pocket, and you collect the prize. The rocking horse blows onto the panes of ice in order to melt the frozen water, but it is not yet hot enough to achieve the desired effect.

Meanwhile birds, including silver parakeets, throw bubble gum at children and tap on a big bass drum. The drum is really a larval hatchery of capitalist tendencies that ferment like a block of blue cheese. Plasma glass floods the interior of the hatchery, creating transparent statues of the greediest of contortions, including tributes to laziness and idleness where barnacles have the silent opportunity to encrust themselves on the legs of pianos and other table legs like spiders. "Yes, the spiders are your friends," say the Sunday school teachers to their students, but the mothballs are the embryos caught up in the web of the spider as it waits in the dark for the correct spatial vibration which will inform it of the prismatic rhythm of leaves, deep within the puffy sleeves of maidens of the state. These maidens of the state also happen to be the ones who punch tickets and timecards with their erotic rabbit's teeth. The cards are gnawed and nibbled until all that remains are suspended sea rocks with heavy guitar eye-lids that reflect the smash of one coming on the left side panel. Hot, eager eyes consume sea lettuce as it grows from rock crevices in the stones of streams in the cat mountain, where the souls of songs are harvested for their optical brilliancy as well as for their archaeological comforts.

As soon as the silver parakeets return to their ritual nesting and mating grounds, they pair off and assume a restful repose in their solenoid alcoves. One more Technicolor week of wooden splinters. A dark shadow of ice is their glove, their light bulb capsule. The glass marbles are passed from one claw to another and obtuse angles regulate the trajectories of freak adult yes-men and yes-women with their mouths sewn shut. With a remote control click of the fingers, church-motels become the stomping grounds for barbecued toenails as they pay their taxes, eat their cancer and eventually die. Babies grow up and learn the same process. All the while, the sideways guitar showers the tree shadows with hydrogen flowers, producing a sensuous carrier tone through a skeleton of a homely giraffe. The illuminated skeleton is an edible book that can be ingested when the guardians of happy-enforced labor are not looking. The skeleton music of hydrogen plumes is what she's been searching for; it is her solenoid casing which will be great for magnetic personalities, forever silver.

Catflesh Countrycide

1

The hospitals were full of reckless family members who had inexplicably, voluntarily given themselves to the solar disease. Rude doctors and nurses pushed visiting, less-affected offspring aside in order to effectively contain the diseased inhabitants, with their sun-scorched, red-splotched faces and limbs. The blistered victims set out picnic blankets in the middle of gray stone ghettos, where the city refuse had been abandoned by a society whose morals had run dry over the course of centuries of humanity's glorious career as a worthy and wise pack of bipeds. It was easy to lose one's way on the dry streets, forever wary of random spiked tumbleweeds that threatened to graze one's legs during moments of distraction and careless sorrow. The architecture of the crumbling habitation was a soiled, discarded tissue. The blisters on the people's bodies and faces were too familiar, too agonizingly close to home.

To escape the horrors of the surface world of blistering mutation, prototype diving suits were developed. Each helmet had seven air hoses on top, where air lines contained filters and were screw-attached to holes in both the front and back of the breathing mask. The suits were used to travel to a mysterious underwater station several miles beneath the ocean, created by a technologically advanced species who had built the structure with oddly cramped doorways and corridors. The body of the first diseased human pioneer was found last week with the seven air hoses disconnected, with some of them partially reattached to the

66

wrong helmet ports in an odd mix-and-match fashion. Did the diver try to conserve air by breathing in a little of the stagnant muck that had flooded the station's primary airlock? The divers who found the body were confused by the horrible spectacle. They repopulated the vulnerable station in greater numbers to learn more.

Unfortunately, not enough replacements were sent. The ghostly first inhabitants cut air-hoses, isolated single humans, and killed them one by one, effectively decimating the diseased human diving crews. Much later, the scattered bodies of the isolated divers appeared all over the station, later discovered to be architecturally vast in size and depth. The primary inhabitants were never discovered in an official capacity, but they made it clear to the humans that they had no space to share with them in their dark, underwater world.

Back on the troubled surface, the diseased populace had been hit by another well-planned economic recession. Business after business obsessively reported a swift and total plummeting of their stocks, as they quickly added prayer-like promises of a better tomorrow, with food and festivities for all. In the schools, the wizened, elderly teachers officially switched over to a more conservative grading system, reevaluating students, with barely composed faces full of mock apology and false regret. The bountiful cheese that had been affixed to the teachers' grade book sandwiches was then cut by half, and thereafter the students' school-cheese report-card sandwiches were much leaner, only half as thick as before in the good old days.

Once the yellow-jacket colony has affixed their parasitoid larvae within the pages of the report-card cheese sandwich, the embryos feed from the recorded information with purely digital voraciousness. The birds, seated on the branches of the poverty-stricken classroom forest, chirp and clack in synchrony with the assimilation process of the knowledge bread. The sunset attaches threads of prismatic light to all of the cornerstones of the suburban ghost town. A meteorite burns magnificent feathers into the cracks of the wood-based concrete, and so new metropolitan fossil-bouquets are created for the bored and hungry children who walk the diseased halls where the initial outbreak occurred. A phosphorescent moth flutters across an electrical conduit, releasing a crowd of anxious circus-goers from a cramped broom locker, where chess pieces lovingly decorate subsonic spider webs spun by the previous inhabitants, who have now taken up residence behind the wooden grandfather clock where the grenade launcher was hidden.

The biochemical foliage is a tattoo of birds in flight, with elbow macaroni as a sheltering lodge for confused ants that left their mud hills for bigger and better things in the city. Friends in the metropolis tickle themselves with coffee and paint images of human ears all over their bodies in the attempt to recreate an externalized museum of prismatic light of the binary code variety. If only this canned history were manufactured inside of flower pollen instead of blue mortar. One street corner attracts the nauseating winds of a hurricane whose eye is a glass palace of rotating hourglasses, whose sands are bleached to an avian pink color. Once the hourglasses have intimately poured their sands into ancestral patterns, a flaring lamp of yellowed antiquity bursts through the weak plaster of the hurricane, invading the primacy of the eye of the storm, who is then forced to look elsewhere to concentrate its microscopic investigation of falling pinecones and other external wooden paraphernalia. The clear storm drifts across to the other side of the street and sweeps away a scorched grocery store reeking of chicken fat. The hurricane continues to scatter winds and pink avian sands across its uncertain, subconscious path, and weak primates run.

The flaring lamp of yellowed antiquity falls prey to greedy dust mites, and the lampshade itches and flinches under the sleepless humidity of mosquito bites. The suffering in the reaction cauldron is unforgiving as forks and knives are smelted down to a molten tumor that adheres to the porcelain beauty spa where loveless mannequins frequent when they go on vacation to twilight strips like Las Vegas, where electronic ratchets pull the silhouettes from closets and shoeboxes, when the clothes of conformity are saved for cowardly Monday gatherings.

The clothes shake like limpid snails that have been decompressed and stretched out like red pencils, which deserve to transition over into the next barnyard, where a lazy ox munches on dried hay. All of a sudden, happy farm hands burst out from behind the inclined hay and throw an angular lantern at the combustible material. The sensuous fire burns behind active fingernails, and so the claws grasp at the soiled drapes of the farmhouse, where the ox family whistles Dixie while staring at the geomorphic shapes in the ancestral wooden wall paneling. The shapes of the resurrected oxen with discerning heads bowed are etched into the geomorphic wood. They resume their diamond stable activities at all levels and inclines. Suddenly a tech-writer falls from a short tree and breaks his ankle on a fossilized dinosaur bone that was growing at the bottom of the tree. Upon being rushed to the electric disease hospital, the tech-writer is pampered by infected nurses with large red blotches on their faces. The infected nurses hold out their hands in sympathy, banshees of the concrete mortar of genetics. A brain pushes a coffee saucer off a waiting room table and so the expensive silver clock of false leanings is broken and re-energized at the same time. A flute plays a somber marching song as a large, unearthly hand reaches from around the darkened corner in order to better absorb the released telepathy with its bared gray skin. The inherent underground telepathy of the large, gray hand has broken the plaster off the wall, and so an exploited, foolish nun is left with an unwanted panoramic view of the world from the luxury of her cloistered bedroom. The wooden splinters of the stone fireplace mantle fall into the large copper soup pot, and so the frog broth is now spoiled and barren, eventually inaccessible to the hydrogen boots that lick the coals underneath the pot.

The cascade of bone fragments from the other end of the diseased hospital's hallway calls out for purple retribution. Ribbons are tied around dead fingers and mangled corpses are stuffed into freezer capsules in the morgue on Floor 13, where only privileged, blistered people may go during their patriotic Coca-Cola flute breaks. Where did the blistered, parasitic hotel come from, and at which date was such a dark building erected? Who disabled the ice-locks that allowed the frozen fish sheep to fall from the egotistical freezer?

A brain pushes another coffee saucer to the edge of the hospital break room table, where it falls to a diseased floor that has been congested with genital dust. A transistor within an operculum flower grows from the muted soil, and the blue desert opens up its gorgeous eyes to the woman that birthed it, raised it, and released it into the world of celibate neon hatchet fish who play invisible guitars with their teeth. These fleets of fish slowly circle the sinking blue desert, and envelop the globe with their forcefully static tails that move even when they don't want them to move. The blue desert rests at the bottom, on a pale bed of sand, and begins to categorize the lost people of the sea with a resilient candor and an opalescent positive cynicism that expels webbed threads made from the creaking footsteps of children.

2

After the laboratory tables are cleared of reaction flasks and apple pie desserts, the experimenters take a stroll through the forbidden bamboo gardens. The running streams in the bamboo gardens yield fresh water to thirsty hands. Bordering the garden are hills of dirt that have been hollowed out to create a horizontally planar fossilized Ferris wheel. Each hollowed-out compartment is a seating cubicle on the Ferris wheel. In some of the compartments hang rope nets with bundles of human skeletons. The bones on some of the skeletons are coated with an opaque mother-of-pearl secretion, suggesting the presence of a rather large and eccentric mollusk. Part of the fun for the amused scientists is that they can pick up small, marble-sized, mother-of-pearl spheres that lay at their feet in the bamboo garden and then throw them at the rope-suspended human skeletons in the fossilized amusement-park ride. As soon as the mother-of-pearl sphere hits the pearly-coated skeletons, a metallic sound is heard, and the scientists become happy. They look at their own hands and then run through the bamboo garden shrieking like stuck lobsters. After the wondrous garden is vacated, verminous mammals crawl out of the shadows to investigate the scene, including the pearly coated metallic skeletons that now have become tortured musical instruments hung within restraining nets of rope.

Throughout the mud-brick hills, other hollowed remains are found, a veritable Pompeii of an amusement park. Entire compartments are opened up to the air, with happy plastic skeletons hanging around within their torture rope nets and lustrous bivalve secretions. A tuft of wood is left behind from one attraction box, and the coated bones fall to the floor in a musical cascade. The walls burn from the new atmosphere, and the precious wallpaper blisters and peels at the touch of a luminescent bony hand that once caressed the labial palps of an extracted bivalve who was thrown out of the water at too early of a young age. The folds of the ear can perceive the slightest sound, and so the mind shall build geometrical castles of green music festering within the dried cracks of skin that used to reside in an emotional desert. This happens to be the very same desert where clams clamored for tuberculosis on a dried riverbed and where flammable goldfish adorned a cursed christmas tree that had lost its needles and was in need of a few medical adhesive bandages. The dryness of the desert was hereby proclaimed too dangerous for clams as well as for goldfish, and so the bluish-green-lit desert with its turquoise sands became a legal deathtrap for any tourists or sea-life within a mile of that oven-like sector. A sleepy child adjusts its loincloth and rises from a bed of dried plants in order to face the arid day. The birds greet the young urchin and the daily history lessons are analyzed while cliché coffee commercials can be heard blaring from a local radio station. Even though ladybugs can alter their spots, it wasn't possible to stop the evil processions of coffee commercials that flooded the blistering turquoise desert separated from the fertile bamboo gardens by way of a fossilized amusement park. It was as if night and day were barely divided by shiny musical wishbones.

As night falls, the blue snails glide from under their rocks and greet the azure sunset. The flammable goldfish and desiccated clams understand this cue, and fall silent from their usual banter and idle chatter. Without the presence of the snails, the clams and fish would remain forever mired in their superficially transparent world of useless coffee and lipstick commercials. As the blue snails glide across the moonlit turquoise sands towards the babbling clams and goldfish, they conform to a V-shaped convoy pattern and brace themselves for reckless jokes and monotone Christmas carols.

The leader of the snails cautiously ascended a shard of petrified wood while his comrades waited behind, still tentatively in formation. The lead snail exclaimed:

"Stop these insipid monotone Christmas carols at once! How can you dare attempt to sing about silver bells, fruitcakes and reindeer with a limited voice in the B-flat range? Instead, I urge you to turn your gaze to the full moon, a competent celestial agent capable of making hair grow on your hairless palms, and honeycombs grow within the nodal branch-crotches of special eucalyptus trees from California (which ultimately leads to mentholated honey). There's no reason why you should incessantly babble about coffee and other commercialized beauty products. Now shut your mouths and get out your party hats and paperclip spectacles!"

Upon being commanded so by the lead snail, both the desiccated river-clams and the flammable goldfish put away their communicative toothpaste, and the mollusks hobbled over to where the snails were encamped. River stones separated themselves from the clutches of blistered wallpaper, and the snails grasped at the frozen splinters of copper seeping from the stones. Meanwhile, the dried clams and paper goldfish produced colorful party hats the size of cherries and placed them on their heads. They reached under petrified wood fragments and withdrew miniaturized spectacles made from carefully bent paperclips. After the dried sea-life had donned their party hats and microglasses, they were ready to partake of the festive species triumvirate. Fish danced with snails while the dried clams played an orchestra of violins. Next, the clams danced with the fish while the snails played banjos. Finally, to be completely balanced, the blue snails danced with the dried clams while the fish played sullen tap-dancing ballads with an antique collection of bronze piccolos. After the last fragrant dance, a degenerate flammable goldfish spoke up:

"Ah, dear friends, the time has drawn nigh for all good jungle clams to come to the aid of their party, which means us. We are searching for a plant-like corridor that might allow us to send telegrams to a Mexican grocery store located perhaps fifty miles from here. Should you help us contact this Mexican grocery store, we would reward you handsomely with some voodoo chicken feathers, which we once collected from a discarded crown of thorns that had been hidden under a naive girl's Dutch oven. These bloody chicken feathers will remain meek and mild for now, but some day they will open a doorway to a stormy mountain top whose trails are marked by painted skulls and crossbones, where glorious sunsets give new meaning to the word "evil," such that evil will become much more sharply defined than Nietchze's moral force that happens to go against the wishes of the cowardly powers-that-be. No, this feathery invitation to evil can only be offered once per lifetime, and not any more often than that. The blissfully wretched mountain to be released by these ticklish, innocuous voodoo feathers shall always remain dark and foreboding, and yet will always contain a superior strain of mutagenic coconut milk. The evil coconuts that grow atop this evilly displaced temperate mountain, with shaky trails marked with colorfully painted skulls and crossbones, are not endemic to this evil region, but were once imported by a shipwrecked porcupine that thankfully was rescued and then conducted back to its dubious place of origin—i.e. these evil mountains of which I speak. When my paper goldfish brethren and sistren obtain translocative passage to this lustfully evil domain, we will access the mutagenic coconut milk and rejuvenate our rather fragile fins and other appendages. You see, this mutagenic coconut milk was once mythologically thought by a pack of heathen ragamuffins to be a sassy fountain of youth, capable of regenerating entirely fragmented and lacerated souls, capable of rebuilding the stones of the musky castle heart. Without the mutagenic coconut milk, all earthbound creatures would remain mired within the insipid shackles of the subconscious holy family, within discontented civilization. There were once many of us who doubted the existence of this regenerative mutagenic coconut milk, but now life has led us to seek it out, to put an end to the droll, drossy lifestyles that we have pursued in times past."

Upon hearing this passionate speech, one of the dried clams spoke up: "Wow, that was quite a sermon, Daddio. Unfortunately we desiccated clams have no means for you to contact this mythical Mexican grocery store. We clams live a meager existence, unhappily neither with good sex nor with mutagenic doorknobs to lead us to corridors of prismatic fluid glass. As we are here, lost like you, in this beautiful sandy turquoise desert, we are mightily tempted to join you in your cause to find the mutagenic coconut milk. Perhaps you will share with us the full extent of your knowledge on this subject, for we, too, find ourselves broken and in need of a mending of the spirits. Every day we rise to greet the blue sun of severe heat that shines down upon us. Every day we meditate upon wholeness, yet the intimacy of fragmented face dimensions draws our attention away from our empty pursuits of sensual denial, and so we shudder in waves of green and blue as a creaking shutter opens and closes with every gust of wind. We see bricks in the wall sliding out of place, and we also hear the din of a rooster eyeball as it rotates upon the diamond needle of an upside-down turntable. We have platinum and bronze keys, but they are useless on these wire cabinets that grow beneath our feet. All in all, we live each night for the snail dance as well as the embrace of your piscine skeleton. You are the chapter two of our lives before the story was taken away by the hot wind that came through this honey-combed gully the night before."

As quickly as those last words were uttered, the hot wind returned and carried away the paper goldfish and dried clams. The snails were luckier by managing to remain adhered to some gall bladder rocks embedded in the sand like a soft mosaic of nausea. In the morning, the shadows of iron railroad spikes appeared as if a monstrous forest became the buoy markers for a new train system to be constructed at a later date. At this moment, the stones in the sand chose to converse with the blotchy clouds above:

"Ooh, your reactor is getting overheated, like a garbled telephone answering machine. I can't see you now, but I feel that you would benefit from exploring the wonders of a lava parachute. You've explored the formulas and equations up until now, and all you've done is boxed yourself in with pickles and cotton candy. Surely there is a better way to translate your alphabet from its soup form into something more understandable, like the soft, furry ears of a mentally receptive cat."

The clouds in the sky responded to the stones embedded in the sand: "Yes, we suppose that you are correct. We would not have been banished from Earth's lowly surface had we not attempted to hike up a mountain that was rumored to have vast subterranean copper mines. You see, we would use this copper, in a purified form, as a focal point through which to arc our green lightning, which seems to entertain beautiful, young maidens long into the night, even after their parents have put them to bed."

Even though the drifting clouds had finished expressing their anthropomorphically complex thought, an epileptic seismic wave shook the ground, ultimately disrupting the bird-like listening behavior of the embedded blue stones. Columns of seawater appeared out of the cracks, and disturbed, displaced lonely sealife appeared, very much perplexed. As a test-tube is inverted, spilling its electrostatic contents, a child's lollypop is carefully wrapped in electric spider web to be kept safe and sound in a taxi's trunk until the day of a Jewish wedding. Only until the glass is broken will a flaming motorcycle appear, bearing the iconical crest of a gray bird from the cosmos who lost its spare wheel while in orbit around the gravitationally greedy body of Jupiter.

Although the strange upward-stepping cycle was momentarily broken, false corridors of mirrored opposites reared their depressing, confusing heads, and within the outer lands, fat-lipped popcorn people continued to scratch their heads. But even while in orbit around the Jovian gas giant, the Jewish wedding motorcycle albatross felt the immanent break-up of the corroding glass bottle cruelly suspended in a shockproof organic gel. The corrosion of the bottle was a welcoming sign of greater things to come, when the electric fuses of eye sockets would take on a secondary symbolic significance that no powerful executive officer could discern with beady, sleep-deprived eyes. Once the albatross motorcycle was fused with the glass in a burst of Vulcan flame, the indigo universe began to peek around one of the frozen moons.

A hand makes a signal that gets relayed to a hopscotch board, which then is passed onto a lamp, illuminating a sickly, faded piano keyboard. The cracked, yellow ivory spells out a written language on the above page with indecipherable runes. The lemon tree burns, and its acrid cargo spills into a godly, forbidden swimming pool of luxury. People come running and attempt to tie tree branches together to make fanciful arches, but their eyes peel, and they stumble into each other, wielding shaky magnetic cans of forbidden pet food. The dogs will lie still today, under the fear that they will be beaten with iron pikes. Surely this was no ordinary albatross motorcycle wedding.

Coconut man raises his iron pike, and demolishes the palm-beach swimming pool, which then bleeds a thick secretion composed mainly of guava jelly. This unforgettable sequence of events produces marked fear in the raven eyes of two-dimensional people made of jig-sawed wood, burn victims of passion and apple pie, and all flowers that grow on the North American continent. When the puzzle pieces are thrown onto the embers, they burn like a library of degenerate cookbooks dating back to the nineteenth century, when mayonnaise and bread used to shut people up for a few hours. Ancestral tombstones complete the code, and so the past is stacked against the future in a morbid, experimental conspiracy. "Let's make as many monsters as we can and then set them upon each other," says papa tree-man, as he caresses his menagerie of smothered wooden children. And so the continuing cycle begins, and micro-history crawls forward, like a plagued crab back tracking in reverse.

This particularly plagued crab, caught in the back track of oppressive fire-hose wooden madness corridors, becomes a nauseating impostor of the child of Mother Spider. Fortunately, Mother Spider returns and squashes her false offspring like a bug. Mother Spider climbs the arms of statues and then creates a web of brilliance, innervating the stone arms as they are weathered by the wind. The webs become veins, embodying the inner fabric of the statues. These statues will pay tribute to their mother, and will also piss on the wooden postcards who tried to pass themselves off as family. A spider on the arm is quite a bite, and so the statue children carry the spiders as if they were special wristwatches that would catch flies like clockwork. This moment of familial bliss is interrupted by a coarse howl that ruptures the air with teeth and nails, erupting from every pore on the statues' bodies. Mother Spider watches over her children with a wink of the eyes, with a closing of an electric moth's wing. The sands travel upstream like a lustful operon that managed to blow a few hydrogen bonds accidentally, releasing a sensuous cassette of enzyme deactivators. The race is on after the sands have finished their fascinating movement across the backs of scaly reptiles with angry tails and dancing eyes, which light on the wingtips of the hyperactive, hiccuping moths. A shooting star arcs over the next hill but the moths don't care.

Your magnified cliché is a tattoo on my arm. Your roses speak but the thorns scratch my watch. The webbing tears at the wrist, but the clock still ticks. I rest under the safety of your skin, like a blanket full of abnormal fruit bats treading upon necrotic cockroaches. Your spectacles are jubilantly removed and I see you through the eyes of a child's fruit bat. Your eyes remove more of the prisms from my fragmented hand. Instead, you set fire earrings upon the steps leading up to the dark house, an intimate homely metaphor for something else unearthed behind an even larger castle, where grotesque, faceless children play amid mold, philth and rotted books, heedless of the passage of leopard-skinned automatons maneuvering overhead during those cold, snowy winters. A place where smiling youth congregate beneath another wooden impostor. The final climb of the ladder yields even more frivolous fruit bats, yet that's the reason why you glide in on an ocean smile.

Now that you have the spider on your wrist, time will always bend backwards for you. Your spaghetti fingers will grasp the key chain, and lights on the floor will show your legs to the dark spiders sleeping in webs in the ceiling corners of the tabloid penthouse room serving as an electrical relay station for flying fruit bats to be someday anchored to your fingers in the form of a ruby ring. The magic ring is a fresh, wet teardrop in the process of falling from your cheek onto the plate, and we shall hold your spidery eyes forever in a clasp of broken glass that will mop the floor clean of all bloodied bandages that used to conceal your hidden beauty.

3

On the roundhouse spiral, the latent tectonics erupt through beautiful bourgeois houses, and the living structures grow new extensions, wings and rooms, all at eccentric, acute angles. The children are roused from their beds with red wonder in their eyes as the rats and verminous insects come through the unstable cracks in the floor. The children discard their sugar cereals, flinging them against the paper walls. Streetlights topple and crash through living-room windows, and fruit bats phase in and out of the paper domestic walls. All houses containing agitated children sprout fire escapes, and so the youngsters grow fangs and descend the ladders into the streets. With the swarming pack unleashed, the rats and verminous insects are no match for the transformed children. Grimy rodents and large, palm-sized insects are grabbed and penetrated with sharp human teeth. Fluids are sucked from the verminiferous corpses, and then the small bodies are discarded, like aluminum drink cans. The rampage of the children continues down the street, carried by a cold wind. The chilling draft blows past disturbing statues and busts of famous bipedal celebrity apes, causing the sickening human forms to glow with a nauseating neon blue light. The wind seems to acquire a mind of its own, purposefully travelling from one blue head to another, causing all streetlights to become superfluous and die out.

The war planes suicide themselves on the city, instead of dropping bombs. The exploding aircraft cause the houses of the blue vampire children to be upturned, cast aside, and ruptured wide-open, allowing even more children, who are sleeping under black dirt with giant larval insects, to awaken and emerge from the putrid soil. Quite a far cry from the average weekend camping trip.

On another continent, war officers hike down green trails in the nude, checking up on their beehives and hopscotch boards. The worn trails have conducted many greedy feet up to the wooden fortress of fine books and morbid paper flowers. The bookshelves carry aeons of degenerate salad recipes, as well as the false novels of artificial lives of unrequited life. So much moldy wood and paper shown off by a sickly blue sun. In the pretentious drawing room, a general bends over to examine the oozing, noxious brain of a block of blue cheese. The bluish-gray creases and folds in the brain of the cheese exhale a rancid odor as well as thick, prehensile hair-like appendages that writhe and grasp towards the peering, vulnerable face of the general, who always maintains a safe distance from the captive, malevolent cheese. After the cheese brain is stabbed with a blade, it is discarded in the sewer where it will multiply to grotesque sizes and new incarnations. The foreboding lamp in the corner, cast in the shape of a human head, looks on with silent obsession, waiting for the right moment to strike.

Suddenly the walls of the war room shed their cheap covering to reveal tier upon tier of cardboard matchboxes. The drawers from the matchboxes slide forward to yield perky grasshoppers that raise their emerald compound eyes to survey the peculiar room, now littered with female undergarments of every fabric and color, thrown to the floor after the departure of the general and his prehensile blue cheese. The curious grasshoppers leap from the open matchboxes, ignoring the thrashing remnants of the blue cheese brain that reside on the weathered table, completely ruined. Once the insects have pushed themselves under the crack of the door, they are free to travel down a fragrant stone path that leads to the inner courtyard of the fortress. Seated in the lovely courtyard is a beautiful maiden with an impish smile and wide, wondrous eyes.

The maiden then said to the green insects: "Ah, I see you've had the chance to admire my unkempt collection of sweaty undergarments. I designed all of them myself. If you will, you might also want to survey the upstairs area of this mansion; you all might find those recreational chambers to be quite interesting. For now, each of you should take one of these candles and then sit upon my shoulders and fragrant, soft hair, so that we might ascend the mansion steps together and illuminate the forgotten pleasures of this forbidden house."

After the grasshoppers chirped their agreement, they took the small candles, lit them, and positioned them on the dorsal part of their abdomens between the backs of their musical legs, and then sat down upon the hair and shoulders of the mysterious youth. As the woman ascended the purple velvet staircase with the young insects, the flickering light of the candles illuminated many a glass cabinet containing strange, well-polished specimens of fine metal shrapnel, as if grenades made of gold were used to tear silver and platinum targets asunder. This beautiful shrapnel would have been best suited as a finely crafted garnish for a set of honeycomb bee hive salad bowls.

As soon as the attractive maiden and her company reached the top of the stairs, the woman touched each of her firm breasts with a copper monkey wrench, causing dim, green ceiling lights to become lit. With the upper level illuminated by a pungent green light, it became apparent to the grasshoppers that the uppermost floor of the house was being used as a feline embryo farm. Lining the walls were giant, clear champagne bottles, with a developing lion fetus swimming in each. An umbilical cord ran from every embryo to a large, centralized pumpkin, from which the developing animals apparently derived nourishment.

The fair maiden said: "You see, due to the shortage of hot lion meat, we grow and raise our own specimens here. Once the creatures are mature, we release them into underground lakes with Styrofoam couches so that they might live a complete and happy life underground. Every year or so we survey these underground cavern lakes to track their progress and assess their needs. As the lions are born sterile, we must repopulate these aqua-caverns twice a year and provide them with condoms and TV dinners. Sometimes they even send us postcards during the holiday season. Therefore, my associates and I who create these underground lions consider ourselves to be quite self-sufficient, and so we have no cares or worries about what happens to the rest of the world. If the masses out there develop fangs and suck out the viscera of giant cockroaches for sustenance, we don't care; we only wish them well and urge them to 'keep in touch.' My associates and I truly enjoy employing these euphemisms; pretty words are what make the world go 'round."

After the sightly maiden finished her green-light explanations, the grasshoppers asked to be left in peace for a few moments so that they might have the opportunity to discuss all of the phenomena they had just observed. The young, mysterious woman left the vast attic chamber and descended the purple velvet stairs, silently. The grasshoppers found themselves alone, with only a few of the candles left. They would have to hurry. As they leisurely hopped to each of the gestation bottles, the grasshoppers regarded the developing lion fetuses who twitched in some cases and were even highly animate in others. After these confused observations proceeded for a short while, it became possible for them to hear the shouting of human adults through the wooden floors. The ruckus sounded like a man and a woman bickering over something perhaps trivial, yet the violence of their voice intonations was unpleasant to the tiny ears in their insect legs, if not disturbing. Eventually the brood of five hundred or so grasshoppers made the unanimous decision to vacate the awesome house, however benevolent or malevolent its inhabitants really were. The green insects knew that they might really be the experimental playthings of these humans, after having been incubated in a matchbox hive hidden behind the war room wall, that their proposed escape plan might have been somehow anticipated by these hairless apes, but they felt that the risk was worth taking. The plan was that they would avoid both the snide, experimenting humans in the castle as well as the surrounding countryside of insect-eating child-vampires. Their alternative was to seek out the subterranean, artificial lions in their underground lakes.

Eventually the consensus was that the green grasshoppers should try to access the subterranean lakes by way of the convenient sewer system. The insects descended the purple velvet stairs and promised the maiden their complete cooperation, after they made a trip to the bathroom, of course. Once the legion of grasshoppers had occupied the restroom and closed the door, they immediately flushed themselves down the toilet, saying goodbye to that accursed house of genetic engineering forever.

The passage of the grasshoppers into the sewer world was a terrifying one, no doubt, but eventually they regained consciousness in a rank cesspool and navigated their way downward, downward, ever downward. Along the way, they encountered many strange sewer inhabitants, some inanimate, some not. After many days of exhaustive travel without food, their perceptions of time became warped due to the absence of sunlight. Along their journey, the green insects had many heated arguments over the usefulness of their mission, of whether they would ever have a somewhat non-dysfunctional life again. Despite their doubts and fears, they stuck to their journey and kept track of one another by way of musical chirps, and so they minimized their casualties.

Eventually after an inordinate passage of time, the grasshoppers reached a glowing computer interface panel that would probably give them access to the lair of the subterranean bioengineered lions. The green grasshoppers had no trouble opening the digital lock; it was only a matter of correctly matching pretty colors with pretty numbers. With the lock released, the door to the lion lair opened to reveal some odd equine creatures no taller than the height of a ruler. Their hooves were monodigital and their transparent flesh was bioluminescent, displaying their intricate internal organs. The divergent flesh horses regarded the bedazzled grasshoppers with a sense of muted indignancy:

"Who are you and why are you here?" [In fluent English, of course—the editor]

"Please don't be angry, but we are here to make contact with the underground lake lions, of whose existence we learned from their human creators on the surface world. We came here to find these lions because we found ourselves in total disgust with the way humans manage the surface world and ruin the experience of life. We have found that if people are not tampering with nature, altering it, then they are piggishly consuming it, as some bipedal apes are in the habit of greedily exsanguinating and eviscerating giant cockroaches, for instance. This is not the type of world we want to raise our brood in, and so we have sought the council of the underground lions, who are accustomed to living external to the presence of the human vermin. Besides, we can play a mean electric-guitar flamenco lullaby, and we also believe in the goodness of wood carving instruction. Please let us pass, so that we might obtain the advice of these legendary nether-worldly lions."

"We will allow you to pass, but be warned that we do not take kindly to those who insult our feeding practices, for we are not ordinary horses—we are Carnivhorses!" The transparent bioluminescent equines then unzipped their fanny-packs and produced a tasty picnic lunch of live, wriggling cockroaches. Their specially adapted canine incisors punctured the chitinous skulls of the roaches and the loathsome insects were completely sucked dry of all bodily fluids. The Carnivhorse who had spoken to the grasshoppers, belched with pride and said: "Buen provecho. And now we will be on our way, as you will be on yours. Give our regards to the felines; gosh they're great neigh-bors to have!"

The grasshoppers thanked the ghostly Carnivhorses and entered the opened portal that led to the lake.

Somewhere up in the surface world, in an ocean, the tail of a whale moved in a self-directed circular motion, expressing lustful inclinations toward infinity. On the nearby shore, the light poles began to dance in the same way a womb contracts with utter and total plasticality. Megacyclers churn out fragrant buttermilk, and the streets are drenched with a parachute rain, melting the heavens to a reduced pool of molten tin that cracks and blisters when doused by a cloud of quinine-laced water. A hiccup from a cash-register spells relief for the carrot-topped molten tin as it regurgitates ingested kneecaps found when exploring the cracks in a flower shop that installs fists instead of light bulbs into the sockets.

The magnetic locks on a honeycomb salad bowl are released, and so the magic flower shop enjoys an onrush of new clientele that flock to the store in order to select only the choicest of fragrant flowers for their nectar. The special flower sweetness will eventually be placed on the salad bar to be enjoyed by the neighborhood people, especially the elderly who live in Florida and who wear leopard skin pantyhose under their wristwatches. An American Indian regards a tree and feels an intense wave of well being. Once the whales have migrated onto the land and begun having intimate relations with the blue skyscrapers, a carrot peeler is hurled by the Indian towards a hotdog cart that plays French music and has windshield wipers, so that on even the rainiest of days, people can still see the hot dogs behind the panes of steamy glass. When the hotdog cart loses a wheel, the owner laughs and slaps his legs. Eventually the wheel is replaced back onto the axle, but the French owner still laughs and slaps his legs while the giant whales are seen intimately coiled around the electric skyscrapers. These particular whales are wearing headphones, listening to eerie, perverted flute music that propels them to drool fragrant trails of saliva that smell of pungent ambergris, a sexual proto-perfume that the grand old gals of fifth avenue will fight over someday when they learn of the latest fads, like the alligator skin walking canes and the beautiful feline mirrors that they will use when they need to look at themselves in the middle of the night. Yet even still, the French hotdog man laughs and slaps his legs, while adjusting the cart's windshield wipers and gently touching each of the juicy hotdogs.

The French hotdog man pushes his cart to the seedy docks of the emotionally incomplete metropolis and watches the seagulls fly over the beach. The seagulls are heedless as they grasp at imaginary motorcycles that burst into flame. After they ignite, they dematerialize and travel to a distant, dark star where they will enjoy their sumptuous and excessive wedding night. The French hotdog man laughs heartily and slaps his legs. He then draws his attention to a throng of gambling people who bet their money on the outcome of a duel between a blue lobster and a crab. The two crustaceans are matched in size, but not in intellectual thirst. The foolish lobster prances on its long legs while the crab tweaks its eyestalks with its strong but gentle claws, removing the annoying seaweed that sometimes grows there. The referee throws a lit firecracker into the water, and upon detonation, the two hard-shells begin to grapple with each other. The fight ends when the crab ties on a bib and has lobster claws for breakfast. The winning members of the attentive crowd clap their hands and collect their winnings from the lobster losers. After the money is forked over, the crowd disperses, and the referee removes the cleaned shells of the dead lobster from the aquarium. The crab is gently patted on the behind and allowed to sleep for a few hours until the next fight. In the meantime, the sky grows dark and Sol dims to a dull olive gray color. A tentacle of solar plasma arcs from the darkened sun to the forehead of the crustacean referee, and her head becomes filled with malevolent solar plasma, leading her to renounce her Jehovah's Witness religion and become an avid solar hockey advocate. The French hotdog man laughs and then slaps his legs.

Down in the dark, underneath the city, the grasshoppers finally end their first pilgrimage. With meandering thoughts of the glowing Carnivhorses still on their sticky brains, the green merry insects meet their first underwater lion, who rises above the surface of the underground lake and regards the former group with abnormally large, bioluminescent eyes. In fact, the entire body of the engineered feline is glowing and hairless, with the same transparent flesh of the Carnivhorses. The lion appears mistrustful and carefully eyes the expectant grasshopper pilgrims as she reaches obsessively into her purse to withdraw a fresh tube of red lipstick. As the bioluminescent lioness applies the lipstick to her mouth in the same way an inept monkey would, she growls a slow, melancholic marching tune. After the red smear of greasy monkey-face lipstick has been applied, the lioness replaces her makeup and asks the grasshoppers why they have violated the underground lair of the glowing biogenetically engineered lions. The grasshoppers tell their woeful story, causing teardrops to fall from the lioness' imposing eyes. The artificial feline reaches for some tissues from her purse and says:

"Oh, so finally you have come. Our records have indicated that some spiritual brethren would someday flee the surface world and come see us for a visit. Of course, my husband, bless his transparent heart and penis, doesn't believe these legends, but I still do, and so do some of my clonal family. Why don't we go meet them? I'll introduce you to them. I think you'll find that despite the darkness, we lions tend to live a quiet and peaceful, rarely disturbed life down here. And because we are bioluminescent, our electric bills tend to be low," explained Madge, the name of the transparent lioness with the red, greasy monkey-face lipstick.

Madge created several boats for the grasshoppers out of hardened, low-density clay that was mined by the lions in their subterranean lair. As she led the small boats with an attached cord, the grasshoppers benefited from the phosphorescent glow of the artificial lioness, which illuminated exquisitely sculpted bas-reliefs in the cavern walls, apparently executed by the felines themselves. After a short stint of passing through winding cavern tunnels half-submerged by dark water, the lioness and grasshoppers arrived at what presumably was the central cavern, currently occupied by several of the bioluminescent felines. After Madge introduced the journeying insects to her fellow tribesman and explained their plight, the other lions had equivocal responses.

"So what if they hate humanity. For all we know, they could be just naive pawns, allowed to come this far just to disrupt our lives further," said one hostile lion who was adorned with a necklace constructed from the shells of red cave-clams.

Another lion spoke: "Sure we don't completely trust them, but at this point our lives have been so shaken up by the monkeys that a little more disruption wouldn't matter. I think that any group willing to escape by flushing themselves down a toilet is worthy of being taken seriously. It's amazing what desperation can make a body do. I, Coldmouth, propose that we outfit these brave insects with provisions and then escort them to the borders of our domain where we will put them on a trail that will lead upward to a tiny island, which is small by our standards but sufficiently large enough for them to comfortably populate."

After a little more persistence, Coldmouth and Madge sold the generous idea to the rest of their comrades. While the two supportive felines helped the grasshoppers ready themselves by gathering supplies, the rest of the luminous animals reclined on their floating Styrofoam furniture and curiously eyed the insects. After escorting the grasshoppers to the exit from the lair of the bioengineered lions, Madge and Coldmouth apologized for their colony members' mistrustfulness:

"You see," declared Coldmouth, "our people are constantly harassed by the Homo sapiens twice a year, where they exterminate our old and weak and replace them with new clonal units. Even though they provide us with comfortable furniture and the means for us to be agriculturally self-sufficient, we feel that through the modification of our parent, progenitor race of lions, our lives are cheapened and nothing but somebody else's experiment, and that's no way to live. Nevertheless, we have been secretly working on a way for us to reproduce ourselves. In fact, we have even succeeded, but have been tragically forced to destroy our new offspring in order to keep our activities hidden from the bipeds. Despite that awful secret, we will someday soon leave this domain for another, faraway location unknown to you and the humans, before they return here again. There, we will still be self-sufficient and self-reproducing so that we will no longer be controlled by the bipeds, and so that our destroyed offspring will not have died in vain. That is all we will tell you. By the time the humans come back this way, it will already be too late to find us. Now go, and may your second pilgrimage be even more successful than the epic first one." Madge nodded, said her farewell, and the grasshoppers returned the gesture. After the gate had sealed behind them, the insects followed the prescribed path, reached their uncharted destination and were never again seen by prying eyes.

Oblivious to the passage of the green grasshoppers, a pair of neon chopsticks falls from a nightclub to the street below, where they shatter.

The rarefied argon disperses and a street lamp groans, as if it had bad gas. The wail of a police siren approaches, but the car passes the club in favor of investigating a crime scene at a public parking lot down the street. All of a sudden, a nickel-plated umbrella falls from the sky and dark clouds appear. The large threads of lightning permeate many of the, uh, buildings and cars, and even a few people who end up falling to the ground in convulsions. Next, the street and all surfaces manifest a half inch-thick coating of ice, which confuses the sleeping birds greatly. The slumbering pigeons and ravens grumble and straighten their 1970's disco sleeping caps. And thus the world is born anew!

When the second clock ticks as the first one once did, it hiccups on the chime of every hour. The clock convulses from time to time, sending out plant-like branches that sprout tiny orange leaves, suggesting that the clock is preoccupied with other tasks of importance. Noisy children come running and hang plastic beads on the branches, as if they were adorning a sleeping god who had just distributed tin commandments written on aluminum foil and then gone to bed. A mason lodge, very well lit from its numerous windows, sits all by itself on an abandoned mountain-side. Its numerical address just so happens to be printed on a label that is stuck to the back of the clock in the city. A breeze of wintergreen interrupts a woman as she passionately kisses the minute and hour hands of the clock. The unknown woman, however, knows her boundaries and so makes no efforts to love the date dial of the clock: that particular component is off-limits to all but a few. Somewhere within the mason lodge, lonely old married men take off their fez hats after saying a prayer and stare obsessively at the old clocks that hang from the wall. The wallpaper is somehow feline in appearance, and exhales the impression of furtively probing whiskers. Once the mason goers begin to fight like crabs with spiked claws, the fun really starts, because each of the wall clocks open their face plates to release a mechanical bronze hand. Each hand opens in synchrony to expose a small bird embryo. The variously colored embryos are not animate, but they all release enough heat to cause the surrounding air to eddy and ripple, creating a mirage-like distortion in the room that induces the Masonic fez-wearers to sweat profusely, and throw bright green pea pods from their over-stuffed pockets. After the Masonic brothers have emptied their pockets and sweat glands, they run like dogs from the well-lit mason lodge, out into the dark night and over a cliff, where they fall more than five-hundred feet to their deaths.

In the morning, the police report states that the crushed bodies of over a hundred Masonic fez-wearers were found smashed on the rocks below the archaic wilderness Masonic cliff, and that all of the milk and cookies within the Masonic fez clubhouse refrigerator were eaten. Apparently whoever had finished the milk had placed the empty container back in the refrigerator.

A meteorite falls from the sky and strikes the earth close to where the shattered Masonic bodies are, and the investigative police decide to take a permanent lunch break, fleeing in terror. Brilliant crabs streaked with purple, orange and yellow erupt, en masse, from a nearby lake and march to the site of the bodies. Even though each crab only weighs one-fourth of a pound, there are so many of them that they consume all one hundred and fifty-two of the bodies over the span of six hours, with just twenty minutes to spare before sunset. The crabs become fat and lazy, and then return to the water to molt, eagerly looking forward to the next meal.

A few months later, a troop of orangutans passes through the woods and reaches the rocky clearing. The sight of the bleached skeletons immediately inspires a wave of fear, but the alpha male persists, and the rest of the troops follow. They examine the skulls and femurs, as well as a few ulnas, and use the bones as percussion instruments. The clicking and clacking of the musical bone instruments are a pure delight to the orangs, while fire hydrants erupt from the ground beside them. The hydrants command: "Put down those Masonic bones at once, or you will reawaken the old fez hat curse that once decimated all life on earth. Put those bones down immediately; you are so warned!"

The orangs obeyed rather sullenly, but did as the fire hydrants instructed. Somehow the orangutans' day had been ruined, and the transparent world now seemed extremely thick and opaque. The trees, heedless of the warning, began to secrete globules of sap that solidified within the hour. The orangs forgot about the bones and paid homage to the sap secretions, hooting and panting with untied shoelaces. When the sap globules expanded and became the world, the orangs immediately were insignificant. With the spheroid sap bodies as the new solar system, the orangs became mired inside of the spheres, in a subjectively inverted fashion. Essentially they represented insects trapped in amber. The primates did not despair, however, and they continued to pay homage to the heavenly secretions even though they had undergone a radical change in perspective. The celestial sap globules collected the proof-of-purchase stickers from oatmeal boxes, and when enough labels had been obtained, the new resinous solar system sent away for a galactic can opener that would enable them to re-invert their reality whenever they wished. Therefore, moving objects from one sphere to another could be accomplished through many divergent avenues: via claws, hands, gravity, sneezing, etc. Unknown to the colorful crabs, the police, the Masonic fez skeletons, the fire hydrants or even the orangutans, the shadowy green grasshoppers picked up the clear resin tree marbles and put them into their corduroy pockets. Finders keepers.

4

Back in the hospital for sun-scorched diseased people, unknown minds continued to stubbornly push ceramic coffee saucers off of waiting room tables, while nurses had their hands full with a viral outbreak of a newly mutated disease spread by pigs, of all creatures. The lead doctor filed a report detailing the first documented case of the degenerative illness: apparently, an airforce pilot claimed to have received orders to fly through a particularly turbulent area over some hills in the Nevada region, and then land on a top-secret runway in order to refuel and then proceed to Seattle, Washington. The pilot indeed landed the plane successfully, but encountered a hideous ranch that was situated alongside the runway. The clueless pilot was lured to the ranch by way of a colorful sign that advertised fresh lemonade. Upon entering the first corral, the pilot observed a peculiar rodeo in progress, with diseased, gangrenous cowboys attempting to lasso red, bloated pigs of all sizes that were in the process of stampeding and resisting capture. In fact, not only were the porcine animals resisting the cowboys, but they appeared to be diseased also, and were even displaying signs of intelligent aggression by biting some of the cowboys that had fallen from their horses. There was one pig in particular that could have weighed at least two tons, and had an intelligence that superseded the smaller minions of violent piglets. This particularly larger animal remained in the background and orchestrated the activities of the others, and proved even more difficult to manage for the cowboys. As if the ranch were an inverted concentration camp, the fat, blistered pigs eventually controlled the behaviors of the weakened, emaciated ranchers, biting them and forcing them into corners where their arms and legs were amputated by the rabid porcines. The pilot responded to the situation as quickly as possible by attempting to search the grounds for unaffected survivors and evacuate them to safety outside the confines of the outer corral of the ranch. Unfortunately, the officer managed to receive a few minor bites and also excessively breathed the foul, diseased air. Upon escaping, the wounded air force pilot resumed course to Seattle and managed to bring the disease with him, ultimately infecting the entire military base. From there, the plague spread to the civilians, who already were suffering from the solar disease.

In a fevered delirium, and before the quarantine was officially erected, the fevered pilot managed to escape from the hospital, and his body was later found slumped over a picnic bench on the periphery of a public park. The only clue to Sergeant Lloyd Harold's madness was the following letter to his girlfriend, which was found crumpled in his breast pocket:

RECOVERED DOCUMENT, 3/15/2024

Dear Jamie:

The pilot light on the stove went out. The oyster sparrow flew to the back of the room and disappeared through the gate. A troublesome kind of mannequin blew its way out to the street whereupon lightning flowers emerged from the eye of the skyscape, which put everything into aqua florescence that grazed through the heart of the octopus.

Lovely youngins flock the skies of the blue cotton that fluffs its way into your heart. The road to the heart of the blue cotton was straight through the shopping cart of the tomorrows of the bronze, gold, and silver tennis racquets that explode, while being used in the Olympics. These exploding tennis racquets frighten the lovely leather guests who wear sweaters and finger Rolex wristwatches, opening the eyes of condors who smoke filterless cigarettes by the sidelines. The green sun that sprays out grape bullets completely drenches the crowd, turning people into the astral pear tree grove that celebrated its left foot the day Rat-sniper exhaled the memory of a magic dragon that sat on thrones of sponge, amid the valley of fruit cocktail beverages that bore many legions of floating cigarette butts, away from the eyes of the elusive tourists with their many-ringed fingers that beheld a massive slab of frozen mercury amid the cold wastes of drugstores. Such things broke through clouds. The hands of the clouds used sign-language to perpe-trate the referee as a mere side-line smoker in the world of an artificial tennis court that was blinded by a peculiar kind of light-bulb with a very off-color that threatened every rusty framework conceivable, among the ruins of the circus freak-show, yes, the circus freak-show that was obliterated with the complete smile of a non-talkative avocado that channeled all efforts wastefully into mere watermelon propaganda.

I know that such things exist; that they are burning holes in our clothes, on fabricking clothed bodies into the most perfect of nudities, so that only streams of plasma arise out of limbs of the lightheaded heavens, spewing starts out of green oceans. A little loose-for-loose honesty. Some of these stones remain unturned as they talk of certain legends and certain possibilities that encode the greenest of forests that come from your hair. All guns trained on the Swiss-cheese monument to the honor-dogs that patrol the useless byways of all sex-police states that carry on with innocent eyes of the flaming Mickey Mouse skull, chopping out the eyes of the cantaloupe. Lucipheromone told us only yesterday of the odd lights that shimmered on the threshold of our measly, pocked coffee cups that hold still in shaky hands and the way the candle put the light on the star knuckles that shifted gears to accommodate a magnetic carbonated soft-drink that the Brady bunch children all drank on Sundays after church. There was no answer besides unknown carbonic rings that ripped up the, uh, buildings with the sweetest of breaths. The cycloptic eye that focused on foundationless, uh, buildings that quivered and quaked in the throes of one of those Friday night kind of Flocos Cornchip orgies that released a knife to the throat of the living-room land, slicing the neural cord of the lamp.

In any case, all is well darling; I hope they will let me go soon—I'm starting to have urges for citrus foot powder, of all things. Supposedly this is one of those artificial-tennis quarantines. The walls around me are starting to get on my nerves. Maybe they'll let me go soon. Aren't you aware of some great turbulence in the air?

Your lover,
Sgt. Lloyd Harold

These pigs certainly left a smear of the human rat race. Even though the outbreak was controlled, humanity was left with many casualties from the plague. There were even a few roller-skating rinks that had to close down. So did most of the dentists.

Aside from encountering a few petitioners and tomato-throwers, the children were not overly harassed by passers-by as they waited in an infinitely long queue leading up the large steps to the marble hall of the dentist's office. The giant hall provided much shade to the nervous children. At the top of the steps was a receptionist who passed out slices of cake to the unsettled youngsters with a curious generosity that went unnoticed by the children. After each child finished his cake, he was admitted through the doctor's office never to be seen again. Around the periphery of the building were fruit trees of an unknown origin, producing fruits of novel shapes and colors, usually the size of a standard apple. The cars of parents entered the facility by way of a guarded gate, and they left through the same manner after depositing their children.

Underneath the giant dental complex, underground rivers flowed smoothly and quietly while the afternoon moon in the sky exerted only the weakest of gravitational effects, only barely affecting the course of travel of the groundwater. While fried eggs were cut from trees by way of a hatchet, the mountain guardians collected rocks into size-sorted piles for later use. Every now and then large crustaceans poked their antennae through sewerage pipes that riddled the pristine mountains and then withdrew, ultimately realizing for the umpteenth time that they were irritated by the harsh sunlight. When cowbells rang around the wrists of plastic trees, their internal skeletons melted, releasing a surge of gray water that was just as fresh as it was dirty. The gears within grandfather clocks erected at the base of those plastic trees moved with non-lubricated agony, attempting to travel from one minute to the next. Apparently the large plants were not comfortable manipulating the grandfather clocks, but their actions were not optional and only cried out with a mammalian urgency that could scare an entire planet off of its axis. Underneath the plastic trees were frogmen who carried billiards cue sticks while they rummaged through packets of vegetable plant seeds in their travelling bags. One of the frogmen opened its hand to show off a collection of smooth red pebbles that was uncovered from a forgotten city submerged by water, only a few years after a major river had been forced by a storm to divert its course. A colony of ants marched up the hand of the frogman carrying the special red pebbles, and their black, glistening bodies were beads of poisonous onyx that foretold of dark, ominous things to come.

The lightning from an approaching squall storm terrorized the frogmen who hid under automatic umbrellas raised through a celestial aperture in the tops of the fine grandfather clocks erected under the protection of the plastic trees. Even though the cold rain wouldn't arrive for another fifteen minutes, the dark frogmen quivered in their tracks and sought out information regarding the alchemy of their smooth red pebbles in a mysteriously small and dry textbook always kept with them at all times. It eventually dawned on the frogmen that all of the animals on the hill had stopped moving and vocalizing, so the company frequently checked their watches to temporally monitor the ominous situation. The hands of the men began to sweat as they remembered similar past situations, where they once observed pineapple bushes grow fruits in the shape of human skulls, for instance, or where on another occasion they opened up their small, dry books to release a million gray pulsating moths from their uncertain pages. Regardless of whatever was about to happen, the frogmen, staked out next to the grandfather clock, felt a sentiment of being lost or off-course from some desired path, and their fragile morale was at stake.

After the rain began to fall, the shivering frogmen overcame their fear of the precipitation. They stretched open their webbed fingers and toes to catch the water droplets. Simultaneously, the dental complex surrounded by a guarded fence opened the shutters of its many garages, and masked workers came through the thresholds pushing wheelbar-rows full of giant teeth, perhaps those from a freshly killed herbivorous dinosaur or maybe of another source. As the exposed giant teeth began to absorb the rain, the frogmen outside the fence watched, and tensely held their billiards cue sticks. After the pineapple skulls dropped off of the trees and floated in the water collecting in a sunken part of the ter-rain, the frogmen used their cue sticks to play a game of pool with the skull fruits. After an hour or so of involved game play, the intensity of the rain increased. The falling water, a true, universal solvent, caused the large dinosaur teeth to melt, releasing the life that was contained inside. Hence, the large teeth transformed into large white koi fish that escaped through the fence and swam over to where the frogmen were playing games. As soon as the colorful koi fish interrupted the game of the frog-men, the molar-fish stood on their root-tails and became exquisite ivory tables that neatly stood on the well-kept lawn, now drained of all rainwater. The frogmen, in turn, transformed into bronze teacups that rested on the tooth-fish tables and had peculiar amphibious markings. The rainwater that was absorbed by the ground ultimately made its way down to the water table far below, where it would someday reach the ocean as a magical run-off.

A Chinese dragon's head erupted out of the darkness and its smooth eyes were small oceanic planets trapped within its green eye sockets. Usually this sort of dragon never made it down to the deeper portions of the earth, but today it accomplished that feat, and its magnificent scales were slightly perturbed. Its streamlined body writhed as a flooded river does, and so the creature polished its teeth with chalk. Its scaly arms were raised to reveal a classy wristwatch or two. A keyhole in the wall, of a most perfect shape, gave inspiration to the dragon to light sev-eral of the glass lamps that were cast in the shape of human heads devel-oped like film in a red-lit darkroom. What happened to the orange industrial paint that you used to hold close to your heart every day as

you passed by display cases of dried flowers that presided next to rest-
room couches that couldn't have been in anyone's budget?

A weasel knows the answer, better than a dragon inside of a glass
house. The dragon in the glass house with planetoid eyes sees the entire
world at once through its own eyes, ad infinitum. After a blender is
attached to the wall horizontally, the door opens to allow carrot people
to perch on hemlock branches leading to the outside world. The outside
branches cut through the glass fabric to reveal a sarcophagus of bones,
dried tomatoes and crap dice, all neatly mummified underneath fiber-
glass mummy bandages. The knock at the window is the dragon, as a
colorful light bulb can begin to laugh at the way the lopsided shadows
move across the wall at four a.m., an hour before the caffeine begins to
flow through throats and stomachs. Needles are blown through a dart
gun, casting even more shadows on the wall, which confuse both the
colored light bulbs as well as the planetoid eyes of the dragon of dark-
ness. The claws of the dragon can sometimes be likened to lovely carrot
peelers that can shear the bark off a tree, or the scalp off a human.
When the tree falls down, it is because its trunk collapsed, utterly lique-
fied to a pulp, because of a faulty notebook that needed tightening. A
fleecy corn material is then overlaid upon the corpse of the fallen tree,
and so the first plaster dinosaur bone is cast. Magnets are used to
remove the cast and then the plaster imprints are hidden away in an
undesirable floor of the city hospital.

After a hummingbird beats its orange wings and says hello to a lucky
doorknob, the lights go out in the house, and the door to a cellar is
opened, releasing the dragon once again for its nighttime prowl. The
feet of the reptile are actually ears with hair on them enabling the crea-
ture to witness birthing events like the dark visitor who stepped over
the poorly lit threshold of the eye of a tarantula that mowed the lawn
with its fangs while the shadow overtook the racing freight truck. How
amazing it was for the truck driver to find his firefly lantern extin-
guished, with only the eyes of the stranger on his back. The ancestral

flute released the dragon from the bottle, creating such a racket that Midwesterners picked their teeth with the bows of violins.

Long before the microscope had banished its focusing dial from the platform, the dinosaur teeth were free to revert to their ancestral fish morphology, swimming away to an ocean dialogue that employed strangely shaped metal implements of unknown functions. These metal implements used to wash up on the blue sandy beaches many years ago, until the factory that made them closed down. This factory also used to bear a coat of arms that featured the dark dragon with its oceanic eyes within the ferrules of hard-cast steel and feathery nitroglycerin. Once the factory released the dragon-fish back into its own element, bones became plants and decorative jewelry transformed into blood. The wings of a lamp fluttered and coated themselves with this blood, creating a blooderfly that flew away, after only once landing on the tip of the curious dragon's nose. The lizard howled and chased after the blooderfly, but the blood-stained insect left the dragon in a trail of dust that became only scaly diamonds clustered around the toes of the creature. Never again was the ornamental blood seen. After a brilliant sunset, ring-tailed lemurs found the diamonds on the ground and ate them one by one. Later that night as the lemurs slept in the dragon's lair, they had strange dreams of telekinetic forces that rearranged their bookshelves for them and planted brilliant vegetable seeds in the family garden, which forged a crooked, dark, stone-laden path back to town. A guitar in the trunk of a wrecked car broke the silence of the night, and felines stopped their prowling to sniff the air and appreciate the broken chords, in the same way a snail can appreciate its own broken shell on terrestrial holidays. Too bad the off-worldly eyed dragon of darkness missed out on the midnight concert.

A blotter removed its legs and splashed water onto its cold body that had slept in a stasis chamber for thirty years. The drapes by the window quivered in response to the termination of the stasis, but the pineapple skulls from the fruit tree still continued to drop. Meanwhile, teeth were still under construction, as if the poorly-charged batteries of the blotter felt the cold mask of an apathetic crowd that misunderstood the troubled meaning of language, not to mention the edible dry books that were secretly hidden in the cracks in the wall. The paper hair of a musician cried out to be burned, but buffalo hooves prevented that event from occurring. More lamps in the shape of human heads were lit and the buffaloes refused to leave the living room of the palace, so they required herding, by force, into the boring den where dads play with inane spinning tops and pitiful forceps that litter a crowded desk of chaos and domestic insanity of eggs and rampant fish-teeth.

With the fish-teeth overrunning the farmhouses, the buffalo hooves aligned themselves in a parallel formation and became instantly wrapped in a pliable cellophane membrane that protected them from degradation by the air. After this sort of impulsive foolishness carried on for an hour, certain spots on the surface of the sun cried out for attention, sending flares and waving patriotic flags which provoked ridicule from many people on earth. The human lampshades, in their infinite pulsations, madly grasped at the plastic chaos, wearing large sea crabs on their chests as a means of identification. When the last fragments of DNA were released into solution, the hyperactive enzymes became jittery and wrote odd letters to their senators, asking them to clean up their messes and to repair the lost limbs of aggressive insects that were reduced to molting cannibalism due to a shortage of food and electricity. The streetlights within the transparent tooth-fish grew dim, and a child's basketball slowly stopped bouncing in the middle of the street where it could be hit by cars. Fires of rage ravaged helpless structures, and some less-fortunate cities were consumed by red flames of passion and eyelid strength. Random female pigs appeared, carrying their infections, and a rural, developing nation was seized with the odd urge to consume miniscule amounts of raw bacon every five minutes. The world of frogs became an aquarium zoo that paid tribute to the fires and the raw pig-hides. Eventually bluebirds in magnolia trees ate the magnolia flowers, causing the skulls of the birds to assume a distended appearance. The mutated birds were happy and visited old-fashioned wooden motels that used to be churches, where the red lights of boredom trickled down the archaic and faded flock-designed walls. People still donated lots of money to the space program, and thus the new space shuttles were out-fitted with wooden furniture and the remains of old vinyl record-play-ers. The cats were then satisfied with their mouse-paw key-chains and used their new brass keys to open tea cabinets which held the gilded eggs of future teleportations to the interiors of magic pumpkins and other rural farmhouse treasures of resistance.

A parking lot becomes decapitated by the flow of the ocean, and soon the chaotic, upturned sea-life returns to an equilibrated state of seren-ity, where rocks and objects no longer fall, assailing the eyes with music instead of splinters. The starfish from the shadows (that like the legs of women so much), calm down and take a momentary reprieve, relaxing on soft beds and lawn chairs with a glass of fresh lemonade next to each and every piece of unadulterated furniture. After a few moments in the relaxing gloom, the dinosaur teeth-fish fall asleep and dream in terms of stacked logs that will build fabulous firewall structures to dream upon when the weather gets cold, forcing people to love each other for their warmth. The full moon in the sky, always a full moon, may or may not affect the dreams, but they certainly appear in the same way bril-liantly lit birthday candles appear to grey, crescent-shaped moths that pulsate within the folds of a magnetic slumber, sending sharp eidetic images of geography to dormitory brains that are lost within their own healing reflections, re-magnetizing themselves with waves of glassy ocean bearing the planetoid stares of subsurface dragons and manta rays. If it weren't for the wide planet eyes, sight would be lost and a rot-ted skeleton would immediately fall to pieces. However, the planet eyes are always present, and therefore no collapses of rotting skeletons are observed. Upon the sleeping bodies of sleeping children there glides a carnivorous snail that removes the forehead portion of the skull to inject a bitter venom that creates cabbages out of their young, virulent minds. Lost in the sub-sea caves, these carnivorous snails are bred under special photosynthetic lights of blue, green and red, causing the snails to grow at an accelerated rate. At low tide, when the moon takes a nap, the snails leave their sandy caves to go foraging for coins dropped by swimming tourists. The salvation from the coins leads to a better understanding of aqua-culture, in what is needed to successfully raise happy, healthy man-eating snails for a candlelit night of pleasure upon a yacht of mean-spirited gangsters who lack consciences as well as common sense, leading high school literature teachers in their late 60s to crow like the uptight geese that they are. Surely Mrs. Stencil has better things to do than forever living vicariously in other people's pasts. Surely the wise and learned lecturers remembered to save a piece of life for themselves before it is too late and hence impossible to climb out of the death bed!!

5

An underwater train caught on the tracks of mirrors is the roller coaster of unconscious aquaria. The glass marbles laid down upon the tracks were systematically shattered to reveal the cat's-eye chips embedded inside. Once the tracks were flooded, the eye-chips became holistic magnetic inserts to be placed within the sockets of eyeless baboons who had ruptured all relations with burning fish that once were limp teeth. The mirrored tracks used their waterfalls to crack the glass windows of obsidian that presided over them, several clueless flights above. Butterfly skeletons fell from the ceiling, fine configurations of dust, and left designs of salt upon the balding foreheads of the baboons with cat's-eye chips inserted into their previously empty eye sockets. The pulse of the reticulated train slowed to a relaxing crawl as the underwater viper disappeared through a side tunnel, never to be seen again, at least until the next chaotic holiday season.

A door opens, disguised as a mirrored panel, revealing a trio of storm trooperettes, dressed in black, of course. These storm trooperettes synchronously raise their left hands to each display a silver ring cast in the shape of a low-cut party dress affixed to the band portion. In the region of the bellybutton, there is a clasped ruby, making the ring sparkle with red brilliance. The dark female figures confer among themselves, while they each turn their rings 180 degrees so that the miniature silver dress and ruby parts of the ring are clasped in their closed fists. In the dim light of the mirrored train room, amid the shattered glass of the extracted cat's-eye marbles, the storm trooperettes clasp their ruby party dress rings, causing the inner light of the gems to reveal the bones in their hands. This display of power terrifies the baboons with the implanted magnetic cat's-eye chips, who run after the long-gone train that sped away minutes before, attempting to flee the potent, muted whispers of the darkly clad women with their illuminated hands.

The onyx ceiling falls in on the underwater subconscious train station, obliterating whatever lingered. Perhaps the whispering women in black were crushed, but then perhaps not. Probably not.

In an alternative universe, a downwardly spiraling gale of gliding seagulls comes near to rest upon a dysfunctional family who are currently obsessing over their hairdryers. Next to their neurotic pencil bones, the x-ray of a gated mansion equipped for the unlimited entry of only cats, exclusively, looms high within the brains of children who sleep underneath developing tanks of orange lighting in the halls of hospitals lined with the midnight scampering of silverfish and transparent geckos. A woman's voice of crystal softness enters the ear canals of the sleeping children who die within their dreams underneath the diabolical developing tanks in a world of nether-emotions and superficial armchair cigar conversations. Old know-it-alls with beards, books and bank accounts exploit the sleeping minds in their icy frozen repose, paused until life might resume again with the wag of a finger or the stroke of a pen. Thank gODD for heart failure. The voids of time open the locked book doors, revealing stale red carpet, useless bookshelves full of useless books, as well as the dusty living-room typewriter. Apparently Santa Claus has been indisposed for several centuries now.

Trauma hounds keep running towards the stopped train that is stuck, mired, hung-up at the turning point between life and death, fallen prey to second-guessing and underwater, upside-down garden hourglasses, allowing the inverted images to breach only small parts of the blood-stained glass.

The oracle at Delphi is really a buried larynx from below, and this fact enables teetering grandfather clocks to dry off next to a comfortable hearth in the shadows of a cinderblock domain, where red-lit developing photo rooms are treasured and enunciated with the greatest of care and refined teeth. The subconscious larynx rasps at the undergrowth of great redwood forests that sink tendrilous roots down to touch the throat, and teeth erupt from fossils, causing the tense air to ionize in a flash of airborne sparks. This commotion causes the train to crawl forward down the mountain, crashing through gangrenous underbrush. A flirt with fire sends the train scampering down the popsicle mountain. Still in the underbrush, the wild eyes of fire peep through the dried weeds, building the cities of the mind, where the duality of existence teases the palate and pate of a bronze-dipped skull. The choking vermin did not know what hit them after the cinderblocks of the train melted into a warm puddle of dog urine. The train burns up from the grand old steepest descent options, a complete ember that rests on a jambalaya shrunken head. The conga drums liberate the fissures of the skull as the train, now a glowing cinder, enters the microscopic world in a blaze of glory, a magnified icicle that didn't make the grade, that missed the train, or boat, rather. Did I say boat? Poor choice of words.

I see you locked up in your baboon house of glass, with lollypop perfection and the invisible, starred wallpaper. Your wooden limbs are organic, but they still don't fool me. Perhaps you made the correct drop at the correct bridge, but the noisy stones do nothing to conceal the type-written terror of a pocket-sized guillotine that you once used on hairy rodents that blessed your fireplace altar where the pumpkins fell down the cellar stairs into the neon blue basement garden. Eventually you placed another rodent's skull in the way of the guillotine blade, and your cruelty became magnificently apparent. No pausing for you.

And you didn't stop there: your collection expanded to include the severed heads of many vertebrates—birds, mammals, reptiles, and even a few invertebrates thrown in for good measure. After a while, you ran out of room to house your head collection, and so you moved the entire group to a museum warehouse where you charged a hefty admission and ran a concession stand in the lobby where your staff sold cocktails made from the fresh blood of a snake. At the grand-opening you boasted of plans to include humans in your exhibit, creating simulated habitation rooms displaying the skewered but preserved guillotined specimens of fine family members in various acts of post-nuclear dysfunctionality. The red curtain draws to a close upon your depraved specimens, and they retire for the evening, fully exhausted, a veritable challenge for any back-scrubbing taxidermist. I have problems making out your shape as your dark form disappears over the next hill. Save another day for your museum.

A few miles offshore, at the bottom of the ocean, polluted scallops hesitantly extend their languishing tendrils to explore the backseat of a sunken, rusted 1956 Plymouth jalopy that perished many years before. Even though the radio was left on, there is no battery power, and the scallops are sorely disappointed. A monstrous floor current lifts the corroded wreck and carries it off the continental shelf to where it falls to the depths of salty black time. On the shore, some primates find the flooded houses of absent Caucasians, perhaps carried away by the flood. Within the submerged houses, the primate divers find all windows and doors padlocked and sealed with a chain-link fence. After cutting through, the divers find swarms of vicious barracuda lingering inside.

The writhing, drifting fish have had cubes of their flesh neatly excised with a sharp blade, revealing a white skeleton underneath. The skeletons of these fish become an ivory chain-link fence, and the fish templates are peeled from the organic lattice. One primate has his fish with lemon and butter, while another decides upon garlic and chipotles. The primates laugh and climb the roofs of the houses, which are above the water's surface. A swarm of fruit bats nears and casts a wingspread shadow upon the breasts of the primates. The monkeys raise their hands in abnormal deference, allowing their chests to open to reveal bronze statuettes of finely toned pornographic squirrels. Each bronze pornographic squirrel statuette has rubies for eyes and is equipped with panoramic teeth that serve as katana blades. Once the bronze pornographic squirrel statuettes have been revealed, the swarm of apocalyptic fruit bats seizes all of the naughty statues and replaces an equivalent weight of sand into the bared chest cavities of the now-deactivated primates. The bats then return to the dark sanctuary of their cave nests after the transaction has been completed.

When night falls, the bats emerge from their caves in search of fruit that have been coated with a fine layer of condensation. On this particular night, the fruit bats decide to forage within a netted vineyard, where the grapes are plump and yellow, sometimes, like tonight, with a frosted, powdery appearance. Each bat selects a choice grape and flies off, holding the fruit orb with both claws, heavily resembling a mobile optic orb sometimes manifested by certain winged, mythical beasts. On a neighboring hill, within the safety of a house for battered children, two girls observe this grape-foraging spectacle and decide to do their laundry. The clothes-washing process takes all night to complete, but in the morning the girls are not tired and they see octopods with unnatural numbers of arms pressed against their sunlit windows, displaying fleshy colors of ochre, purple and red. The vision of the many-legged octopods amuses them greatly, and they refer to anatomical textbooks to gain a better grasp of why the bulbous cephalopods have so many extra legs, and why they might enjoy basking in the sunshine. In the distance, the view of Chesapeake Bay is visible to the girls, and they ask permission from their therapist as to when they might be allowed to go mingle their toes with the warm, brackish water. The therapist shakes his head and gives them a wad of cash register receipts, indicating that they might never leave the house. The paradoxical beauty of a Saturday for slaves.

Under five feet of stratified water in the bay, male blue crabs spindly march over rocks, nervously flexing their pincers and snapping at all things that swim by, acting as an underwater army of ants. A microcosm of shopping malls and all things civilized with yowling babies and leaking car batteries, even the nose of a man who laid claim to a concrete shower stall in the amphitheater for the isolated wealthy. The fashion of past decades reigns supreme under these fertile waters which the orphans admire from their sky-lit windows with adorning octopods. Unknown is the full extent to which this truly brackish subculture exerts its tidal influences on the lungs of the orphan sisters who learn algebra by day and rewash clean clothes by night. In the end, all that remains is a pile of rusted horseshoes that will supremely challenge the reality principle, slapping it on its backside and tossing out figurative bones for it to fetch.

6

The fireflies jump over the fence and over the moon, and faraway paradise lunar caverns open up for the seismologists of the wooden hotel. The caverns of the moon house a comfortable velvet couch on which sits a family of yeast biologists who tie yellow ribbons around their fourth digits in order to remember their children who have left home. With the children of the yeast biologists gone, the cats roam free and sleep all over the various corners of the unconscious mansion where rain constantly falls in the form of moist, purple snapdragons.

The snapdragons fall and adhere to your soaked sleeves, releasing flower catapults from the secret bamboo towers that erupt through the grass in a rolling pasture behind the psychological mansion. Underneath the manor are inverted mountains that exert the gravitational pull of a swirling gas giant that is cold but riddled with frozen lightning.

The swirling gases convene at the site of a half-buried brick of iron placed on a magnificent serving platter garnished with parsley and violet snapdragons that whispered softly through microphones planted around the platter in a wide circle. A pair of panda eyes wears a tuxedo as it examines the world in terms of a dark inverted hourglass that uses the shifting sands to reveal an icy, frozen face that can look through the darkness at galaxies in the beyond. The purple snapdragons flex their jaws and the panda eyes insert themselves within the pollen chambers of the flowers, observing the black and white splotches of wildness that burn through metal and lead to a spilling of human seed on the hot concrete. The panda-eyed splotches on the fur are a masked desperado clasping a hot and fervid hourglass that shakes its tail like an overheated sidewinder that scrapes its way through sands that go cold at night.

The moving sidewinder becomes splotched like the panda, and it burrows through horizontal layers of shadow, cracking its stones like a cobbled street hat holding rusted keys and crawling legs that move sideways across the glistening black stones. The forest of stones allows the panda sidewinders to twistingly migrate across them, in the way a needle points to important directions on a compass. The panda serpents flick their tongues, smelling the ozone and freshly cut buttercups with their yellow, sweet pollen. The snakes continue with their migrations across the panda bricks and then disappear into a dried river cave, running down through underground waterfalls where the leg-shadow starfish—that special kind of echinoderm that attaches to the legs of the unwary, casting them in the shadows, covering the legs with suction cups—appear with a green brilliance, sending light through the watery depths.

After the descending panda sidewinders reach the muddy bottom next to where the green shadow-leg starfish are reclining, the snakes coil themselves into balls of thick rope and assume a dormant approach to life. The hibernating panda sidewinders dream of disheveled rainstorms and the nostalgic sigh of a pond that exhales airborne algae and a humidity that softens the hands. The dreams touch upon the algae as the cells combine to form plant pyramids that greet the air with a gasp and plaster themselves to stained glass windows of yellow and orange tiles, mingled with droplets of a blood-red glass made from gold.

The coiled, dreaming, sideways panda sidewinders shift through restless dream sequences as their physical bodies are transferred to a weapons factory on top of a sand-covered pillow. The dormant snakes do not rouse from their slumber as they are gently placed in cylindrical tanks well lit by glowing gases. Meanwhile, the soft tones of monotone male and female voices puncture through the haze of filmy vision in certain places, casting the shadow of uncertainty on the dawning collective unconsciousness of the coiled vipers that are now awakening from their wet slumber. In their holding tanks within the weapons factory, the sluggish panda sidewinders struggle in vain against the chilly air to rouse themselves back into a state of activity. There are many rooms in the foggy weapons factory, and each room has its own set of voices, with strange premonitions recorded onto vinyl albums by the mentally disturbed restaurant association of southern Alaska. The rooms are interconnected and frequently communicate via iconic representations of the emotional subjective experiences of the human race. The high-speed interplay of images is confusing to most, including the snakes who have uncurled but still remain thoroughly sluggish and immobile. The crawl of absorbed legs next to obsolete pelvic bones sends a cry of feeling across the ripples of time into the lower bass ranges, upsetting even the earthquakes that rattle the earthworms bumping into the concrete underneath the weapons manufacturing facility. The voices from the building are one-sided, unidirectional, as there are no sentient ears to hear them.

Portraits of rats with oblong skulls hang from the central office walls of the factory, and plush leather chairs sulk next to the coffee machine by the company president's desk. As if autumn blood were seeping from the ceiling to drip onto a textbook of mangled body parts that rests, open, to an inviting page on the president's desk, the voices of acoustic guitars can be heard from only a few of the oblong-skulled rat portraits, exquisitely executed in only the finest of Dutch oil paints. The floor gives way to reveal an underwater, always underwater basement containing the sunken crystals of time travel that big bruisers seek when their verbal clichés don't cascade and careen from the steep walls of icy hypnosis that capture lustful, wayward eyes when they scan a young face that searches the rat portraits for flickers of real feeling.

Anomie House

1

Clear eyes in water, honest eyes in glass. A chandelier swings like a pendulum to catch a plummeting feline who stepped out on a book-swivel ledge trying to capture streaking blue fireflies that sprung from its elbows. The cat adsorbs to the glass, and the moving, glass house flies through a bird's nest into a warm skull-cottage on the fringe of a safe forest. Little Red Riding Hood would never have had time to prepare for the kitty chandelier, but her teeth were certainly sharpened.

After the cape swung and the blue cottage bricks shattered, the kinetics of the forest primacy were altered, changing them forever. The cat chandelier hissed like a meteorite in its melted state while the disoriented feline emerged from a pool of molten glass. The cat sniffed at a breeze and then scaled a tree that had been lightning-struck several years before. The cat in the tree was now a lizard-flower opening to the approaching nightfall, and a mysterious woman of tap-dance persuasion orchestrated a midnight storm of thunderous propensity, barely veiled behind her wet eyes. A tower in the crook of the cat-tree now sent its fire tail down to the damp ground in a cold puddle, waiting for the air to rise.

The cold puddle is shocked by the thunderstorm, as flying pebbles etch the claw-marks of razor clams into the folds of brain-rocks that festively erupt from beside the older boulders, left behind by innocent glaciers, which sometimes annoyingly prompt the brain-rocks for information. The rain obliterates the rocks with splashes and yowls of cow communication. The rocks couldn't have melted, but they at least could have remembered a blissful infusion from the cracks of industrial floors. They spun dizzily into each other and broke ripples through the large glaciated puddles that infested the landscape with interest and a sense for where exactly the orange juice was being hidden. If that secret were known, then many an aquatic anaconda could have returned upstream for a visit to the discreet orange juice depot secretly stationed within the wings of forest obscurity, of pine tree electricity that could tickle just about any random light bulb under consideration. The orange juice spills across wood, and the games have begun.

An old LP melts and enters into the folds of reverie as its etched groove approaches the moment that silenced it in the beginning, when a stray pulse ripped through the filaments of permaflame lanterns burning with a hot and heavy fuel. Your hands are cold as they shiver across my arms in the ice-jungle of, uh, buildings, that rain like ticking clocks across my vulnerable back. You take advantage of the moment and initiate the mystery of a solar kiss that burns the sneaking shadow into the wall as it rose across the wallpaper in a rickety cascade. What a solar flare it was to behold. Tomorrow's hopes still nestled within the hive of crystalline pinecones that are only an effigy of the superstition of older minds from previous centuries. A missing face, lost by only two days, spells agony on a photographed retina. The exposed film is dupli-cated by lightning, and a short-circuit breaks a mirrored cycle that has insidiously seeped through an innocently flowered toaster whose touching decals bear the names of Asian warships, having a special way of dropping rose-petals into a bowl of milk to calm the senses.

Waiting for the dark bird takes the minutes and twists them into eternal pretzels, confusing the air-currents, making eternity a genie stuffed into a bottle. The agony of the lightning-wait spells the symbols of mythology across the dark forehead that rests on a woven pillow in Reno, where the archaeology of sign language reposes within crouched ear-bones of a black-bear cat preparing to wake up, rising through the protective fog of sleep, the only domain impervious to the barks of techno-dogs regurgitating moose meat for their pups when antlers become satellite hands reaching through the din of the wake-up call. Feline confusion results with the rise in consciousness. Birds of day mate with birds of night, and painted light bulbs put shivers into the shoulders of dancers that approach a discarded box of crayons left behind by the flippered inhabitants from previous years. Somewhere in the south of an electric raygun, a flipper slaps a refrigerator that hoards the prized tropical fruits that someone abandoned. This someone might have been in league with a certain other someone named Coconut Man. And so the key was pressed to the lock, and silent hands fumbled with a reticent door latch that prevented the entry of snakes at the threshold.

Any paradise can be threatened by loving gestures, but it's the permanent ones that become bronze-coated chicken bones in one's pocket, especially after billiards racing and other pleasant hand-clapping distractions. Several couples seen mowing their lawns in the distant, well-irrigated suburbiaside pause their lawn care activities momentarily to take off their hats, and wave to a parade of passing crocodiles who respondingly take off their singing hats to greet the happy lawn couples. The crocodiles continue with their uncertain parading behaviors and disappear behind a bend in the road. Meanwhile, the happy couples return to their houses to continue their readings of big books that tell of magnificently detailed protocols for the rearing of prize-quality carrots and other useful life skills when the stork is on vacation. The house library does contain its useful manuals, but it also carries the photographic histories of generational legends in the making, especially when those legends breath the cold air of icicled branches that have previously penetrated even the most tightly woven of socks. No mercy for the icicles nor the socks.

The perfect wooden floor melts, releasing the bands of wood one by one. This element of surprise squirted lemon onto the sushi brains of the wood, and the house was consumed. Fortunately, there were no observant magnolia trees in the vicinity of the melting house, which might have reduced them to plumes of pink fire. This action might have spelled disaster for the tree-and-house relationship, and so the house was later resurrected with the help of generous snow trees who happened to be passing by that winter. But for the present moment, the grand house was now just a muddle of wooden memories cut from preformed diagrams cryptically imprinted underneath their unsound beams.

The collapse of a house can never be taken lightly. Fortunately, houses are shells, and shells can always be remade. A wide-open sky rippled in its blue clarity, and a vast countryside reached out in all directions. There were many houses to be seen, each with a unique flag billowing from every spire. Somehow, the heat of the day caused the world to be illuminated more radiantly than normal, and so all mundane activities were halted in order for various irises and retinal parts to adjust to the increase in light. Even the birds flew erratically, frequently dropping to low altitudes and terse trajectories. Every bird knew that the heat of the noon sun was deafening.

A close galaxy expelled a bright blue comet that approached the world at a high speed, which would barely graze Earth's atmosphere. Fortunately, the people alive would know how to keep a greater distance between them and the gorgeous comet. Even though all sentient terrestrial creatures knew that life would change forever with the passage of the comet, they still looked to the skies for answers to questions of the heart, which were usually but awkwardly considered at peculiarly long lunar hours. Passionately beautiful female humans emerged from the shadows to secretly observe the approaching comet while amorous gentlemen suddenly appeared beside them completely oblivious to the sad memories of the melted wooden houses with the limp wooden annuli rings. While male and female apes smolderingly embraced, the wooden starfish that represented the remnants of the melted houses appeared and crawled along the legs of the heedless humans. Eventually the starfish understood and decided to have a gala dance party under the weirdly lit moonlight that appeared next to the light of the blue comet. The women laughed and clapped their hands, while the men held their arms to the sky, foolishly attempting to grab what was too many miles away. The aroused humans began to bark at the odd celestial events, and the sky took on a purplish color, which enhanced the natural beauty of the moon, making the universe look like fabulously chaotic velvet. A traveling skeleton appeared from the smile of a scheming goose, and removed a lantern from its satchel. The lantern cast a warm green glow over the surrounding rock formations, and the amorous couples paid no heed. The traveling skeleton drank from an obscure coconut and then replaced the milk flask in the bag. The skeleton surveyed the area, as well as the reproductive wildlife, and then turned to the shadowy paths leading away from the ritualistic forest clearing created almost exclusively for midnight romance. The bobbing lantern-light cast elusive beams away from the receding traveling skeleton.

After a few miles at a brisk pace, the traveling skeleton paused again for a drink of the obscure coconut milk. The skeleton turned its hollow eyes to the moon/comet source of light and drank the cold, blue rays that closed in on its eye sockets like a warm, purple sock immediately pulled from a hot dryer. The skeleton resumed its course towards the top of the mountain, holding the lime-colored flame high to discern the dark, twisting branches of leafless trees. After encountering a few wayward voices over the span of two hours, the traveling skeleton arrived at the top of the steep hill and rested its dry bones on a vast, flat glacial deposit of wet, nocturnal coldness which chilled it and reminded it of less desolate days. The primate skeletal figure located an opening that led down into the cold, dark earth and then entered it.

As the bony figure passed through the entrance, the lantern gave off its last cold rays to the outside world as the traveler entered a new phase of its nomadic life. Once the aperture sealed itself shut, the skeletal nomad descended many miles of stone-cobbled road to some of the warmer, lower areas of the earth's crust. The dark passageways had not seen any form of light for perhaps centuries, and so the walls glistened with wet mineral deposits that were as beautiful as they were anthropo-morphic, revealing the limb anatomies and skull casts of mammalian creatures of a conservative cuteness that gave pause to many of the romantic encounters to be initiated that night. The passageway walls indeed went with the flow and so became a river of animated life that proceeded in eternally slow motion. The skull eventually reached its temporary destination: a low-ceilinged cavern bearing a table fashioned from local geology, with chairs and magazine racks concealing heaps of dust under them. The traveling skeleton sat down, rested its weary bones, and put its thin legs on the table.

The endoskeleton napped in that position for a year before it decided to inspect the ancient writing on the walls, which contained detailed records of a governmental organization that spied on country-folk when certain royalty were in the area. Such texts were purely frivolous, and yet they brightened the traveling skeleton's evening to a great degree, which encouraged it to put a spring in its step and a sparkle of reassuring teeth to the lower areas. What was particularly disturbing were curious scenes of common daylight, depicted with an off-worldly quality that would have made a great insignia for dried squid that could be used in place of stained-glass. The skeleton paused upon examining these latter images and pulled some brilliantly polished jade marbles from its frayed coat-sleeve, tossing them at the bas-relief image of alien daylight, which could easily have been mistaken for a translucently iri-descent, dried, giant squid. The spherical minerals smoothly clacked with the rock wall like velvet. When the marbles fell to the ground, innervated craters appeared, sending out tendrils to grasp the precious marbles, which were now a transformed variety of optical sensory organs enjoyed by some folks. The stained glass, dried squid images reverberated overtones of an alien dawn from many years ago before apple pie was invented. Monsters in horror movies grasped at the bars on the window, shaking at solid beams of immovable metal. Yet the influence of these monsters was like a dark lantern that the mysterious traveling skeleton found in a refrigerator tucked away in one of the underground geode outcroppings. The small caged ghouls snarled and drooled out decayed fragments of flesh, but their gnawed arms were too short to reach further than a few inches from the lantern-cage. Eventually the slime-dribbling monster miniatures gave up their reaching efforts and concentrated on more mundane aspects of caged lantern life, such as uninterrupted cable television and knitting. The ghoulish, filthy monsters behaved themselves for the duration of their time with the traveling skeleton.

Once the traveling skeleton had rested itself and recovered the dark ghoulish cage-lantern, it resumed its cryptic mission to the deepest existing parts of the earth. The caves lost touch with the traveling skeleton as it receded into the deepest domains of the earth's vast crust. After the traveling skeleton had passed through, the stalactites celebrated by adorning themselves with paper cocktail parasols that bore the printed images of various flowers carrying a strong flavor of sexual imagery. The stalactites continued to crawl to eternity, their stalagmite mates. Needless to say, happiness generally brews through the eons. The dampness of the inner earth caverns dissipated somewhat, with the passage of the mysterious traveling primate endoskeleton. Somehow, the voyaging skeleton took the moisture with it as it moved on to lower, forgotten domains. The artifacts of men and women seemed like a distant comet bent on passing over the moon, on a starry midnight sky that served as a poetic and intellectual bed for the sleepy.

Giant birds grasp at the planets, but they prove too large for even these flyers. Suddenly, cantaloupes are kicked and squashed by leather booted feet. The flying cantaloupe pulp soils the soft linens that cover all of the ergonomic furniture, and obsessive feline informants arrive on the scene to observe the behaviors of the violated melons as they blend well with lime juice to make a fragrant throat beverage of aromatherapeutic proportions. The cautious felines sniff at the fruity pulp covering the various pieces of cozy furniture. Their eyes fixate on different portions of the sky as well as the furniture, seeking the telltale motions of liquid sidewinders that will ultimately coalesce into the rhythmically tapping tap shoes of a soothing traveler with a sixth subliminal sense. The dancer can hear the luscious sighing of a bright candle that could turn any one pocket into a sentimental and romantic coliseum from a waking moment in the early morning, when shivery breezes kiss necks in the dim softness.

The felines made a playful response to this rhythmical expression by affectionately snarling and blissfully drooling in the direction of the magical tap shoes that came knocking on a loose window. In fact, such near-total bliss was highly contagious, and so the whole universe shuddered with pleasure for a brief moment in normal time, and the feline informants began to feel a special affinity for sand-castles. As soon as the feeling mounted, it just as swiftly dissipated, leaving the dark feline creatures to ponder their fifth digits and their prehensile tails, sometimes with rings of an off-color. The smashed cantaloupes actually paved the way for great things to come to these not-so-lower depths of the earth, and afterwards the quiet feline creatures slipped back into the shadows of the caverns, mashing their soft fur against the moist walls.

On the surface world, seagulls with consciences muttered to themselves on a sandy boardwalk, and picked at wriggling worms that had somehow been displaced to the beach area. Heedless children darted across the boardwalk, incessantly humming and singing child-like spelling tunes capable of exciting even grandma and grandpa. The singing children eventually found the hotdog stand, and a revered quiet fell upon them. With the children preoccupied with hotdogs, the seagulls began to create a new form of life out of precut fragments of plastic very cheap in construction and yet everlasting in emotive potential. The plastic constructs would eventually take on lives of their own, but until that moment, they preferred to remain quiescent on sandy operating tables reserved by the seagull artist-doctors who would reanimate the slumbering plastic. With the plastic life on the certain road to animacy, the seagulls celebrated by pitching stones into the sea, watching them skip across the possibly dangerous waves. By receiving this monstrous surge in spiritual hope, the maritime birds commenced a touching episode of collective preening and pecking that culminated in an ocean rainbow caused by the spray of saltwater into the air by large, untiring waves. The birds moved away from the breaking seawater and concentrated on their plastic obsessions.

Underneath the beach, the feline informants could feel the crashing of the waves, and could almost sense the new twitchings and stirrings of life within the artificial limbs of the plastic life forms. These tremors could be perceived within six miles of the seagull plastic factory, and they helped the surrounding beach area (and the caverns underground) generate a new sense of hope that was lost when humanity had attempted to apply to its own existence a two-dimensional conception of reality that in all truth deserved to have been a healthier four-dimensional concept. Nevertheless, the arrival of these new plastic forms of life was expected to be a highly cherished and celebrated event, almost of the same caliber as the adoration of a pasta box with bells and whistles for happy-slap musical festivities.

Even though the plastic life objects were temporarily inaccessible, they were still within reach and could be seen through their small, illuminated blueprints installed on a panel next to a very inviting telephone. Apparently, all outgoing phone calls triggered the illumination of the blueprint displays for the plastic forms of life being cultivated in fervid, dark rooms across the country. Eventually the plastic was to be released into the environment, but until that day arrived, the plastic life forms gently hibernated, completely submerged in their maturation buffers. Sometimes they were cared for by a group of hardware store advocates, but during other moments they simply floated within days of perfect silence.

A tour bus accidentally crashed into one of the depots containing the developing plastic life forms, and the plastic creatures yawned and realized their premature awakening. They threw a temper-tantrum and were kindly bottled up by the confused bus-driver, and after that gesture, the people on the tour bus resumed their tour chatter, card-playing and post-industrial flirting. The bus-driver sat on a bench at the curb, wiped some sweat from his brow, and pulled a flask of warm, green tea from his jacket. He swilled the tea, and then pulled the bus from the flimsy, barely disguised wreckage. Within four minutes, the bus was back on course to its final destination: an igneous cave hotel. In all truth, the hotel was embedded within the bowels of an old igneous lava arrangement that had solidified many centuries ago. The naturally hollowed caves were a result of gas being trapped within the rock, causing many interconnecting cave-ins. The tourists were happy to be living inside of once-molten rock. It made them feel good, especially when they rubbed their feet on pumice bath rocks adorning the pricey spa, which was available, for a fee and a little skin of course. Little did the tourists know that their memories of the plastic life-forms were to bunk with them in their dreams that night, revealing the secrets of avocados and other light bulbs that would naturally overload, creating electrical outcries that can move through metal at a disturbed pace like a tattoo made of echoes.

Although vivid, the dreams revealed themselves to be short in duration. The sleeping tourists yawned and muttered, hugging pillows and avoiding the light of day, which really turned out to be a dream of daylight. Within the vortex of slumber, the tourists were unaware of when the plastic life forms would return, but they knew the day would arrive eventually.

In the waking world, a sea bass dives beneath a boat, intent on catching the vehicle. The soft wailing of fluffy kittens reaches its ears, even beneath the water, and yet the sea bass chooses to ignore the infant feline cries and pursue other interests. Once the sea bass reaches its final resting place—a bed of shredded green onion and ginger—the large fish reflects on how tasty its eyeballs could truly be, and it breathes in the flowery cilantro that lulls it to sleep.

Aside from larval writhing and twitching, the sleeping fish-cocoon grows nicely beside some boulders and harvested firewood in the desert sands. The nightfall cools the air, and the fire burns well in the darkness where only the shiny eyes of animals dimly illuminate the surrounding areas of darkness. Meanwhile, the hibernating sea bass barely displays the rise and fall of its slowly breathing body. Indiscriminate mousetraps suddenly snap shut, causing the vigilant fish-audience to shudder as they peer at their sleeping comrade tossing and turning in a bed of onion and herbs, with only a pregnant geode for a pillow. Lightning can be seen in the background, suggesting that the arcing electricity is striking the sand, causing veins of glass to flow under the burn-site. The fused grains of sand marry to make glass, and this nocturnal development causes the watcherfish to wring their nervous hands as they eye the cooking pot of tasty pork 'n beans on the campfire. After the lightning subsides and the last rolls of thunder reach the uncertain ears of the terrestrial watcherfish, there is a great relief, and the fish cheerfully consume their beans, looking for those imaginary cubes of pork that show up on the picture on the can label but never make it into the canning process. Sometimes life can be cruel that way, but the fish understand that life isn't perfect, and so they continue to obsessively stare at the slumbering sea bass sleep talking to the geode pillow while touching delicate but redundant flowerets of broccoli next to its eyes.

Underneath a world of metaphors, the big fish wakes and quietly slips into a whirling pool unnoticed by the other members of its kind. As the fish sinks to the depths of the dark water, it melts into a multi-lobed specimen of a bio-engineered tomato with blue spots (formed when the UV light content happens to be excessively high on certain days of the week). Such tomatoes never last long into the cold season, but they at least have the opportunity to show their spots during the warmer months. Sometimes these bizarre tomatoes were featured on salad bars across the Australian continent, but due to superstition, these special love apples were shunned by superstitious apes who scratched their armpits while looking at TV screens and wearing comfortable yak-fur slippers. All of the newspapers in the world couldn't do any good for the loss of this genetically modified organism, the spotted tomato. This GMO got caught up in the upswing of highly orchestrated paper trails, leading to its firm unpopularity in the inner grocery circles. Sometimes the grocery-club personnel would plot and scheme regarding these suspicious but colorful tomatoes, but their twisted musings never led to any substantial sort of action, other than heated, mock-serious gossip that was vicious as it was entertaining. Nevertheless, even though the Blue Spotted Tomato fell out of favor with the Australians, there were certain determined individuals within that territory that insisted on secretly cultivating the delicious strain within the hidden confines of secluded backyards and sinister dead-end paths within camouflaged gardens, allowing small quantities of the fruit to flourish even in an all-inclusively hostile environment. Despite the hard fact that the tomatoes came from a sleeper fish, they suppressed all fish characteristics in order to survive, in order to someday chew on electrothermically fused, venous beach sand of a pale blue variety.

2

A schipol of dust streaks across the frozen air, and the hibernating molecules of the frozen surface of the wooden cutting board are not aware that an evening's salad is being prepared upon the solidly suspended molecules of the sleeping wood. Eventually, the plaster tiles of the ceiling begin to cascade in annoying patterns across the beautifully tiled floors that house the frozen cutting boards. The ceiling tiles were in the shape of maple videotapes mysteriously growing from a lone trunk that spurt forth from the center of the cold floor of the den. Those tiles somehow were afraid of the cold and so missed many a collision with the block-frozen cutting board that lay awake for the strokes of the solid cleaver lurking in the dusty cupboards amid the spider-lairs and the dulled cans of freshly-cut green beans. So many lazy pumpkin-heads that were so ready to get smashed by the colossal swings of sledgehammers and other heavily industrial implements. And so the pumpkinseeds went flying during that particularly easy moment.

Those troublesome seeds landed in a left-handed pitcher's mitt that had been carelessly discarded among some old onion-sacks left behind by the previous inhabitants who faithfully rented the present flat for at least two years previously. Yet they decided to stay, even though the threat of the flying plaster tiles and nefarious pumpkin seeds that sub-consciously threatened every thriving youth in the greater area of "civilized" society managed to get into their minds and remind them of plaster-ghost-tiles of the past. Or so most of the plaster tiles thought, or at least half-suspected, as they measured the lengths of their tacos by the widths of their burritos, and sent in their cryptically-numbered answers by the early light of the half-busy morning. At least enough time for a half-corrupted cup of coffee, and maybe even a peek into the depths of the backyard blue-crab cultivation underneath the feet of the wayward exercise freaks who distracted the world with their feet, while their visions gave rise to a very photogenic farmyard of blue crabs with their claws in the air, saluting an odd form of urban Dixie. Such oddness would be paid for with blood.

The cylindrical pipes of plumbing surrounded the daylight of the feet that were seen too many times. The sunlight burnt the images into the wall and the preserved concrete photo was cherished by many successive generations. This sort of tunnel vision kept some sleepy folks sane in their television-watching hours and rocking chair adventures. The rainy flowers outside of the house hugged the concrete walls, and the interstitial spaces within the concrete managed to connect in a porous fashion so that rainwater could civilly conduct itself through the space of the concrete blocks, only to emerge on the other side of infinity as its distorted images stretched out onto a plastic road of ceramic atrocities and misshapen human-like figures. The dead, iconized ceramic forms were pure cliché, and would have fit nicely into the trunk of a taxi destined for the bottom of the ocean. This ominous formation geographically made certain faces nervous because of the strange resemblance to figures of people made out of charred wood that occurred previously on a rainy street in a foaming city under interesting urban pressures. The painted ceramic city blemished under the heat of the day, and all vestigial baggage fell free from wandering bodies. The baggage of ceramic burden melted into pools of frog piss, and a swaying tree spat rain on the ceramic rocks, who absorbed the spit and internalized it. The tree moved its crinoid form on top of a large slag of ceramic and sent its roots within the cracks of the heavy mass.

Within seconds, the tree dissolved the thermally compressed clay minerals back into their previous forms, and then absorbed them as photosynthetic nutrients. The tree then rested and prepared for its next jump to the next ceramic residue. The tree's name was Pluroid; it lived for certain nights where moonlight mixed with streetlight and the result was an urban aurora of purples and reds. Only some of the alleyways and back streets were receptive to that kind of hungry sky, and mostly cats were able to view the phenomena, while the apes were beneath acorn blankets within dormitory hideouts.

But the sky was instantly slashed to ribbons by a ribbed tool that had corroded electrodes behind its blade. Flashes of light rocked through the night sky and all transparent octopods dissipated with the breeze caused by the light. Their suction cups were encased around trees, and yet bodies continued to fade, writhing in compressed gases in the process of burning the night trees guarding various caves in the back alleys of shell-strewn litter tunnels where degenerate bipeds hoarded various devices made of plastic. The plastic devices would eventually oxidize, but not until the morning when such life forms were clearly visible. But only the owls knew about such activities as they transpired in the silent early morning hours when the darkness kept life at bay and yet not all asleep. Annoying hornets crawled from wooden crevices and began to journey among the various urban horror-sculptures that served curious purposes. Their teeth grew like rats', and yet it was not cheese they craved. The hornets took advantage of the fact that it was summer solstice that night, and they attached finely spun wires of particular thinness between the tips of their teeth, creating the primal makings of musical instruments that would soon be shaking the world on the subsonic level. The hornets forgot about their multi-use stingers as they carefully tuned the new tooth instruments. In the act of being caught within the slow passing of seconds, the teeth molded themselves to the high-quality wire and became receptors to the wires. The hunger of the stinging angry insects flowed from their newly erupted teeth into the tautly implemented metal, which could bend to any mold. After attaching all of the musical wires, the fanged hornets sullenly gazed at some carelessly strewn copies of *The Shouting Chicken Skin* and began to read the non-specific words of animals grasping at logic. This was the moment, at the point of looking at oddly discarded textbooks, that the sky began to fill with powdered doughnuts that could tempt even the nastiest of cave dwellers. Nevertheless, the musical hornets ignored the doughnuts, and the evil books, and propelled themselves through the dense air that served as more of a distraction than a source of life. The air was a symbolic representation of presumptuous condiments that only hid what was underneath all of the mayo. It was a commercial that could only have come from an intellectual armpit lurking out there amid the garbage and other suitcases and handbags that were now hanging dangerously from the branches of the sentient Pluroid trees. Somehow these trees sunk their branch tips into the ionized liquid of red and violet auroras that had plunged to low elevations, engulfing the tops of houses in a grip of color that diffused feelings into the inanimate objects. It was the tearing of the sky that set these developments into motion and would eventually release the altered hornets into an atmosphere that would bathe raw skin with a lick of the hidden sun, bleeding through the pores of the wood.

The night trees were suddenly ripped from the ground and were prevented from becoming magnolias, which would only attract cannonfire from some secret weapons kept out of sight behind a conveniently nearby hill. The trees were gently conducted into sumptuous bedrooms with lavish bedding and appropriate accessories. Before the trees were put to bed for a hundred years, gentle hands placed the moon's orbit through the heart's of these trees as they began to dream of their secondary lives that occurred invisibly among their various knots and other wooden infirmities that warped through their trunks at sometimes unpredictable angles. The moon would not pass through the hearts of these trees until one hundred years had passed of variously arranged summer solstices ultimately spelling the bloodlust of wolves who knew the hair of the trees intimately. The day would arrive, eventually, but not until that special moment predicted by wolves and musical hornets alike as their new voices reached through the knots of the wood and tattooed the trees with alien patterns of writing, creating nocturnal books of them for others to read only when the candlelight was at the right intensity. Not until that mood was set would the wood reveal the written secret that was sullenly initiated by alien hornets that had no understanding of the primate fauna riddling the continents with their plastic empires and carved objects of insectoid hunger, which was a puddle on the sidewalk. Nevertheless, the parched Pluroid trees slept for their allotted hundred years, dreaming of the day when the moon would wake them from their dreary slumber. It was more like resting an inch beneath the surface of a mud puddle rather than a steeply descending drop into the universe of everything.

As predicted, the Pluroid trees eventually emerged from their queasy stasis and re-entered life as the new century passed. They resumed their usual nighttime, as if nothing had ever occurred, yet they still awoke to the questioning eyes of the wolves and the musical stinging alien insects. And yet the trees said nothing, since they couldn't really say much anyway, and they passively migrated across the night fields in a total silence reminiscent of floating candles on a pond of pink happy-lilies—that special breed that can float even when the sky is upside down in a freeze-dried container kept in hip pockets by hip astronauts who are working late out in the cold wastes of outer space.

After the silent but now reanimated Pluroid trees drifted off into the distance, off into their mysterious lives, the rest of the world resumed its long hike up the mountain in search of the burning bush, or at least some kind of cerebral artifact that could be instantly classified and comprehended for later contemplation in symbolic form when the lights were low and sparks were easily generated from the contact of two objects in mutually close proximity. This condition of reality was spelled out upon the sonic pages of hibernating auroral branch-books. What was written on those pages told of icy crystals that could slip through one's fingers, and of how green glass vases could spontaneously crack, bleeding out red droplets of silicon all over the floor. This inorganic, evacuated material almost represented a slaughter in itself as other vases made of glass shuddered and attempted to resist fractures that might lead to the uncontrollable bleeding of red-jeweled glass droplets. The information regarding the blood-red glass droplets from wounded glassware was then transcribed from the recovered auroral space books of hibernating night trees who mutter foreign languages in their sleep.

This perfected knowledge remained within a library of wood and glass, all tucked away within an intergalactic truck stop situated on the edge of a nebula. Sometimes the library would be duplicated, branch for branch, word for word, and then the library visitor would take a vacation to another nearby planet for perusal and permanent edification. But for the most part, the library wasn't often filled with patrons, just old spider webs and empty plates with cookie crumbs, red droplets of glass, and empty milk glasses. Could the Christmas cockroaches have passed through this sacred valley at least once over the eons of desolation and abandonment? No one really could determine that, at the present moment, and so the intergalactic library visitors made their duplications and then went on their way. It was possible that as soon as the intergalactic library patrons left to return to their home world to disseminate that special knowledge of ice crystals and inorganic blood-fossils, they would slip into obscurity along with the library.

Even though time passed very slowly for the library, it happened very quickly for the musical alien hornets who had been discretely observing the peculiar glass-dropping activities and decided to home in on the commotion of the few intergalactic patrons as they left the intergalactic library book depot. The alien musical hornets began to sing their mating songs and danced in intricate flight patterns, confusing a few vacationing polar bears passing by with their umbrellas and Goldilocks porridge picnic baskets (imported from France). The hornets paid no heed to the happy polar bears as they waddled by with blood on their chins and fish in their thoughts. The song of the insects assumed intricate patterns as the clicks of their antennae were attuned to the minute air compressions caused by small flickers of lightning grazing the hill over which just passed the vacationing polar bears. Once the insectoid music had coursed through every pore in the surface rocks, praying mantises hopped over a neighboring fence to study the peculiar wasps that represented a territorial threat to the praying mantises.

Once the mantises had eaten the entire group of alien wasps, wire fangs and all, they seized reeds of bamboo and played organic flute music. This result was probably due to the digestion of those musical fangs and metal strings, which once comprised the vocal mandibles of the peculiar wasps who came from beyond earth's home solar system.

The mantises produced pocket mirrors and regarded their own newly formed singing mandibles and shrugged their insectoid shoulders, utterly perplexed. The praying mantises bored into some large baobab trees and created very quaint cottage-style bedrooms within the discreet hollows of the giant trees. A squirrel skull, attached to a string, dropped from the higher branches of the baobab tree and landed within reach of the praying mantises. They ignored the proposition and resumed their tunneling activities, stretching their graceful wings from time to time. Once the task was completed, the mantises began a very laborious task of cataloging all of the different sound varieties, through which they were capable of producing from their newly developed organic musicality. Eventually the catalog was completed and stored in a very safe place, and the praying mantises started to sing to the trees. The uttered music forced the cavernous trees to assume new organic conformations, with repositioned branches and other small adjustments. The new tree home of music was a true piece of data, a testament of the waking world. The tree was able to migrate as a cloud would, due to its connection with the song-codes of the resting mantises who ate plenty of large black ants for dinner. The tree now became a world in itself and would drift through any and all obstacles.

Eventually the tree assumed the shape of a curtain and permanently resided next to an open window, blowing in the breeze. The curtain-house was multidimensional, allowing the rather large insects between the inner folds of musical reality to rest peacefully in a paradoxically compressed form, like a vacuum tunnel created to house certain wooden organs that preferred the absence of atmosphere in contact with their bodies. The only entrance of this multidimensional construction was situated between eyes of an iron wolf frozen like a statue in the wastes of a cryogenic meat locker. This meat locker was safely hidden in the basement of a mutated restaurant that placed little treasures close to the hinges on all of the large and small doors. Once in the meat locker, all one had to do was to place one's hand between the glowering eyes of the frozen iron wolf. Its irises sparkled as they caught the light of the large torch placed next to its sharp ears. With such a process, it was possible for the musically adept mantises to come and go as they pleased within the multidimensional house-curtains that were billowing in a cold winter wind, blowing through the rooms of the chilly restaurant.

Many of the small rooms within the cold restaurant were permanently occupied by comatose, savage trees in the process of lunar hibernation, forever serving in the creation of instructional runes that might someday be useful to other drifting trees on vacation from their usual routines. At certain times of the year, there was even a small group of ex-nuns who would come for worldly visits in order to inspect the tree-like instructional runes, comprising a useful library. The ex-nuns would finish their chocolate smores and then turn their moist eyes to the runes so that they might be able to go camping in rugged mountain areas where mountain men with big phalluses dwelled, at least during the off-season. The ex-nuns were a very tidy group, speaking in perfect English and forever in awe of the variety of worldly pleasures available within the odd confines of the cold restaurant. The mantises were always very happy to see these ex-nuns, and so extended their every courtesy and male flattery of their endearing grace and spontaneity.

These ex-lovers of Jesus Christ of Nazareth enjoyed these traveling experiences and grew accustomed to receiving the nocturnal visits of some of the more daring mantises in the odd midnight hours when most creatures were asleep. With their souls satisfied, the once-lovers of the man-of-the-soiled cloth slumbered in utter serenity, dreaming of trees and other roomy plants. Every so often an unconscious hand dangled with uncertainty, but eventually all was peaceful, even in the throes of subconscious metamorphosis to new insectoid levels of development. The ex-wives of Jesus slumbered very well that night, awakening the next day feeling solidly refreshed, with firm limbs and sharp minds. They had an energizing breakfast of raw mango pulp mingled with the juice of a sweet lime alongside a plate of unleavened crackers with twelve-thirteenths of a mutilated sardine upon each. These meager rations left the ex-nuns charged with life, and they sauntered out into the worldly world, in search of husbands and families and other quaint and altered acoustic-guitar feely-thoughts. Through such behaviors, the ex-nuns established certain patterns of force, which the sentient mantises came to expect.

3

In ways that were hard to predict, the hours of the clock demagnetized and began to creep backwards, ever so slightly, in response to the seismic waves that shook the public phone booth. The clock in this phone booth took a beating earlier when narrowly avoiding a stampede of ostriches who had heard a televised commercial for dental hygiene products. The ostriches seized upon this consumer potential by rounding up their spare change and rushing off to the corner store where such things were usually sold. But the current seismic waves, which were a challenge to the phone booth, were not showing as much mercy as the ostriches did. The skeleton of the booth began to buckle under the moving forces, and the clock and the other phone booth accessories remaining inside exhaled a firm sigh of despair, as they watched through the dirty glass of a Coca-Cola truck being raided by electrical repairmen in search of a breakfast drink.

These developments might have been alarming to some, but to the clock inside of the phone booth, the display was routine and somewhat boring. The clock looked down at its own thin arms and noticed that the black-painted metal was starting to look like painted bricks of clay. Within the bricks were cement adhesives holding them together, even when the ground shook. But on this day, the bricks were knocking in their joints, ready to go to horse races and other checkerboard events where even one's steps leave multicolored tracks on the floor. This sort of foot-ambiance was recognized by retina-scanning doorknobs that were irregularly placed at various angles in the witch-house that recently erupted through the tracked floor within the disproportionate phone booth. The foundation of the phone booth held together quite well through the short but surprised appearance of the witch-house next to the old grandfather clock.

As if by chance, the house chose to come through the floor so that the clock would be facing the backdoor to the basement cellar, where pumpkins and other well-preserved artifacts dwelled amid spider webs and discarded robotic dentures. Within this small backdoor cul-de-sac, there was also a small, discarded plastic radio emitting sinister hypodermic music. This suffocating music seemed to worm its way into the cracks of the witch-house, inspiring visions of a foreboding conflagration that would consume everything within the public phone booth. Despite the terror of the hypodermic music (that was attempting to torture the isolated grandfather clock), the witch-house did not provoke much of a reaction from the rest of the besieged phone booth. Within the witch-house, warlocks and witches peered out of the dusty windows previously opened once or twice in another life. The witch-creatures spoke among themselves, discussing in a heated fashion the latest developments, including the captured grandfather clock that had been taken prisoner upon the majestic arrival of the witch-house.

Once the grandfather clock had been dissected and all its metal organs categorized, the witches and warlocks all held hands and began to chant a spell to be effective as of midnight. The chanting was louder than it seemed, and the entire spell could be easily heard by those ostriches who had now surrounded the public phone booth.

4

When sewerage boys plant mango light bulbs at every street corner, a wealth of tickertape fallout is available for viewing. Library tables are arranged also in response to the planting of the mango light bulbs, and these activities are delightfully festive distractions for people with pet alligators who are bored with the more mundane aspects of life. The owners of the alligators are on the verge of senility, but they curiously protect their pets as well as the mango light bulbs that they furtively seek with inept claws. On the dreamy city sidewalks, the light bulbs rise from the concrete at dusk and pneumatic riveters cause entire brownstone buildings to fall. The rising dust causes many an eye to be inundated with soot, but that event wouldn't force too many observers to retire early to their well-stocked, inflatable homes. Once the well-stocked, inflatable houses are occupied, narcoleptic toothpaste donors arrive with suitcases stocked with toothpaste and other oral hygiene products. The toothpaste is then gently smeared all over mirrors, allowing vampires to remain from becoming frightened at not seeing themselves in the reflective panes. This kind of Friday afternoon activity can take the greater part of six hours, and nostalgic pelicans shed tears in order to be involved with the toothpaste-mirror gang.

As suddenly as the toothpaste-mirror gang arrives on the scene, they and their followers immediately become self-obsessed, as they usually do in their busy public lives that revolve around mirrors. Even though they might be doing a great service for the vampires who cringe at not seeing themselves in mirrors, in the end they create chaos for those who must shave in the morning, or apply cosmetics to lips and other areas. Once hooligan politicians create laws that might someday abolish these self-obsessed toothpaste-mirror gang members, then the future might be more easily absorbed by the eagerly spying satellites who have managed to reach the cracks of the door like roaches.

But at least the children know wiser than to waste their time with toothpaste mirror gang members, and so they quietly tip-toe past the oddly lit crack under the door, declining to peer through the key-hole at certain groups who claim to owe their existence solely due to their collective images in mirrors covered in a toothpaste pastiche, which could be better executed by a ring-tailed lemur from Madagascar, where all of the fun stuff happens anyway. Meantime, in bathroom-land, perverse primates carry out their toothpaste worship oblivious to what their children chose to witness in the outdoor areas of the world. This sickly inequity is toxic even to the moping fruits that grow on backyard patios next to croquet lawn constructions. Sometimes Jesus even crawls out of his ant hill to survey the toxic fruits and awkward croquet arrangements, yet he always yawns and goes back to doing better things, things worthier of attention than just limp fruits and dysfunctional sports equipment.

Nevertheless, the wandering children pass through the backyard of anonymously yet sinisterly positioned protein drinks on immaculate picnic tables (of a disturbing blue coloration), and manage to make their collective way into the alley, where all of the wild peppers are growing next to the dens of camouflaging lizards who treat the sun like a lover. It is in the alleyway that the border between night and day is indistinguishable, and this bridge represents the full spectrum of all feelings and techniques of tactile reassurance that members of the primate taxon really need. The alleyway, now a barnyard of wooden statues, brings its will to its knees and then rips the roof off with a very well placed burst of wind. The summer of the barnyard becomes apparent, and communicating telephones present themselves in odd corners of the barn facilities, glowing with a green plastic cheapness that makes the roosters laugh and the cows begin to shift their bony stances in boredom.

As if the boredom wasn't enough, the cows endure a marked resurgence of sinisterly positioned protein drinks in odd corners of the haunted room. One brave rooster approached one of the protein drinks and peered through the jagged metal aperture at the oddly stewing hurricane of clover within.

A cow also comes to look through the opening, and saw the following white street-backs hurry over fields of hurricane clover, where young women frolic when their clothes turn invisible behind a lemon-juice candle that they used to keep at the back of their abnormally large closet in the dusty bedrooms of their grandparents' neglected mansion found close to other neglected mansions in the neighborhood. Immediately, the aroused girls disappear behind an antique red velvet curtain and make love to the portraits that are secretly hidden beneath the curtain. Due to the fact that the naked, lovemaking young women spend a lot of time with the secret portraits, the bemused butler of the mansion can only conclude that the paintings indeed are very well hung. Once the girls have emerged from behind the curtains with sweaty brows, they sit in the plush fancy chairs to have their tea.

When the young female lovelies rise from the couch and dress themselves, they eventually answer the phone that has been ringing for at least six minutes. The butler is the caller, and he asks the young female lovelies if they have done their mathematics homework. Of course the young women say "yes," and the butler is soothed by this simple answer that fortunately did not become complicated, like it so often has done in the past, especially when red velvet portrait curtains and earl gray tea are involved. The butler, now calm and finished with his nervous perspiring, wishes the young ladies a good evening as he prepares to have some exciting curtain portrait experiences of his own. After the butler finishes pouring his earl gray tea, he rises from his fly-swatter couch and dons his most expressive butler uniform. He marches throughout the velveteen house, opening doors and windows for imaginary visitors, so that he can be ready for when the guests come to the neglected mansion. In the meantime, all the butler has are his telephone, feather duster, and a skeleton key that can open and lock all rooms and secret compartments throughout the house. These tools are all that he requires to weather the elements of dustful neglect seeping through closed fists like a delightful mass of blenderized avocado flesh. Once the butler has unlocked and then locked the last passageway, he calls his young female lovelies to verify that they are completing their stuffy literature assignments. Once verified, the literature assignments are stuffed into literary recycling bins.

The dawning sun pours over the neglected, dusty red velvet house, and the young lovelies and the butler writhe in feverish dreams, each in their own separate bedrooms, of course. With the morning light, the house becomes comfortably flattened and promptly inserted into a Ziploc evidence bag for further processing. Where the house used to stand is an underground beehive of tunnels and chambers used only during the warm summer months. Now that the house is gone, symbolic trees erupt and obscure the pleasant summer catacombs so that no prying hands of neighbors might enter. The trees bear bloody berries that are wet with blood. These berries are so engorged with animal blood that they seep down the branches like tears. Even the birds leave these berries alone. These burnt fruits might be harvested at nightfall, but uncertainty still lingers regarding that particularly desirable outcome. With the removal of the berries, the tree would be enabled to generate more bleeding fruits, and these might serve useful to the neighborhood canning plants that are located on every corner.

Humorful time melts the canning plants down to the ground, eventually, leaving behind a sallow magnesium ash. That ash is made into a paint that coats your walls, where the lights are not electric, but of the awkwardly homemade type, where the moment of the annoying flicker is unpredictable. But time moves on and the sun rips through the room on a daily basis, inducing the painted ash to sprout neurological tendrils maintaining a natural geotactic tendency, sending down roots to underground streams of untainted mineral water. The neurological plant thing drops the roots as far down as it can manage, forcing aside walls of rock bursting with dull but perfectly shaped octagonal rods. In this manner, the sallow walls drink from the ground.

Nauseating blemishes shudder throughout the plaster walls that support the neurological plant thing with its newly burrowed roots. The roots can dig very far down, constantly weaving through new fissures in the rock and dodging those octagonally crystalline rods. Although inert, the rods are a nuisance and their unseeable beauty only fogs the corneas of observant mammals with furry fingers and dripping noses. Once the roots have managed to reach the desired underground water supply, they quickly absorb the water and minerals at a phenomenal rate, forcing the plant to burst through the seams of the house, spreading neurons through the shell of that which used to house it. The discarded house was now a discarded substrate that was embryonic filth within the tendrils' grasp.

Giant, white shoes lurched forward, and a large figure stooped to collect the neurological plant still perched within the remains of its infantile mnemonic house cradle. With the main root severed, the overgrown neurological tree was quivering upon the floor of the collection vessel. Fortunately, the container was equipped with water tanks that opened once the neurological mass was transferred. With the transfer complete, the colossal figure with white shoes closed the container, leaving behind a few shattered two-by-fours and the newly chopped initial root mass, still quivering.

In a few days, a white truck approached the area to excavate most of the surrounding yard in order to extract the root, which had begun to decay, releasing a putrid odor that scared away most of the wildlife, including the raincoat fish. The remains were burned at the site, and after the ground was neatly packed (thereby closing the hole to the subterranean groundwater), the white-shod work-crew left and never returned. In place of an empty lot next to other houses perched among lurid rock outcroppings, the planted seed of a new house was already beginning to grow, sending down roots, attempting to reach naturally occurring water. A bird with sickly purple feathers flew overhead, emitting a shriek that could only have come from a mouth that loved the taste of blood. The bird landed on a nearby tree to observe the newly formed house at a closer distance. Already the features of the backyard had erupted like fungus, with inflating organic picnic tables covered with sinisterly placed cans of an unpronounceable protein drink. The sickly purple bird squawked and rubbed its gnarled talons through mangy, unkempt feathers. The bird was joined by other members of its kind and they conferred among themselves regarding the new house, including in the discussion whether or not the warehouse might some-day have those juicy termites with which they so often loved to engorge themselves. After the conference, the mangy purple birds each flew off in their own home direction (due to their competitive territoriality) and stayed away from the new house for a day or so.

In the meantime, the house grew to its final size within hours. With all domestic organs in place, the house looked almost like the surrounding ones, barring a few design innovations which the older, neighborhood homes did not have. In this manner, the house could function well along with its brethren, absorbing newspapers and spewing out x-mas lights. As the years passed, the house grew into a fine, model specimen, grab-bing eyes from all around to gaze on its touching rustic qualities, its organic picnic tables, its swimming pools replete with burnt-on foot-prints, and last but not least, its attic that bore phosphorescent teeth spurting from every beam and joint of wood. These intimate places were the rave, and were well documented by the newspapers that continu-ously fed into the homes at all hours, even when the sun was down. Such a solid metamorphosis frozen in time, such a magnified process.

Once the intimacy of the houses had been breached, systematically, the flow of incoming newspapers became sporadic, and of their own volition, the folded packages of regurgitated current events fled from the site of the punctured metropolitan suburbia. Houses became soft, and strange hands began to throw coconuts at refrigerators and microwave ovens, conveniently dislodging electrical currents with the kinetics of eyelashes. Moments were labeled with numbers, and a time of autumn bliss remained fractionated into guiding rocks that fell from the precarious wall of a damp canyon. The misplaced wall spelled the end for the variously arranged houses with their backyard organic pic-nic tables with those curiously positioned (yet seriously misplaced) protein drinks. With the wall in a state of fuzzy dissolution, unknown hands were able to free themselves from cul-de-sacs where they were sequestered for the last neural coffee break. With their fingers free and able to move throughout the maze-like catacombs of the fibrous walls of the melting houses, hands arrived back into action—a movement they hadn't seen in at least half a century.

5

At the rip of a stretched wing, the formations of castles were shattered by an abrupt clap of thunder. The impinging weather asserted itself with the gravest of rolling thunder mimicking the spinning lightning of artificial turbines, which are sometimes found besides lakes and small country houses off-limits to foxes and unkempt staircases. The friendly lightning was intended possibly as a flashing beacon to scare away paranoid travelers, or maybe a living tissue in search of healthy cells to pop into the complex, touchy-feely architecture of unplacid skies. The falling raindrops seared the frigid skin of the land-animals who crawled and skulked amid barely swaying limbs and branches, marking a dark nexus every time a bolt of lightning penetrated the lower atmosphere. The fervid animals groped around in the dark, making themselves comfortable from minute to minute beneath bushes and other dark objects of cover. Fortunately their eyes did not glow by themselves, but were only briefly reflective with every arc of electrical current. These reflective eyes sometimes gave their positions away to some of the other faceless creatures, but those sorts of accidents happened rarely, like when certain juvenile creatures dropped their candy-machine flashlights next to their nighttime running shoes that they saved for desperate incursions into rock walls frequently located next to moving water currents. The darkness of the murky ravine was nearly complete as the moon began to hide behind a thick cloud. Even the Pluroid trees quivered in their peculiar brand of ancientness.

Suddenly one of the animals dropped another candy-machine flash-light, and for a brief moment, the form of the creature was illuminated to show a fumbling wretch grasping for the fallen device. All of the dark wildlife in the ravine paused to consult watches, horoscopes and baro-metric pressure in order to make the subconsciously unanimous execu-tive decision to flee one of the world's darkest crevices in search of higher-grade candy-machine flashlights, which only rumored and grotesquely fabled privileged beasts had achieved through their mortal efforts. After the cheap device struck damp, rotting, fallen plant mate-rial, the entire swarm of the light-starved creatures of blindness effort-lessly dashed away from the scene in completely divergent trajectories, in the way the spores of the night mushrooms disperse in the early hours of morning. The running beasts tasted their own blood as they left their temporary ravine and perceived the beautiful terrain of a world at night. Their sensitive eyes registered the barely-red shades of dark apples, clinging to branches, right next to the gentle swaying of the artichoke spikes. Delightfully dark picnic tables still asserted themselves in the shadows behind well-kept houses, with abandoned but full pro-tein-drink cans positioned on every corner of the outdoor furniture. The form of the moon was present, and it provided what little light it could give to a land that was asleep. The night beasts marveled at the mysterious purpose of the derelict cans and made a cell-phone call to any receptive relatives who could provide explicative information within the short span of thirty seconds. The march of the insects was apparent.

Once the insects were noticed on the walls close to the garbage cans, the royal skateboards were hung from backyard gates, and all of the apple crates were stacked for the coming morning that threatened to crash open within the approaching hour. The day was to be the sword that was to cleave the sweating, throbbing darkness into halves, which would finally eliminate a twelve-hour folly of candy-machine flashlights and mythical protein drinks abandoned on outdoor furniture. The spear through the glass that would become the morning.

Ripping up the glass, the morning poured in (as was expected), and appropriately froze all liquid forms. It soon became visible that the branches of the stationary trees were embedded with very smooth pebbles that might have come from a stone-tumbler. Fortunately, the trees were not concerned, and spent their time dealing with other issues. Every now and then, beautiful women would emerge from houses, pass from tree to tree, and mutter things to themselves. Although it was never determined what was being said beneath those stone-encrusted trees that might as well have been tombs, their roots feverishly grasped at rocks at all hours of the day and night. This action was enough to distract all observers with the shaking of the ground caused by the unstable tectonics that created many valleys and ravines in what might have been smoother terrain for settlements to occur.

The sun shone on everything within the hour, and the now-defunct world of the night exhaled a cold, misty sweat that spoke of sleep. Even though the picnic tables now displayed a coating of homely blue paint, they still faithfully carried their symbolic protein drinks at all corners and edges of the structure. And even though birds sang at the encroaching tables, the chirping had no effect on the integrity of the paint, and so they remained a homely blue color until the next paint-job, perhaps five or so years down the endless temporal road. Until then, they would remain as they were, and continue supporting the asses of those who sat on them, as well as all of the plates, card games and plastic record players.

Suddenly, enormous grandfather clocks erupted from the well-manicured grass, and their limp clock-hands fell from their attachments with a sultry brunette clatter. The front doors of the grandfather clocks violently swung open, as if in the throes of an uncontrollable purge, ejecting an infected pendulum of some inner genetic condition that disrupted the purgatory of the timepieces. With the pendulums repulsed, the clocks fell over with relief and slept amid their neatly abscised clock-hands of many colors and cryptic markings. Even though the clocks fell into instant slumber, the rest of the world did not follow, and so the morning activities of the world resumed after the clocks had gotten the chance to settle. The once-open ravines and treacherous canyons were now neatly sealed, impervious to the daylight, and they conducted their perpetually dark activities with snails over their eyes and combing forks moving through their hair.

The sun followed neatly planted rows of pine trees that bore much pollen and pinecones. Once again, there was the question of the evilness of the pinecones as they looked down upon the ground with its matted grass and discarded teeth. Also on the ground was a carelessly discarded book of matches bearing the image of a cheetah in mid-flight over a burning tree-stump with a suspended hatchet on its upper edge. Those oddly blue picnic tables suddenly became ready to receive barbecued plates with plastic politics and neurogenic teeth that were like cerebral fish crammed into the fissures of broken metal.

After the barbecue festivities have begun, amber staircases appear behind only a few of the largest oak trees, and openings to secret professional workshops are revealed to the naked eye. At the advent of the secret professional workshops that are now made public, there apparently was a barbecue, and yet there was more: wheelbarrows full of hot coffee, tambourines, bean-bags and tarantulas with very sharp teeth. These offerings bespoke the inner nature of the secret professional workshops that just went public; they said something about the types of things that used to go on in private at the bottoms of those amber spiral staircases that were dug down into the earth.

Once the professional private workshops were available to all creatures, the libraries began to carry some of the manuals that accompanied the workshops, and so the simple people were happy for a while, at least until the seasonal storms would arrive. When that happened, all of the secret professional mists would be cleared and swept away like scattered popcorn on a sticky movie-house floor. Such a spilling of corn seed represented the ship trapped in the bottle, and would foretell of many cosmic bouquets to come.

When the neurotic brooms rose from the dirt to begin the clean up of the spilled popcorn seed, a lone cowbell is knocked off its window-peg by the wind and it oddly smacks the ground. Remove one seed and then there's another to take its place. These kinds of developments can only transpire when the hidden ice and holy, mythical fossil bacteria on the moon are taken out of their storage lockers by moon people who don't really care all that much about earth, due to its brightness that burns their retinas, forcing them to spend their solar days under boulders where they sculpt words from rock that get shipped to a central sorting area. Within the lunar complex of alien musical gibberish, a big crucible is melting the solid words down to a liquid form to be used for an unknown purpose, unknown even to the moon people, but presenting dire circumstantial evidence for the lapses of lunar madness within the brains of terrestrial warm-blooded animals. Lunar lexicon is never stronger than when one can see the craters secretly bearing the hidden, frozen ice and the holy, mythical fossilized bacteria that was already pre-categorized by the folks back on the steamy earth.

After the fallen cowbell released the wrath of the moon, the pine trees dropped their pollen and the previously fertilized seeds that spiraled down to the ground. The seedlings were happy, and they celebrated by becoming magnetically attracted to pipe-cleaners and well-formed cubes of plastic explosive which would provide much joy and entertainment during the building season when certain forges created spiked garden implements ultimately making retired people happy. Of course, the spiked garden implements would make others happy, too, especially when the red maple leaves of autumn were the last umbrella of foliage before the frozen winter would set in. Past that point, the metallurgical workhouses were converted to hotel suites containing multiple televisions and archaic flyswatters. The pine seedlings knew of the repercussions of their actions, and yet they still stuck to their pipe-cleaners and plastic explosives.

When the next day broke, the metal garden implements were neatly folded and stacked within a potting shed by careful hands. Those tools were to remain there until spring, when the children were let out from school and paper dragons were released from repressed lunchboxes. An ominous sky spilled open, bidding the moon to do its noxious exercises on a landscape that would not sleep until bow ties were unwrapped from paper boxes and attached to stone hands of invisible statues. These statuettes were cautiously positioned behind the vigilant pine trees who had just left a strong period of fertility, which bespoke a vague sentiment of happiness and completeness that no tombstones could fracture. Uncertain wind-currents extinguished all open flames and the stifling sleep was routinely dodged by all of the night plants erupting from cracks in the nocturnal tombstones, inverting the claws of black tigers who gnawed at leftover bones from previous kills. Green, unripe tomatoes were hurled at the tombstones, and the firm flesh of the tomatoes made hostile noises that disturbed even the black tigers, interrupting their teething activities. Phones rang but remained unanswered while preoccupied teachers poured over their books of mental boredom and premature, prepubescent career-building that certain people were deeply concerned with in their idle, non-working hours. Of course, there were always those dark, professional workshops available to attend, especially when there were so many of those important buzzwords and superfluous acronyms to toss out obsessively and compulsively, close to the time when the last train would pass through the pine forest. All lights would have to be extinguished then, and all workshops would have to be paused until the sleeping hands could regain control of red pens, grade-books and desks in order to format the coming day into a predetermined template, which only linear minds could easily follow without having to deal with the subconsciously-buried, rationalist guilt that threatened to surface during mild, randomly occurring natural events, such as the falling of pinecones and pollen. These actions were considered by some as over-stimulatory, and the sooner that lists could be checked with red pens, and that outlines drawn out on left hands, then life could return to a predictable pattern which even socially-shocked minds could handle. Thank gODD for bits and harnesses.

Once the busybody social engines have gathered their niter and applied animal by-products to their bodies, arms are unzipped. The skin from the unzipped arms is lifted to produce well-grown honey-combs within the bone-cavities that leak only the purest of green blends of honey. Such a cache of corporeal honey is dangerous to surface com-munities, and so coffee and cake are produced for atonement, hopefully convincing all regional powers that no danger is to be introduced at informal social gatherings. Meanwhile adolescents longingly gaze at the potting sheds that are mercilessly sealed off for the winter, or at least until brighter skies are opened, scaring off the sultry, overcast mists.

We will sever the roots from the tree, as we have been asked. Our pocket-sized church laughs merrily inside of a filing cabinet crawling with hungry ants that search for honey (vestigial drippings) from the exposed honeycomb bones that were offered by the purveyors of con-fusing social gatherings. The ants resist the frustration of scarce honey-blood, and continue their futile search for crumbs left behind from the feast from a few days ago, when the flesh was still freshly killed, and razor clam comb-cases were neatly installed on top of plastic explosive attachments dutifully cemented to the lunchboxes of loved-ones. The guitars of the loved-ones also have frets made from razor clams, and this additive gives a distinctive sound to the chords that move from one instrument to another, in the same way fungal hyphae are linked even with natural obstacles of stones, roots and plastic fish skeletons that, despite their factory-induced odoriferousness, are hardy, firm examples of the phonemes of feelings, the building blocks of a spontaneous emo-tion. The magic guitars cringe with every passing hour and numbers rudely insert themselves within wooden cracks that were once free of all musical contaminants. Every now and then, strong arms use the guitars to slap incoming sports equipment venturing too close to the honey-combed skeletons of humans who assemble the sweetest of bedroom furniture, especially when merciless reproduction is initiated within the claws of angels and disconnected eyebrows. Surely the eyes of frogs were meant to reflect more than the sickly chords of a semi-professional workshop.

The ants will return to cash in on their honey-combed animal bones, and they will accordingly get to work, completely leaching all infused flower nectar from the hollow crevices and pits. A mother cat licks her kittens, noticing their red paws and sleepy eyes. Even if they were to stretch out in the sun for an hour, they would still retain the hairy vision of sunset within their ears, among the dust mites and other verminous nuisances that had entered without knocking. An unearthly cowbell is hurled down the ear canal, and so the kittens dream, twitching within their visions of knee-high grass and elusive rodents with glowing whiskers. A knock at the back door has the roughness of a freshly shorn beard, and the cowbell is regurgitated through the keyhole, revealing red eyes with bluish-green colorations that observe the end of life with a piano-wand, magnetically tantalizing all electronic equipment.

While doorknobs are polished and red paws scratch under the threshold of the front door, the lava within the basement quietly stews in the soup cauldron. The hot soup has the ceramic fingernails of windy trouble, and so the peanuts of knuckles are disjointed and unattached, moving in a wraithlike fashion under the skin. Hired hands paint exquisite portraits of the rats who make their beds in the corners of the dirty cellar. This lower room has a record player that lost its needle many years prior to the generation of the hot lava soup. In the basement, wooden sculptures of sterile people collect dust but remain aware of their inactive condition, in the same way other wooden sculptures of people around the globe engage in the same sort of mindful inactivity, at least during the night when they regard their artificially created families that are pocket-sized amulets of deformed coral encrusted with beads and a cheap brand of shellac. Perhaps artificial air is harder to breathe than the naturally occurring variety, but its easy availability is what captures these sleeping souls who remember the first ten years of life before their wooden eyes were chewed out by nest-building insects. Eventually the basement will be sealed off cryogenically, creating a refrigerator of leftovers to sit upon cakes of baking soda that will reduce the offensive odors. In the kitchen, mindful hands wring out soaking rags of honey used to clean seeping orifices in which bone-dwelling honeycombs were strategically planted when the original insect family was created with peanut butter, string and glue made from the kneecaps of rotting horses. These same equine creatures were also the ones who littered the large storm drains after the fall deluge that washed away the minions of the chlorine epidemic. Hands are inserted into libraries in order to procure advice on how to deal with such a pleasant surprise around lunchtime, where idle minds contemplate the maintenance of their daily illusions and accustomed activities. No need to even try teaching old horses new tricks with glue and other agglutinated strands of colored yarn. These washed out bodies, once cleaned off and polished, make nice display pieces to be positioned within the corners of the main foyer, so that visiting livestock can appreciate them from the narrow perspective of horse hair pillows that engender sweet but languid dreams of apocalyptic eggs boiled with every color known to man, so that they might test their fickle theories of life.

Great oak trees grow up through the tender throats of women who value the taste of galaxies on their lips. These special women take the washed-out bodies and mummify them with gauze bandages dipped in plaster of Paris. After the mummification process, the sarcophagi are sealed in liquid latex and inserted into the hollows of the female throat trees where they can passively catch falling stars as the earth enters meteor fields from time to time. These women then migrate through soft forests of horse hair, using the mummies as lanterns that last longer than even the most highly endorsed of copper-bottom batteries, (true rejects in a pile of pre-programmed copper-tops). The newly inspired throat-treed women then proceed to notice that the shapes of their neatly wrapped washed-out sarcophagi, used as lanterns, happen to uncannily coincide with the shapes of the open windows of the fortress to which they are drifting. Therefore, the dead-body lanterns are easily thrown through the congruent windows of the fortress, facilitating the decision-making process of the sequestered warriors to open the gates in order to greet their long-lost wives. These long-lost wives now bear trees that grow from their tender throats, and their long-lost husbands stare at them, as well as at the washed out body-lanterns that were recently hurled through the window by the unknown women. Such an off-key reunion gave all three parties pause; while the body lanterns remained within their bandages and appropriately dreamt of cephalopods with plastic colors, the men and women bickered among themselves over interesting things like can-openers, egos and other interpersonal issues, oblivious to the moat of the fortress that was beginning to overflow with noxious coffee, which would someday represent the blood of emptiness to the arguing people. When the blood of the hourglass mixed thoroughly with the blood of emptiness, the resulting fluid was uncontainable, and so the men and women with throat-trees used their dead-body lanterns as a stepladder via the precise layering of bodies that were now teeming with invasive tarantulas. In fact, the spiders were beginning to feel that they had bitten off more than they could masticate with their sharp fangs. With the stepladder in place, the flustered humans generated a piñata from the uncontainable fluid created from the mixing of empty blood with hourglass blood. This piñata was equipped with taillights and so could navigate the early skies of morning, if necessary. After the warrior husbands and throat-treed wives had descended the steps of the dead-body lanterns, they moved their party to the washroom where they began to shave stray hairs from their bodies (especially from their backs and feet) and talk of coming nuptial card-games where the betting of money was involved and where all of their friends would be present. After the hair was shorn, the fortress monkeys inserted their fingers within the dried shells of razor clams and began to tap the music of their ancestors upon the skulls of their attentive dogs. Once the dogs received the complete, uninterrupted message (via the head-tapping), they immediately became frenzied and went off on a month-long bloodlust episode that culminated with the arrival of a thick stack of razor clam research proposals, which were ultimately approved by the university parrots with black tail feathers and concentric blood markings around their keen, avian eyes. The frenzied dogs returned with the squirming proposals between their jaws, and the fortress monkeys removed the razor clam musical instruments from their fingers, wasting no time in the preparation of their romantic submarine, to be used for their descent to the distant bottoms of the moat where the razor clams once made their first appearance. After the fortress monkeys embarked upon their razor clam search, the dogs sighed, stretched, and reclined upon the now-silent stones of the fortress. They wistfully opened their eyes at the sky and thought about the perturbed hairs on their heads.

Oblivious to some crows that had landed next to the moat in order to stare down into the dark water after the receding fortress-monkey divers, the dogs napped in the gentle afternoon sun and every so often beamed a lazy glance in the direction of the watching crows. After a second of further contemplation, the crows looked up from the moat and asked the dogs: "Isn't there anything else out there to hunt than just this accursed sea life? We've been waiting for this moment now for months, and yet now that the dream has been realized, why isn't it more exciting than just this?"

"Your eyes keep you from getting the whole picture, you fools. It's not just the clams themselves that are desired, but the hunt for them.

Without the ritual, then everything gets boring," responded the dogs who scratched at fleas while they spoke.

"Well, we're not really concerned with pictures or hunts. All we care about are the clams and what we can do with them once they have been gathered from their rocks. Whip us with horsehair violin bows, but we won't rest until these razor clams are breathing straight air. When their secreted shells become seaweed cigar holders, then and only then will we be able to rest."

And so the crows left in a sudden gust and did not return until hours later when the men and the women with throat-trees arrived at the surface, covered with hundreds of razor clams strapped to their bodies in a crude but important psychological gesture expressing the eternal infinity of the universe with its infinite varieties of objects. The monkeys of the fortress lifted their arms in greeting to the now completely roused canines. The shells of the living clams made clacking sounds when they hit upon each other with every motion the primates made, and the dogs looked up, entranced.

"Now we will speak with the cosmos," said one of the throat-treed wives who directed her comrades to neatly and meticulously deposit each of the clams within a surface holding tank with inclined bottom areas. The razor clams were positioned so that they resembled a crowded badminton stadium. With the clams safely seated within their brackish theater, the mollusks forcefully closed their shells and began to make pearls, while singing bold country songs and clacking on tambourines that were abandoned by flower children long ago. The clams were allowed to engage in these pearl—and morale-building activities for several weeks while the men and women of the fortress contemplated the best way to use the clams in a hypothetical battle. They decided that the razor clams would be most useful as elongated, very sharp swords comprised of the externally sharp clamshells. The viscera (and pearls) inside would bring a mortal stability to the sword, so that it would not fracture in battle. In this way, these razor clams would truly be the key that would allow the warring fortress monkeys to worm their way into other fortresses, in order to build even bigger strongholds, like, with waffle irons and unlimited shuttlecock service.

Eventually, the razor clam was to become synonymous with the concept of the upward fortress, and so the descendants of the warring fortress monkeys adopted the razor clam as their coat-of-arms. In fact, they even slept in bunk beds (with pink satin sheets) made to look like giant razor clams so that their dreams of war might be more easily effected in the highly popular currents of reality. Analogously, they had razor clam toasters and razor clam bookshelves, and many other bivalve adaptations to life. With these changes in place, humanity was altered forever by the effects and influences of the razor clams. After this cultural modification was documented, it was neatly covered in white paint, dried and then rolled up. The rolled-up change was neatly slipped inside of a white ceramic clam tube, replete with the razor clam icon.

Once the white ceramic, razor clam document-tube was safely put away in the hollows of the haunted bookshelves of the nearby library where playful distractions were available for the taking, the clam document guardians appeared in order to collect the indicated container. The guardians shuddered when seeing the neatly tiered bricks arranged in front of one of the numerous fireplaces that only served to confuse and not to warm. The guardians sat down in plastic fabricated lawn-chairs and relaxed while their razor clam documents were being festooned with limp clamshells that were boring rather than intriguing. As they waited, they scratched at their shoulders while poring through books made of mica. The silicon-based pages of the books showed them the portraits of maidens frozen in time within the silicone leaves of the moments, and the crystalline features of faces overturned the kinetics of the basement crystals that were growing underneath paint jars from several decades ago.

Usually the paint jars were lifted periodically to remove the dust growing underneath their nitred clay surfaces, but on this day, the clay from the pots was instead fired underneath the kiln from the stranded seaweed that washed up on the beach, which had serviced the erosion of the discarded paint jars. With the annoying seaweed cleared from the garden pots (with pointed brushes), the cupcake vessels then visited the clearing reserved for the cozy barnyard squirrel-chases conducted during those off-hours that were inserted into the cracks of ordinarily faceless, seashell oblivion.

6

Even though an evening in front of the fire might be a blast, there are nevertheless certain concerns that must be touched upon, even if ever so briefly. These fireplaces are truly excellent specimens of living room cannons, and they do well with wallpaper. Sometimes they even light the living room cannons with pocket-sized packs of strips that can be used to peel dead flies off of glowing mirrors that were deftly lowered into wooden crates in these questionable living rooms. The crates shall remain closed for a few hours until the mirrors die down with their incessant glowing and pressed fly collections. The mirrors in the crates only reflect darkness and remain heedless to the living room cannons that must remain ever so busy in the dwindling early morning hours— usually when the snow is falling before lunchtime and the loggers might return to claim their crates. The loggers use the pocket-sized packets of fly peelers to transfer flies of various hues onto their drivers' licenses, to eventually become laminated, capable of informing any inquisitive pair of eyes that these special fly licenses allow the loggers certain privileges that not all loggers and ordinary civilians might have.

Nevertheless, the loggers fall to the floor during their lunch break in a near-total state of collapse after moving heavy trees across agonizing distances. The great distance, however, is not the only cause of the exhaustion; there also exist porcupines wielding oyster forks that make the loggers nervous and protective of their ankles. Even though the porcupines do not attack, they force the loggers into defensive postures as they carry their payload above their heads while staring at the ground below. Once the loggers have left the traveling field and have entered the safety of their forest living rooms, the porcupines laugh, spar with their forks, and then return to a cave located on the side of a public library with roosters foraging in the front yard. The porcupines have their secret cubicles in the library where they read about chipmunk species and sometimes about how to better speed on the open highways. After reading a few volumes, the porcupines put the books away and stroll down to the water fountain. To the side of the water fountain is a bold cabinet containing several neatly arranged power drills. The porcupines arm themselves with the power drills and squiggle out through the front door of the library, oblivious to the Coca-Cola jukebox that has been recently installed next to the front desk and which continuously plays music that sounds like a perfect flute and tambourine duet to be listened to in a crowded elevator on a humid day.

Out on the sidewalk, fried eggs are cooking on top of the cobbles with the roundest of shapes. The porcupines are perplexed by this amazing road of fried eggs sizzling on a summer-scorched sidewalk in both directions. They choose the path that will take them back to their logger friends, all the while curiously gawking at the cooking eggs that have somehow managed to selectively find the right cobbled cooking surfaces. The porcupines take care not to step to close to these various cooking cobbles, madly sauntering in the direction of the loggers who have recently taken an intense liking to cutting away large areas of forest. The porcupines are surprised to find the forest newly re-grown, with a monolithic bronze chessboard hidden behind one of the more senior trees. On top of the board are playing pieces in the shapes of loggers, some of which are holding telephones, fishing poles and even cake-mixers. The porcupines continue with their feelings of confusion, and they curiously eye the odd chessboard monolith with the wooden figurine pieces carrying the finely sculpted, metal implements. Since the pieces are not in motion, the porcupines are not concerned, and they resume their activities down a hungry yellow road.

With distance, the porcupines find that the road narrows, forcing them to fall into a double line, being hemmed in by a rusted urban chain-link fence. One of the porcupines takes a wooden chess piece with which he absconded at the site of the monolithic chess table and lights it on fire. The small blaze is enough to disrupt the chain-link fence as it collapses in different places in order to surround the flame and extinguish it with a rusty vortex of metal. With the porcupines in a recently sprouted alfalfa field, they become obsessed with nitrogen and collectively assume the form of a metallic C-clamp holding the earth in place between pads of cue-smeared velvet. The metallic monument faces the monolithic chess board, and little helper elves appear to carry messages back and forth between the two monuments by way of carefully arranged rusted nails manufactured by delicately soaking some fresh ones in a glass kitchen bowl.

After the lines of communication are connected, a lake roughly five miles away spontaneously explodes, showering fish into people's laps as they calmly besport themselves at happy picnic benches within the confines of a radioactive ski resort on the outskirts of the young cornfield. The communication between the forest and cornfield monuments doesn't stop for a second, and for days the disturbed lake continuously spews out writhing fish into dining people's laps.

When news of the invasion had spread, the loud scampering of running squirrels could be heard as they raced through the vast premises between the lake and the monuments, triangulating the area with fast scampering that eventually created a din that almost sonically resembled the feel of a hot, bleaching wind. With so much rapid traffic, the entire area ultimately became a vast, hilly terrain covered with fur, so that any other travelers in the area would walk through in style, on a carpet of soft fur that was constantly in motion, moving in perfect rhythm and vigilance over the covered scene below, now entombed in a perpetual darkness, like a spontaneous stratification of diverse luxuries. The fur carpet rippled when seen from above, luring even birds into commotion. As they tumbled down at right angles to each other, they noticed some ostentatious jewelry growing from a vine that dipped into a shallow pool where butterflies dwelled amidst the discarded root beer bottles. With the fur carpet fully animate, the mass of squirrels carried the entire monument/lake set-up a full twenty miles until they decided to take a break, choosing to listen to whale song.

Suddenly a fox materialized, and threw down his hat upon the cobbled ground that had reappeared when the animated squirrels decided to take a whale song break. With all of the squirrels reclining against various forest objects with sprigs of straw jutting through their teeth, the fox looked down at his hat and sighed. The hat responded by transforming into a black praying mantis wielding an equally black violin that was perhaps just a bit too heavy for the praying mantis to comfortably carry. Despite the weight obstacle, the mantis managed, while shedding no light (upon the now-dull cobbles of the fried-egg highway) to nobody cared where. The Fox and the Mantis looked at each other. It was the Fox who broke the silence:

"Say, Charlie, do you suppose that we should talk to these squirrel folks, just to say 'hi' and exchange local gossip?"

The Mantis hit the Fox over the toe with the black violin, and then responded: "Well, I suppose that we might as well. We usually don't get the opportunity to see any mammals other than just you, and actually, I see you a lot more than you do. This could be interesting, but then again we might have to deal with their bureaucracy and other forms of collective madness. It might be nothing more than a minute cacophony of cerebral garbage cans rattling in the night that will end once the sun has risen. But I guess I'm curious enough, if you are."

"Well I am, Charlie, and so I believe that after we make a few phone calls, we should see what those animals are about."

Spring arrived, but it brought with it a disturbing wave of confusion that manifested itself in the form of parallel wings of feathers insidiously taped to the back of a hand-held paper fan. Even though the inexpensive brand of tape was used, the feathers still held very well to the back of the fan, which had been innocuously deposited within the cracks of one of the picnic tables that had spontaneously erupted for the squirrels' use. With the fan in place, it served as an instrument that would cleave the wind, creating a set of air-currents that entertained the squirrels greatly. While the squirrels remained occupied with the paper fan with the feathers taped on the back, the Fox approached them with his old friend, Charlie the Praying Mantis. After a few heated words, the Fox and Mantis backed off and decided that they would have no part in the flying carpet of squirrel fir and felt that concentrating on the trees and other forest paraphernalia within was a waste of their time, when considering that their mission for the next year or two was dedicated to being library helper volunteers. In fact, one of their contract obligations was to entertain young children, acting out demonstrative skits and other highly valuable tidbits of advice for young people. Charlie and the Fox sighed as they made their way to a distant metropolis covered with a cloud of pollution.

Meanwhile, the squirrels managed to somehow consume the entirety of the feathered fan without leaving behind any tell-tale signs, and yet their eyes had red irises that managed to rupture a jellyfish obstacle that had always seemed to get in the way especially when least expected. The sky then fractured, and the heavens began to import a flood of auroral haze. The squirrels celebrated these developments by braying at the skies in their tiny, squawkish voices. At that moment they believed they had somehow understood the aurora, but nevertheless they were able to start a forest fire that only consumed but four trees for some lucky reason. The squirrels tunneled through the ashes, eating them and becoming more intimate with the collapsing skeletons of the trees. Once the black ashes were consumed, the alchemy of a dripping saliva trail from an oak leaf activated the roots of the dead tree, causing them shrink into some form of underground mobile life which then disappeared, leaving four holes that led down into the earth.

Within the hour, some internal terrestrial pressure sent out a wave of cat brains floating in a sea of a viscous and transparent red sauce. The squirrels shrieked songs of carbon and fled from the advancing wave of cat brains. The cat brains never bothered to follow the mist of squirrels carrying their pair of megalithic forest icons, still shrieking as they disappeared into the darkness of a spring night briefly punctuated by auroral appearances over a Mississippi forest. For a brief hour close to midnight, the night side of earth was having fun with its own weather, channeling it into rock, and then back into weather. It was a lopsided game that broke lots of things, but all who played it enjoyed it immensely. During that night there were many people who woke up in their beds to find some lazy starfish enjoying the body heat from their legs. Sometimes these starfish would spontaneously fossilize in some people's homes, and these new fossils were kept in the bed at all times, in lieu of the usual fare of teddy bears and other fluffy effigies.

The whales in the ocean could hear the stories of the starfish as they returned to the sea later that morning, and their whale song became fairly compacted, their version of chatter as they laughed and reveled in the fine stories of human legs. As the whales laughed, they sprouted stubby, little feathers on the tips of their fins, ousting a few barnacles in the process. These feathers were red-tipped with yellow highlights, and were probably only truly visible at close range, due to the muting effects of the reduced light. The whales found themselves curling up into rings as their voices arced through the water much like electricity. With their new feathers packed in a goose-bump formation on their extended fins, the throats of the whales took over, being the dominant organ in their sleek bodies. But the sounds never extended above the surface, and so the whales drew no attention to themselves and spent the greater part of a whole day completely focused on their harmonic conversations.

The vines were glad to be free from their oppressive greenhouse, as their slow persistence eventually popped out several panes of glass. The rattraps in the greenhouse were already sprung, with the floor littered with squirrel fur, but the plants paid no heed as they concentrated more on the sunlight.

The old greenhouse just so happened to be next to an old hotel, and was frequently used by the guests for recreational purposes. The hotel management was friendly enough, and they daily brought milk to some dog skeletons who lived on some of the upper floors. In the dog skeletons' bedroom windows there grew sunflowers that had petals of a deep crimson shade. These flowers were happy to live with the charming dog skeletons, and they spent many an afternoon together playing checkers and making plans to renovate the hotel on account of its dustiness and other odd anomalies, like the breathing coat racks with flute appendages. Within a ground level room of the, uh, building, there was apparently a religious alter constructed with bricks, boards and x-mas lights. This room was frozen in ice for at least ten years, and showed no sign of any change over that ten, or so, years. Floating within the frozen ice were crucifixes moving in odd orbits. That all was from the day when the old hotel management decided that a bad ice-cube had to be ejected for the sake of the good of the other icy parts of the, uh, building. With the ice-cube gone, the room was converted into a brand new area ready to be occupied when the need arose. The halls of the old hotel were filled with old foes out for a stroll to stretch their legs. Despite the potential for a seriously menacing situation, the colored glass and porcelain marbles remained within their pottery hut altar.

When the cold winds of the afternoon sweep through the old hotel, the old foes find that there are staircases forming within their arms and legs, in a way that would make one feel like a corridor. The old ones stared down at their arms and legs, seeing different staircases forming from their flesh—human tissues transforming into blocks and sheets of well-bred wood, forming the furniture of a great flavor of transmutation from flesh to limb, and back again. The wind was freezing everything, but the old foes knew of their future in furniture, and braced themselves with freshly sprouted walking canes as well as fishing poles. After the freeze, fresh, young red leaves sprouted from the leading edges of the thawing people. They stretched and resumed their stroll down the dark corridors of the hotel.

Every now and then one of the old ones would stray from the hotel into the springtime weather and go missing, at least in the books. Usually the person would grow like a tomato and then bud off into something people could tolerate. When this happened, it seemed like the air got a little warmer each day. Once, when all of the cars on the street were going in reverse in slow motion, certain people burst from their houses in order to grow as the tomatoes do, and so the person always walked with more energy afterwards, like some sort of vegetable energy plan that would dictate to them the true avenues of metabolism, especially from the standpoint of freshly grown vegetables that are always available in spring. This plan enabled many people to enter into new currents of life that led them outside of the two hundred year-old hotel. Like tomatoes, they grew well in society and paid all of their taxes on time. The only flaw was that these people had the tendency to ride their horses to the grocery store. But besides that, life went well for these people.

Every now and then, these hotel people had staircases form on their arms and legs, but through having the metallic voice of a spider available, the staircase eruption usually subsided, and life returned to normal. In fact, many people had spiders living in each of their rooms at home, and this helped them maintain their corporeal integrity. Their theory was that certain types of night storms of cold wind (that only occur in the beginning of spring) would cause their flesh to become transmutative, but unfortunately they had no solid evidence to support this idea. It only remained a mystery. Out on the sidewalks, the people began to have pet weeds that would crawl through the sidewalk, up their houses to beg for food. The friendly people obliged. It was then that humankind's second best friend became the leggy crab grass.

Thermometer spiders appeared on the scene at the particular feeding moment, and both crab-grass and friendly people paused to insert the thermometer probes, which jutted from the under-abdomens of the spiders, into their ears, enabling them to instantly hear the sound of the ocean, even if they were standing on a mountaintop, or been in a cave in the middle of a continent. With the thermometer spiders in place, all parties involved paused for roughly ten minutes just to hear the sound of a large body of water that was many miles away. After those ten minutes, the people and crab grass removed the spiders from their ears and placed the hybrid organic objects into specially designed velvet cases that were regularly available from the local, neighborhood sporting goods store.

A bowling lane of avian totems is knocked to the side by a fast-moving ball, and then the people sitting in their living rooms next to the sewing machines and the televisions rise from their narcoleptic slumber to answer the door. Many salesmen are turned away that night, proving that chain-mail pants aren't really necessary at that particular hour. In the backyards, silent but radiant calla lilies erupt through various unused little spaces, creating a set of radar that draw perplexing data from the moon. Droplets of lightning seep from under the lilies, and the liquid form of electricity moves like spilled blood, and tastes of it as well. All devices placed in the liquid spontaneously operate and then deactivate upon being removed. When the plants have absorbed enough information, they wilt and become a fine dust on the walkways, perplexing the neighbors in the morning. But in the meantime, the night plants manipulate the gardens, creating new forms of floral arrangements never before seen by blinking mammalian eyes. The stepping-stones on the walkways become more salient in the dimness with the crisscrossing forms of the night flowers.

The owls were able to notice the flowers also, and grimly and coldly blinked their large eyes. From the owls' perspective, the flowers were really miniature wooden barns, complete with hay and an extended family of feral cats. The cats within these flowers occupied even the out-ermost peripheral nooks and crannies of the barn. The cats would always know where to find the important parts of the barn, and analo-gously, within the lily flower. These young cats peered out through the windows of the barn at the owls who were still impassively observing the barns/flowers. Eventually the barn/flower complex fused back into a more integral form, and resumed its previous life as a jolly Easter bas-ket, filled generous heaps of monkey wrenches, of all sizes. Of course, everything is finite, and so the backyards are covered with a universal dust by morning, seeming to bring fertility to the beautiful rose bushes, shrubs and plastic pink flamingoes.

Reality crumpled like a lead horseshoe, and vertical vines of a green color streaked with youthful red fibers extended themselves into the atmosphere from above space. These vines forced their way into the soil, the houses, the backyards, the swimming pools and the outhouses, just like a pincushion, and the earth became a grid of finely spaced vines, forming a new kind of lawn that no homely creature had even seen with conscious eyes. As soon as the grid was established, the vines braided themselves chaotically. The main question that all sentients were asking at the moment was: where do the vines lead? Yet the origin of the vines still remained a mystery. There were some who advanced a beanstalk theory or two, but essentially the new additions to the gar-dens ultimately provided a nice matrix to walk through on one's way home, for instance. The persistence of the vines was the new teeth of the earth as it hurled through space. Eventually the plants were able to secrete some excellent orange seeds in order to plant a few groves here and there in the more permissive areas.

A cicada reached out and took the earth into its mandibles, consuming its salty oceans first, and saving the continents for later. Apparently the molten parts of the earth didn't seem to annoy its large taste buds, and so the entire planet was consumed, down to all but the core. The cicada reached into its maw to remove some stringy vines wedged there during the feeding event. Satisfied, the cicada looked toward the sun and relaxed. Headless snails were singing Broadway songs nearby, and the cicada turned its attention to the inspiring music and decided to go through an extra molt, something unheard of for a bug like this one. The deed was done, and on one fine afternoon, the cicada emerged from an encapsulating membrane with great vigor and health, with an extra set of mandibles, even. The insect shivered, and its outer appendages became some finely sculpted chairs. The middle joints became flesh carpets, and the innermost ones created some rather handy coffee tables littered with Shirley Temple trading cards. The body portions of the cicada became condensed into a prized racing car on its back, screeching at full acceleration. Careful applications of rulers to the exposed tires in full motion provided only temporary roads for the racing car, and yet even the inches were considered significant. After the rulers, some of the cats from the flower/barn complex appeared and danced their way along the treads of the tires, getting up to full speed and dissolving into clouds that twisted and weaved into comets. After the cats had departed, the shadows of birds seeped through the finely sculpted chairs and etched their own images onto the corresponding seats, then congealing into a frog that hopped away.

Meanwhile, the cats enter Saturn's orbit and penetrate the murky atmosphere, realizing their own gaseous, jellyfish potential. Even though they might shed their fur, the follicle cells in their skin evolve the ability to secrete gelatinous ribbons capable of fully withstanding the gravitational effects of the large planet. These cats (which have now become floating jelly beasts) move through the cold methane with ease and lose the memories of their prior terrestrial life. Their watches become sprigs of celery, and their padded shoes are replaced with golfing slippers. These changes in the cat creatures are recorded through some of the strongest telescopes, and the rest of the universe becomes excited, making imitative gestures.

In a distant gopher hole, a horde of dancing butterflies moves with reticulated motions, with odd pauses, as the insects encounter one of the worst summers in their extremely short lives. The butterflies momentarily close their wings after landing on a piece of displaced driftwood, and certain nefarious water faucets sprout from their legs, making their lives difficult with the added lead weight. The lead faucets are opened, but no water emerges. The butterflies still find relief with the leg faucets opened, and they resume their perilous migration across the hot wastes of a somewhat oppressive desert. A coyote with houses in its eyes encounters the butterflies, observing them curiously for a moment. The coyote moves on and disappears over a hill of sand bursting with twigs of bleached crab grass, but the butterflies are oblivious.

At nightfall, the dogs emerged and searched for their special something among the various pieces of glowing driftwood that fell from the sky at nightfall. The dogs encircled the masses of driftwood with their numbers and every so often took a vicious bite at the inanimate glowing wood. Suddenly one of the female canines leaped on one of the smaller fragments and held it in a death-grip that could have snapped a turkey leg like a lollypop. The wood was strong, however, and the dog eventually gave up. The dogs manifested symptoms of boredom, and they resumed their hunt for food. Magical hotels sprang from the sandy wastes, and within minutes, the dogs beheld the lights of casinos, cars, and cranky massage spas, all with pure befuddlement. The dogs entered the newly erupted city and peered within the open, public doors in all of the various, uh, buildings. Oddly enough, the inhabitants had apparently departed in a hurry, given that many devices and appliances were still operating. Cake batters continued with their mixing. Local newscasts continued to be broadcast, and the skeletons of fish were available in odd areas resting on beds of their scales. The dogs of night languidly turned their heads to see nothing but empty chaos. Legs that couldn't dance on tables somehow communicated their presence to the dogs, and so the wary animals avoided the tables at all costs. Eventually the canines found a shrine in the center of the town, completely representative of their religious identity, perhaps. Within a carefully chiseled archway were nebulously inscribed diagrams displaying graphically representative instructions on how to carve a pumpkin with what appeared to be a cross between a screwdriver and a spatula. Such incomprehensible instructions from another distant society only made the dogs restless, as a soft rain of cosmic mucous began to fall on their backs. The universal snot was shaken off, and the canines found the kitchen of a casino where they ate the raw steaks mysteriously abandoned in a wide-open cold room.

In an upstairs room, an aquarium shatters, releasing certain kinds of hermit crabs and lungfish. While the hermit crabs move in circles, the lungfish use their lungs to crawl throughout the hotel, sometimes even on the walls. Since there are no other guests to scare, the lungfish make great progress in their goal to get to the elevator, at the end of the long hallway with many doors. A few of the bricks on the south side of the building fall out, and the walls begin to seep fresh rainwater carrying small, fallen leaves along with the bleeding current.

After the dissipation of the secret source of water, an ominous silence fell upon the deserted, glitzy boomtown. Even the birds (who had been threatening to begin a round of healthy squawking) closed their mouths and intensely eyed the glowing town with its bright silence and a recently evacuated hotel standing on a raised hill perhaps two feet above the other, uh, buildings. The three-dimensionality of the town became a stack of folded paper in its bright transparency, which forced it to disintegrate in the same way rubbery candy-striped squids did when in a restrained state of crystal trinkets, of a bold and daring flavor. These other caves, in which the squids lived, were on the same folded parchment sections and seemed to coexist rather well, constantly corresponding via telephone and through exchanging certain highly prized celebrity trading cards imported by a twenty-four hour shipping service-truck and warmly distributed to all of the shops and businesses within the glamorous, deserted boomtown. When the squids decided to rise and do some legwork with their tentacles, they'd often visit the hollow of a giant oak tree that somehow reminded them of home.

From the sky fell celebrity trading cards, and within shallow pools of clear, evil water, appreciative squids made of plastic organics looked up to receive the hallowed images. While the squids maintained their pools with deadly force, a dim shadow wandered from pool to pool in its eternal quest for certain items that only arrived in firm, wooden crates. The squids were oblivious to the above-surface shadow, and vice versa. At nightfall, the water caves closed their roofs, and the dream pools were illuminated by phosphorescence from the algae coating the bottom surfaces. The squids were accustomed to this ritual and intermittently hibernated, sending out telepathic signals to a certain pack of dogs that decided to camp out in the hotel's pool hall. Eventually the dogs began to understand the squids' concept of the endless escalator. The crowded movie theater was the same one that everyone attended on the sideways signal of a cracked television viciously leaking rainwater when looked at the wrong way by a dog who momentarily awoke in order to scratch its ears due to the falling cold air threatening to leave a layer of frost on everything for miles around the deserted, glitzy boomtown. And the dog eyes kept twitching in their communal dreams of synthetic forms.

A cold rain froze, and little flecks of ice fell upon everything. In the morning, the ice would become a flood, but for the evening, it was just frozen rain that made the glitzy sidewalks too dangerous to tread upon, so most creatures simply made their camp in the ice and shared their body heat. Even though the night was cold, the moon was out, transforming the ice into a glistening carpet that covered everything in the vicinity.

Once the ice had a few hours to settle, the sun began to rise. The ice turned to slush, becoming newly liberated rainwater that made certain sleepy cephalopods twitch down in their reproduction cave pools, adjusting the odd rings of color that alternated on top of their pure white flesh. A tentacle writhes in slow motion, as if a muted groan were just released. The evil cephalopods reveled in their languidity, while their minds reached into the mental tap water that would eventually reach the brains of humans with the odd passage of time. Suddenly large bunches of grapes were flung in the direction of the pools, with some pieces reaching the cold, clear bottoms, to the annoyance of the plastic candy squids, who were much more interested in what was beneath the large, algae-covered rocks in the pools forever bathed with a re-circulating cave water which came from the depths of the planet. This evil, clear water was usually turned away by those who lived in the lights of the surface, and so the water always flowed back into itself, creating a perpetual loop that was perplexing as it was dangerous.

The squid farm, as it was called by some brave souls, had been around as long as there was sentient life on earth. Throughout history, various individuals had unwittingly made contact with the subsurface squid biomes that always randomly appeared in various parts of the world, always at different times, though. As a large coin tumbles through the air into the cold water, a light bulb overloads and melts into a hot iron capable of burning anything to the ground in less than ten seconds. The light bulb resembles a certain nasty brain snail once bred in an underground cave pool very much like the squid reproductive pool. Nevertheless, the molten light bulb eventually slows to a crawl and then solidifies into a nice piece of glass slag that almost looked like a couch that was sat upon excessively.

A squid in one of the evil pools reached up and grabbed the wad of glass, taking it down to its bottom lair to reconstruct it into a vial in which it could hibernate whenever necessary. The running shoes are put away in makeshift furniture rocks, and certain squids wrap their arms around some of the stones, creating a coil of orange tentacles where the rust pigment was a behavioral cue signifying extreme concentration. The coil of tentacles moves the rocks great distances, as if the plastic squids had their own lawnmower of humming sparks that followed on the wings of a merry locust's journey into a beehive.

Someone had set off an insect bomb, causing a massive explosion of locusts with purple wings, with the alarming likeness of ex-presidents of the United States of North America on their mandibular, mopey faces. These locusts momentarily disrupted the underground cephalopods' party, and the squids vehemently darted back and forth in utter frustration within the confines of their breeding pools. Eventually the highly frustrated mollusks left the pools to make the attempt to talk some sense into the locusts with the ex-presidential faces, but to no avail. The squids stared at the ugly purple insects and managed to scare most of them away from their cold, evil water, but a few remained as unwanted fellow travelers *for forever how long*.

The origin of the insect bomb was a mystery, and the rocks in the pools grew an excessive amount of blue algae in response to the locusts. It was only a week later that one of the evil, underwater squids found some bomb-shrapnel, suggesting that the explosive might have been produced in a mannequin factory located out on the edge of the spooky glitz-town. This factory's only function was to produce anatomically complete mannequins to be sold to the various department stores in all of good capitalist societies. The trucks would come daily and then each one would depart with a packed cache of anatomically complete mannequins. Every time a batch of fresh mannequins would commence their long shipping haul, the ghost of the factory celebrated being in business for just one more day, just to revel in the glitz and hot lights of a neon reality, possibly comparable to a fresh plate of mutated walnuts.

Faceless animals, fearing a link to a name, crawl among the salamanders who delineate the confines of a room nestled within the folds of a library catalogue. This sculpted information is the breeding ground for a pack of wild hyenas who yap when they see telephone numbers falling from a black book placed side-by-side with a red leather-bound volume spelling out binary recipes for desserts made with a glut of bananas—how creepy could that get?

Gosh your hair looks nice.

7

Several green velveted mannequins fall over with a resounding thud. The youth of the staircase travels along alternative steps that once took the plastic mannequin parts to great department store levels. These Martian, plastic mannequin artifacts reveal their existences over the course of many years and locations, including within the steep oneiric fortresses embedded within the sides of jagged tongue-cliffs, or perhaps within the cement, urinal chambers in the many different Martian cities studded with human and feline life. The mannequins always come wrapped in a sinister velvet and have the tendency to make some of the earth animals (like cats and dogs), very nervous and apprehensive, especially if they've been shown pictures of common butterflies prior to the mannequin encounter.

Suddenly a busload of mannequins slammed into a misguided French hotdog cart, forcing many green mannequins to fly from the open windows of the bus and into the frozen street.

The mannequin bus comes to a complete stop and is unable to resume its previous direction. The mannequins do not move, but the green velvet covering the mannequin bodies remains unscuffed and even looks rather festive when appreciated underneath the lights of the perturbed velvet mannequin bus. A streetlight uses its freeze-ray to turn the mannequin bus into a green-velvet, iceberg Popsicle, delighting the various plastic forms strewn across the pavement (with their lopsided wigs, of course).

It appears that this particular busload of green velvet mannequins was a religious one, because each of the sprawled pavemental plastic automatons was still tightly grasping a bible with red-leather binding. It was highly unlikely that the leather was made of human skin. Each of the bibles had a hollowed-out compartment in which a collection of frozen dragonflies was housed. Even though the mannequins refused to comment on the purpose of the secret compartment with the frozen collections of powdered, sapphire-blue dragonflies within the bibles, the false, pseudo-bibles radiated an uncertain harmony embedded in a permanent state of flux. Every so often, one of the blue frozen dragonflies would fall from a slightly open bible compartment and become affixed to the ears of the fallen mannequins.

Sunny days shine down upon ankles and toned calves. A beach umbrella topples over, completely overtaken by the brisk ocean wind. Despite the fall of the umbrella, the race for a lost, bronze iguana key is fully underway, and this search has been ongoing for at least five or six years. An unwinding fern drops onto a magnetic desktop, encasing it in a gluey secretion that brings tears to the eyes of all curious raccoons peeking at the peculiar spectacle. All of this just because of some old bronze key that had the rare carving of an iguana with red, encrusted gems for eyes and green ones innervated throughout the animal's body. For all that the umbrellas and raccoons knew, this key could be resting at the bottom of the ocean, or within the freezer of a cranky, marsupial kisser. The absence of the iguana key was disturbing to the creatures involved, and yet they managed to live their lives to the fullest, playing with sand and collecting valuable seashells, in their ongoing, obsessive search for the jeweled bronze metal.

After this variety of communal life had progressed for a few eternities, the ground, with its well-manicured lawn, became a billiards table with transdimensional pockets into which the cue ball would periodically fall. Nevertheless, once a creature had learned to avoid some of the more dangerous pockets, it became possible for it to sing of trees that grew to majestic heights, and then the chorus would sing back to the particular initiator of the song. This kind of change seemed healthy enough to all creatures involved, and so the moon began to fall on opportune places in the middle of the night, disturbing the porcupines greatly, yet tending to pacify the rest of the neighboring terrestrial life.

Once the librarians learned how to condemn the cardboard castles that hinted of sea life bearing pentamerous radial symmetry, all of the aquatic phobias were overcome, and so the sinking cue balls that had by now multiplied beyond measurability were allowed to drop and feel the gravity, in the same way solar atoms are sometimes pulled back into the maw furnaces of stars. The librarians created a soup from this furnace maw, and plasma was the main dinner-course as it slipped between fingers and created echo images of bone growing sheaths of cartilage. The plasma even overtook a randomly flying coconut that could have only been released from a secret factory on Mars, one of the many hiding places of Coconut Man, who regularly took weekly excursions to some of the nastiest key islands of Florida, under the guise of a fakir who used knuckle dice to determine how many cents he would put into a parking meter that day.

The release of the tidal flood was no help in times of crabbing, when strange soups were bred between the midnight filing cabinets of folks who created a synthesis of many stray wind currents, generating a pocket-sized hurricane with the peculiar tendency of blowing through inhabited towns. The maelstrom continued with its rampage, in the same way Twinkies are squashed on shuffleboard decks when hailstorms are immanent, also in the same way when a ventriloquist's doll recites the synopsis of a predictable sitcom that would have been better suited to being used for coconut paper-mache. Who was laughing when the visiting moon caused tidal waves over the more innocent landmasses, which could have been synonymous with athletic bison legs? What was the special time that we were supposed to check our watches for when the leg police created an ingratiated pomegranate that could sing songs capable of shocking adults back into tarantula-thermometer primality? Abandon the tinker-toy ship just yet? Not until yesterday's synopsis has been soaked in liquid wax and tossed into a rhythmically active kettledrum.

The lullaby drones on and on. The synthetic forms of the music permeate the wall like lice, and the sheer repeatability of the musical sequence is grating to the ears as it blocks the pathways to real feeling. Frutopically topical rhetoric in some countries, but within the loose teeth of the piranha, the mutated bananas fruit quickly from their axes and drop their mischievous seed onto the fertile soil, in the same way an adorable sidewinder is coaxed into puncturing the latex stretched across the noxious maw of a toxin-collecting martini goblet, conveniently deposited next to a gambit receptacle.

The obtained venom is symbolically kissed by some passing silver parakeets. Their trailing squawks show love in a sinister way, and the flowers of the moment are made of fired clay ready to be glazed with pigments of uranium, casting a hot wavelength that creates some really toxic mashed potatoes. The drooping liquid metal is the goblet that never made it, the breadbasket that caught fire from the hyperactive yeast. After the venom has been meticulously and safely channeled into the right-sized ampoule, the sidewinder accepts the augmented venom from a curiously shaped dropper and resumes its merry, twisting road to the land of heavy metals, including that of molybdenum.

This chain of events evoked a heavy windstorm, forcing many tons of sand into the atmosphere, knocking out all communications due to some of the annoying habits of certain airborne minerals.

Random geo-activity is amusingly recorded with many lengths of videotape, as well as the mutilated recollections of the earth when placed under the control of malevolent sunspots affixing informational tassels onto legs like the troubled fangs of the hyperactive sidewinder as it mechanically regurgitates venom. The tired, venomous arms of Atlas weren't even able to decipher the speaking volumes that lurked underneath the continents as they moved across lace conversations safely filed within strong-boxes installed behind nauseating family portraits. These catalogued facial representations spelled awkward lineages of culture, never surpassing the stunted phylogeny of a deceptive clade. There was definitely another object in the next hand.

The Oxygen Bird Hive

1

Limpid sofas on display in the windows have regurgitated price-tags on them—"very disturbing," said the doctor to himself while checking the reflexes of a disoriented patient's leg. The doctor finished the examination while nervously eyeing a stethoscope that was mysteriously attached to his desk lamp with a frayed string. After the patient slithered out of the room, the doctor cut the stethoscope from the lamp and nervously placed it in the top, left drawer of the desk, next to the tissue boxes and rolls of red ribbon sometimes used when the sun was temporarily eclipsed during certain unprovoked moments.

Fortunately, though, there would be no eclipse today. After lunch, the physician spun at least five yards of radioactive shoelaces, and neatly wrapped them around conical templates to be used in the future when the price of shoes went up, just like the closing notes to an advertisement jingle. Fortunately, a majestic fleet of ships (in the perfectly replicated shapes of violins) pulled into port, and the scientist, as well as his neighbors, were relieved that these floating instruments had arrived. With the flight of children's laughter, bronze bees landed on the musical instrument ships and took a nap underneath the shade of the strings. While the bronze bees slept, the sun sank under the horizon, but upon their awakening, Sol returned to give its brief afternoon colors.

After the nap, the bronze bees descended to the lower chambers of the violin ships, and undertook the task of building hives, so that the instruments would now be occupied. The violins appeared to be happy with the arrangement, so that by the time they reached the sand, the nests were complete.

A few days later, the docked, bee-inhabited, violin ships were visited by curious sailor people who never saw such tiny boats, in all of their years at sea. Perhaps only a meter in length, these violin boats were very compact and yet internally diversified. The bronze bees had access to great kitchens, bedrooms, as well as workout areas with aerobics and bug juice. The sailors weren't small enough for a grand tour, but they were at least able to peer through the windows with magnifying glasses at the intricate equipment and furnishings.

Suddenly a message in a bottle conveniently floated in, grounding itself next to one of the outlying violin boats. The bees on that particular ship were shedding their wings in order to begin a laborious process of reverting to a more ant-like style of life. So far the metamorphosis was going smoothly, but in a month from now? Once the bottle had been furtively retrieved, it was opened and the message was read:

Further to the left.
Curled locks of black on your shoe. Mannequin display cases filled with plastic. Your sleeve is a transforming hurricane ripping apart even the strongest of metallic weaves. With your red sleeve afoot, eyelashes are teeth, and the annoyed lion bursts from a premature pumpkin. Sweaty rain makes this place a jungle storm, maybe a livable hell ultimately folded up somehow over the course of its transoceanic voyage. The molten hell of brighter days is in the Madonna's hand, in jest, and the world circulates its currents in the same way a blender makes a nutritious gelatin salad. Once the molten hell is released, it fuses with the ground like globs of thermite. This fruitful event leads to a certain flavor of fertility, making the plants grow and the insects reproduce in harmonic patterns. The special fertilizer from the Madonna's molten hand turned our backyard into a test-tube. It's completely amazing when those television-headed boxes come over for coffee on only the

odd-numbered days of the month, but if molten slag will do the trick, then perhaps everything can return back to normal, just like before. My, how the days have expanded themselves within the cup of your hand. The fire you're playing with that you left in our yard has changed us somehow. Somehow your arms and fingers are more than just that. Now our backyard is a bird factory, thanks to the intervention of your hands. When will you come back? Why didn't you leave the bricks where they should have been? We thought that you had already put them together. When will we hear from you again?

Cordially yours,
Your Local Coed Roller-skating Club

After perusing the contents of the touching note, the ants returned the message to the bottle and sent it floating down the industrialized shore of the modest-sized fishing town. The ants were bored and decided to take a nap. While they slept, their metabolisms slowed to a lower speed, and their bodies assumed the shapes of collapsed ironing boards. With the ants neatly stacked in columns in the corner of each of their majestic and heavily equipped rooms, their bodies resumed the process of redeveloping their legs for strenuous exercise on the ground instead of in the air. Every now and then, their bronze skin would glisten as organs rearranged themselves inside of each carapace. When the internal clock struck six, the ceiling fans within the ant violin-ship came to life, and cool air began to circulate within the ship, reviving the sluggish, hibernating ants. They were swept up by the fans and positioned on the ceiling. The ants laughed and then dropped down to the floor, whereupon the telephone rang:

"Hello?"

"Hello there. This is the governor of Alaska, and it is my pleasure to inform you that you were selected as a winner in our local sweepstakes. I am pleased to announce that you are now the proud owner of a new

monkey wrench. With this wonderful product, you will be able to flaw-
lessly change your poorly shod tires from time to time as the need
arises. We will be sending you your package by way of special delivery.
We also hope you'd come visit us during the summer. Some of us here
like to play cards. Hope to see you!"

After the ants replaced the phone's receiver, they conferred among
themselves about the potential value of such a wondrously described
monkey wrench. Even though there was no official end to the debate,
the ants returned to their usual activities. While they were having seri-
ously pilgrimolytic obsessions, the bronze ants decided to remain
within their violin ship during the day. After nightfall, they went ashore
and disappeared, abandoning ship, as well as the rest of the bees who
were more intent on creating cells of honey.

Next to the grounded ships, light posts spontaneously protruded
from the sand, and the beach became a dead-end street, not even with
signposts at the end. The street led into the ocean, becoming more and
more popular as time passed. After a month, the bee ships left, and the
area became inhabited by the local population. Later, a tollbooth was
even erected by the road, and the cost was minimal. Next to this con-
struction was a pine forest that glowed with a red, nocturnal brilliance.
The forest was easy to navigate during the night hours with the help of
the phosphorescent red trees. Some parts of the forest were inhabited,
but others weren't. From time to time, night birds would utter distant
squawking and shrieking sounds, but there was quiet, for the most part.
When certain logs were turned over, the bottom surfaces had become
covered with a gently polished, alligator hide. This revelation even pro-
voked Jupiter's gases to jump, offsetting years of hard work in the for-
mation of swirling bliss. The logs were replaced as they were, and the
cosmic alligator skin remained hidden to all eyes in the nearby forest
vicinity. It was as if all of the lights in a planetarium became ropes that
could pull one in many different directions. In the future, after many
lessons, the understanding of the cosmic alligator hide would become

known to all, but for now, it was up to the local travelers to provoke great cosmic hiccups, thoroughly disrupting everything within the solar system—including the comets. The shudder could even change the color of the leaves, in the same way chameleons can blend in with their surroundings. In this manner, the red phosphorescent forest was not immune to the effect of the alligator skin—even when rolled into plain view, whether underneath the moon or sun. Thereafter, until the lesson of the hiccup was learned, the forest would remain as a collection of reflective trees capable of misleading the unwary during the night hours. But during the day, the forest looked like any other. Meanwhile, the highway to the beach still functioned, and all travelers dutifully paid their tolls as they returned to their lairs offshore.

The offshore domains were kept in a ransacked condition, but the barnacles still held to the right places. Synthetic ocean water was pumped in from a neighboring plant, creating an odd scenario, which was confusing to much of the local wildlife, and yet the system worked, in the end. Fingers from the water streamed forward and grasped at the sun above. The whole game was a narrow tightrope walk piercing the exterior windows of all neighboring houses. This connection was even visible in certain instances, and managed to serve as a great source of instruction for the youngsters when they came home from school. Once the windows were opened, a cold ocean breeze followed. Birds from the wall became apparent, and they jumped over variously strewn pieces of furniture to perch on some sinisterly placed cactus plants commanding the corners of the house. The birds closed their eyes momentarily until they removed some rather large items covertly tucked under their wings. These items included fishing-lures, triple A-batteries and lava lamps. However, all of these objects became semi-transparent from the influence of the birds, and so they were abnormally lightweight. With the items shed from beneath their wings, the birds stretched their entire bodies and then merely sat down and observed. Periodically, hordes of motorcycles would pass through, usually every two hours, for some reason. The sun shone unreliably, and dark clouds opened up to allow the light of a setting sun to penetrate. The salamander of the next minute cast a feeble blue glow, managing to attach itself to every doorknob in every house, simultaneously.

The birds remained relaxed and diligent, perched atop the sinister cactuses. Every now and then, one of them would open up a piece of mail to find a printed honeycomb shelter inside, and begin to squawk and gesticulate in an unknown language. But despite the distractions, the birds grew attached to their new house and created quite a place to live. With regularity, new tarantula-thermometers would make their way to the house, sending new oceanic signals to the birds, who avidly learned each of the new waves. When a package arrived earlier that day, the birds ignored it for hours, due to their propensity to take catnaps. But upon opening it after sunset, all of the avian creatures were flabbergasted to discover a beating, three-chambered heart, replete with intact veins and arteries. This living organ drew their attention immediately, and it caused cylindrical bridges crossing nearby cliffs to shudder for a moment.

Uncertain of what to do with the mystery heart, the birds allow it to roll around on the floor until they decide it would be better suited swimming in a kitchen wading pool normally reserved for lobsters, brain-clams, and the like. In this pool, the three-chambered heart can take music lessons and practice the Lobster Cha-Cha during those dreaded off-moments. With their new pet-three-chambered heart, the birds are happy to have another life form to nurture. They feed it various broths, and this usually insures wonderful health.

2

Stars embedded within snowflakes collapse into their respective roses, becoming finely etched tattoos on the flanking muscles of the three-chambered heart, and this organ is turned upside-down, creating a vase holding only the freshest of freshly cut orange roses. Immediately nervous zoo attendants rush forward to measure the girth of the vase with some old, sticky measuring tapes. Their worst fears are confirmed, as they rush to the tailor's to give him the new dimensions, preparing themselves for their worst-case scenario: a bleeding rose vase that held too much blood, creating a senseless blood glut that would distract forecasters for many years to come, perhaps perturbing all football predictions as well.

Aside from the covering strata of muscle, the interior had a ceramic skeletal plate that followed the internal form of the vessel. This discovery was made by the tailor who noticed the disfigurations caused by ceramic bone fractures from prior violent events.

A puppet hanging on a nearby hook (only by its hand) begins to twist and squirm, precipitously releasing itself. There is no need for concern, as the torn hand will eventually regenerate. The freed puppet rolls across the floor and under a bed. The tailor decides to throw the heart vase at the rolling puppet, sadistically breaking the vase's interior, ceramic skeletal plate. The tailor then telephones his friends, and they are invited over for a resetting festival. With the ceramic bone fragments set, the heart vessel vase heals within minutes and is once again able to contain a generous spray of freshly cut orange roses.

Thunder and lightning are forcefully directed into a corral where they will spend the night together in the darkness of an automated ranch where the stone foundations of, uh, buildings are really obsolete fossils. Red clouds flow from around the bend in the road, and the past is turned into a tossed origami salad made from highly cherished road maps buried within automobiles for several years. The blood-red clouds integrate with the road-map origami conglomerate, and the wispy trails of atmospheric blood attract the sharks.

Unfortunately the clouds and origami forgot to bring their yellow swimming trunks that day, and so they suddenly became shark-bait within one hour of their new life in the thunder and lightning corral. The circling sharks became a necklace of deadly fish erupting even on well-tended grass lawns that were completely dry only minutes before.

Once the sharks had burst from the well-kept grass lawns, their circling forms rose to enmesh themselves within the road-map origami salad whose porous nature was suffused with the blood-red clouds. While the sharks fed, some neighboring picnic benches occupied by some nocturnal fruit bats were brought in with the sunset. The nocturnal fruit bats were rousing from a restless sleep in which their mammalian dream centered on the feverish pursuit of fresh fruit under the dictatorship of a time-clock—ultimately enslaving them within a pattern of numbers inside the confines of the seething dream. The fall of night not only freed the red blood sunset clouds and origami salad road-maps from the verminous grip of the circling sharks, but it also freed the fruit bats from their oddly occurring, oppressive dream that had fallen like a misguided meteorite into an ossified primate living room. With the remnants of the dream now but a molecular smear on the tiny neocortices of the fully awakened nocturnal fruit bats, the flying mammals consumed a jolt of pineapple juice-concentrate and then dropped into flight over a dark cliff where they would remove certain talking varieties of rock that night, storing their findings in a large urn made of dark carbon residues.

Tomorrow's hope flew in like a gust of wind, disturbing the hairs on the backs of the fruit bats as they rested within the cozy spiral of a large snail fossil. After facing the cold vertigo in search of their artifacts, the bats shrieked fast songs of loaded air currents. Their talking rocks were neatly stacked within the large urn placed within the shadows of a tree next to the cliff. So precarious was the situation of the fruit bats that they rested with their eyes wide open and quickly resumed their work, paying close attention to the straying wind eddies that would sometimes send the careless flying into walls.

A mirrored image of the cliff was removed from the scene and taken to a black box where it was studied in the same way unknown substances are allowed to drip from opened test tubes. The two-dimensionalized cliff almost made a great postcard, but instead its value was determined by its compressed rock strata that hid certain malignant honeybees inside, along with the blueprints of some hideous and useless tables possibly kept in the basement. After some minor shifting of a few rock strata, the mirror image of the cliff was reinserted into its slot. This rejoining of the two parts helped prevent a possible landslide into the dark canyon, and so the bats relaxed somewhat after finding the last of the talking rocks. Afterwards, they flew off into the night.

The assembled talking rocks began to glow with the tail-edges of butterflies, and this activity was deconstructed into liquid cardboard every few seconds. Despite these fluctuations, the silent chatter of the talking rocks silenced even the frogs, and they became a swarm of horseflies with green abdomens and pretty, red eyes. The lithic horseflies buzzed around the carbon urn, attempting to bite the charcoal, but with severely limited success.

While the horseflies munch charcoal, the urn thinks of nothing but pencils. In fact, the urn usually only thinks of pencils, but on this night, it was beginning to think about green horseflies, also. Rotten tomatoes were pushed into the crevices of the talking rocks, and this gentle application stimulated the nearby soil to sprout some dormant night-flowers. When the flowers were able to unfurl themselves after a few hours, their luminescent colors cast a violet glow over the talking rocks, causing them to quiver and then sweat frozen droplets of water. Somehow the rocks were still holding back, swallowing their words like every daily-occurring cave-in that excites certain journalists when they have the time to do some hiking. A flaccid front car tire causes the machine to wobble as it pulls up to the carbon urn. The engine idles and eventually becomes silent. A displaced cowboy in a black ten-gallon hat emerges from the jalopy and shakes some crystalline blue dust from his gloves. The cowboy just finished his meeting with the local coyote chapter, and was on his way home when his tongue began to taste the presence of the carbon urn with the talking words, out in the dry night. After having adjusted to life outside of the car, the black cowboy shakes some blue mechanic dust on the words, and kicks open a spill-trough on the urn, allowing the talking rocks to roll to the ground. The cowboy shakes more blue mechanic dust from his gloves, and he resumes his night voyage in the shaky jalopy with the soft tires, possibly in search of pink and green mucous fish-birds.

Upon being released, the talking rocks sprout several pairs of legs, and promptly hibernate. The sighing forms of the sleeping rocks confuse several nearby cactus plants who were watching them with intense curiosity. An Eskimo shaves off his beard and resumes his walk towards an ice-fishing locale in order to besport himself of the lovely sea life being transported to the surface.

3

Explosive sparks were erupting in people's pants, even the kind of pants made of fabricated cotton dyed with certain colors, which bleed when people wear the trousers in ponds above sea level. Once the pants have been charged with static electricity, the frayed ends hug the walls of a phone booth made of kryptonite—that special mineral that can debilitate certain people wearing S's on their shirts and other undergarments. A logical crow could stare at each S and come to forcible conclusions lacking deep contemplation, yet which carry the stamp of the eye of the crow, managing to validate most theories that revolve around the anthropomorphological mysteries of post-industrial dog fashions. How far to push certain cars until they jump time, or at least, until their belts do?

Canine mammals etch their paw-prints onto doormats, and so the feast has begun, with carnage flying into exquisitely chosen directions.

The mystery of these directions is a perplexing fly that melds with the prints, in a computer Xerox format that knows no trademarks or other industrially inked forms of identification (meant more for an annoying convenience than they are for describing the eidetically buried symbols of light, which would immediately identify family lineages and other biological records of important cultural processes). These various industrial ID cards are praised in history books, yet most people confusedly lavish their bitterest of optic teeth capable of brushing even the smallest of crumbs from the table. These edible phonemes are guttural and have the tendency to speak louder than what the family lineages say. What would mommy have said?

Your lineage grows on my arm like the pelt of a deer that spent two hundred years moving backwards across a shedded-skin desert. And yet, the lineage continues further, innervating the entirety of our bodies. Our histories intertwine and the unlocked cache of verbs and nouns multiply. Simple mixtures of different flavored Jellos? The psychological polyphyletic feline thinks not, and wags her majestic tail of motherhood over everyone's heads, regardless of the relative odoriferous young ferns that erupt over arms and legs. You are mine and I am yours, and the mutual solar eclipsing dissolves.

Where were you now, in an artery that moves your cells through forward-reaching fingers reticulating around the bend of the dark-maze rat race? Your walkie-talkie drops from your belt, along with the soup crackers you used to save for later whenever you had oyster chowder for lunch (made with roux) on those rainy non-days when you sat next to windows looking at the light reheat the salad, all at a communal table of communicating vessels.

The life boat of soup-crackers in a wayward smile that stretches the sky for just a few extra unexpected degrees. This cascade-within-plastic returns the pre-packaged to a state of fractured cracker-carbohydrate windows, purely spelling the lurker at the threshold that so many past minds perceived so clearly within the arrangements of intimate rocks, speaking languages that would only show off the brain beneath your hair. These languages were prized for their ability allow certain, unidentified out-worldly feelings to enter the equation, causing the hollow book-shelves to glow with a love that was unseeable (nor even perceptible to molds that happened to house the dead grandfathers and grandmothers who were in those readily available family catacombs that we all used to keep beneath our cellar floors, when ideology was philosophy and when we held each other's hearts at night, with the routine cardiac rhythms that spelt the butterfly of infinity, at least when it's being suspended within the volatile media of artificially orchestrated cell-growth).

Your eyes shine through, a beacon through enshrouding foliage that is annoying as it is laid with caterpillar eggs, spelling the promise of many young larvae that will someday become butterflies. This sequence of micro-evolution has the thunderous power to remind all of the psychological, polyphyletic felines who burrow beneath the sunflower soils, even in the extreme heat of summer when armpits sweat crystals.

The Polyphyly of the Feline Mother is disruptive, and it manages to permeate even the sweatiest of armpits, with all of those special crystals. Nevertheless, the clade lingers, drawing the innocents in even closer to the core of the feline heart, with all its teeth and journalistic rubbish. The naughty steepest-descent option laughably becomes available, and so walking people with artificially impaled metal implements (like hammers, staplers, glass-cutters and monkey-wrenches) immediately drop their metal, once the sun shines overhead, creating a reversal of their daily cycle that used to dictate to them the backwardness of dead bodies which mothers used to chant to her children on those peculiar sunny-day afternoons. A kitten's paw pulls the spider webs away from the wreck of this dead caterpillar, and so the eyes of raccoons direct the phonetically unwary in the direction of an open moon in the day sky, telling of a moment of unwary silence in a dark afternoon sky, only moments later, loveably inexplicably.

4

A drenching wall of rain pushes its way through your majestic arms as you fling seawater upon the floating igloo. The rain sets off alarms in your arms, and this result has its equivalent in a pinball machine that has reached a tilted status, with broken glass and pretty, flashing lights. A curl of coffee splatters upon the start button, and electronic munchkins seep from the unattended game. When the coin drawer of the pinball game is pulled forward, many coins are found soaked with seawater, in the first stages of corrosion. The installation of this machine was haphazard, or so you said as you swung your cosmic arms in the direction of my face. Carefully directed rain pushes the game to the back of the log cabin, and the watching butterflies lay strips of glass in a special ceramic dish that will eventually be fused in a hot kiln maintained in the basement for those whale-song occasions when the neighbors pet their cosmic beetles on the head and bid them a successful foraging season.

Your walking legs don't even know why they walk, and yet they contain the trees of a later time when a forest survives a level-five hurricane, creating a tidy little storm in a leg-shaped bottle to be kept next to lifebuoys and flotation vests. Falling metal implements from the sky cause a distraction when landing in a neatly ordered pile which feeds the watching dogs with signals of bird-calls liberated when holding hands in the right way. Nevertheless, the storm is safely contained within strong wind tubes that push the moving atmosphere in a guided direction: into a nearby bay so that the concentrated force of the storm herds the water to the sea, resurrecting the wrecks of sunken ships once lost after futile confrontations with sea-scorpions and abalones who told off-color jokes, especially the green ones.

The confrontation of the leggy storm with the newly revealed shipwrecks produces waves of history that put their footprints into the soft, squishy mud surrounding the wrecks. Up from the mud, squirm flocks of young birds who push the dirt and salt from their eyes, attempting to sing but only coughing up streams of silt originally deposited on the bottom, over the years. Since the birds cannot sing, they produce home-assembly violin kits to bring warmth to their cold claws. While occupied with the building of the violins, the birds enjoy the energy of the sun on their backs as a few clouds scatter, allowing more light to fall upon the scene of a massive water-removal caused by a level-five hurricane generated within someone's legs. The hurricane inspired hunger within the stomachs of the occupied birds, and so they hurried on with their task.

The intimacy of the silt was a different world that normally didn't breathe this kind of fresh air. The wrecks of the sunken ships began to attract green horseflies with beady red eyes, and so the birds made every effort to remain upwind of the rotten ships who jutted corroded beams and girders encrusted with living barnacles. This silty wasteland remained as a prison, except until the ground opened up, and out popped several large octopus-like creatures with vulgar wings and other foaming appendages. Upon sniffing the air from the rotting shipwrecks, the giant octopus creatures pinched what appeared to be their noses, and they carried giant picnic baskets (complete with the red and white checkered tablecloths) from the threshold of their sub-oceanic world. They crossed at least a quarter mile of muddy, exposed ocean floor terrain until unearthing a second door, and then the creatures disappeared inside of it, closing it behind them.

On a nearby hilltop, in an almost-deserted house, the lights within an office study clicked off, and the opening of a bullet chamber within a magnum revolver could be heard, with a dark figure disappearing into some bushes near the open window.

5

The stairway that led downstairs was carpeted with the images of unblinking reptilian eyes that seemed shallow. The bottom of the stairs had a tantalizing table next to it, complete with toothpaste and sandpaper. The clouds on the walls were gray and gave the foreboding image of a nearing downpour, perhaps only minutes away. Despite that warning, the lower stairway was operational in the same way a can of spray paint is so easily used on certain festive occasions, and the stairway smoothed its carpet just for the visiting storm that would arrive momentarily. A facade of wood predicted desolation for the narrow path that led away from the stairs, perhaps leading to the next basement (rumored to contain self-realizing and circular glass lenses exquisitely placed there for the magnification of dark gems, which certain teenage heroes carve within the cartoon waves of their early Saturday gratification).

Interconnecting spider webs create a chorus of memories representing the forest located within the sock, and the eggplant within the meteor shower. The spider webs support sagging bricks, holding back the pressures of a massive land-shift. Once these spider webs are established, a fossilized cocoon is available when wheelbarrows full of roses are brought in by the jolly dozen, carefully selected by breathing florists who navigate the night rocks of a cold mountain stream. The spider webs are snorted and sniffed at by hungry wolves who brave the oddness of their condition but who feel nothing but their hunger (which speaks to them in monotone languages). The wolves arch their backs, feeling the tension in the vertebrae. This magnetic response represents to the wolves a calling of blue lakes with oddly mangled fish washed up onshore. The equestrian potential of this shoebox bay-shore multiplies the number of trees like hooves, and every light pole out on the vague streets carries posted images of baked frogs' legs encased in barbecued belts of sea kelp which are flown in daily and artificially deposited on the shore of the wolf lake. With the newly planted trees growing baby horses from their branches, clones of snails infiltrate the occasional mud bath, and the wolves return from a moment of foraging. They remove their metal teeth and use their canine paws to lift the fangs into a particular tree that has a twisted knot resembling a closed fist, which internally contained the universe in a pre-big-bang state.

An army of saddles was thrown over the branches of this peculiar tree, yet the plant could not be ridden. Wolf fangs couldn't even precipitate the opening of the wooden universal explosion, and all of the combined highways in the world couldn't take a long enough car race to an infinite length of pasta in a Las Vegas convenience store. The wooden fist remained closed, forcing the present universe to await the next big bang, perhaps over an eon. But did the felines in the present universe lick their teeth at the thought? Did the fossils of frogs dance with joy between the rock strata? The wolves stared down into a chasm that opened up in front of them, creating a well of deep falling in-between them and the bizarre tree with the cosmically explosive fist. For now, it seemed, the closed fist had nothing really inside of it but the gnarled layers of wood surrounding the core of the knot like the layers of an onion. A sickly streetlight began to reflect from the chasm, reducing it to a puddle of frozen rain on a deserted sidewalk that reeked of ozone.

Once the water had evaporated, this rip in the universe was momentarily healed. The tree with the closed, cosmic fist began to gallop its roots as waves of solar energy bathed it in warm, morning healthiness. The galloping of the roots never displaced the tree in any particular direction, but it did send blushes of color up and down its thriving branches and diffused a briny ocean smell into the air. Every layer of clothing mimicked this blushing pattern, and the ocelots in the trees winced their noses and extended their tongues with intense curiosity at the motion of the colors within the various forms of organic flesh. The morning air turned over a few paper-thin picnic tables, and the empty, abandoned, meaty protein drink cans attracted the attention of some rats with oblong skulls who happened to visit this area.

The rats decided to avoid the odor of rotten meat that was coming from the cans, and avoided the whole picnic table scene altogether. In the way a rickety pair of stairs collapses into a subterranean basement, a pineapple dropped from the sky and was subsequently thrown into a tree-shredder. The resulting spray of pineapple juice evoked the odd orbit of a wayward spaceship fighting the orbital pull of a small, green star. This lopsided pull, enacted by the vaporized pineapple, is what the green star does to its twin, making a binary system that is exciting for spaceships as it is for streaming sunspots.

6

Your arms move alongside the express train like a sheet of rain trying to imitate a rolled-up living-room rug. Tired fingers connected to the arms disperse as droplets of water sometimes do. Why is that sideways cynicism leaking out of the treads of your shoes? Suddenly freshly-cut branches of evergreen trees are viciously thrown onto empty living-room couches, as if in punishment. This fear of the backwoods goes well with the dull brown of the weathered couches, with frayed uphol-stery. After the tree branches are thrown at the television set as well as at a sultry bowl of ornamental coffee beans, delivery agents arrive who carry with them large crates of unknown objects to be deposited in the living-rooms.

The dance commences, and the floodgates are opened, allowing a fresh mountain stream to send its waters through the inviting house. The water level never rose more than a foot, but it managed to dislodge a few family photo albums of elephants in various states of fashion crises, which had led them to take many volumes of repetitive poses, yet which ultimately would enable them to navigate the labyrinth of their daily chores. Coconuts couldn't have been crazier.

The motion of the water moved into a boil, and the development of the iconic house became a rigidly sweeping kinetic clock, forever in the middle hour, forever expanding. Eventually the opening agents arrived and released the plastic cargo from the crates, allowing the artificial, organic polymers to come into contact with the water. This contact coaxed the amorphous pieces of plastic to dream, allowing their nocturnal encounters with endless streets to weave the concept of spare time into a mannequin's leg. This was the necklace left upon a rock that had been deposited as a footstool in front of the frayed and now-soaked, old, brown couch, complete with floating branches and watchful fish who never took their eyes off the sleeping plastic, who also managed to split into pairs of bicycle tires tied together with rope made from peanut shells. As soon as the chair leg fell asleep, the water became populated with floating peanuts, completely intact. Through floating on the surface, the peanuts could see the sunken, symmetrical forms of iron nails that would not rust, regardless of however much time passed beneath the turbulent nursing baths that nourished the impoverished living room with its parasitoid plastic forms and swift undercurrents.

Faster than an orangutan can consume a 4-pak of light bulbs, the thorns of the raspberry bush puncture a careless foot, causing musty candles to be lit and strange colored marble games to be played in the dim light of an uncertain establishment, where the dogs howl at night and where the backyard is a convincing trompe l'oeil permanently attached to the shady retinas of ornamental mannequins who have been left in awkward positions—in sinks, on bookshelves, and in toilets. The wintry raspberry thorns thrive in the heat, with the oppressive humidity and the sunken roofs of the faraway houses with their giant weather balloons and receiving radios. Multiplying saxophones leave trails of crystal bones that spell the promise of the icy mountain made of black stones and excellent reading material for those slow moments which occur during a parachute fall over the next hill, all in search of a runaway station wagon.

Pumpkins are kicked to the side, and coiled vipers are discovered to be waiting beneath them, in the way a coin is flipped onto a hot frying pan. At last the can of sardines is opened, and generous fractions of the curious fish are distributed in variously occluded directions. The vipers swim across the flooded green floor of an oddly lit living room, now a toy-house attached via chain to a set of house keys resting upon a jeweled pillow. The vipers continue with their mission, and they stalk the moment of time where the raspberries were crushed upon the dried surfaces of an empty swimming pool whose dead leaves hide the game of horseshoes neatly tucked away in a cache of oak canisters. Your falling sky sends plumes of sunset onto the pavement like blood, and the pool of light becomes the eye of a nervous bird looking down from a hollowed oak tree at night. The sunset-eyed owl reels with the crack of thunder, which promises a sudden rain that only a witch could have conjured when released from a grimy soap dish. Once the owl's eyes have leaked enough azure, crimson and orange, the sky tears are shed from the eyelids, dropping a wave of penetrating heat upon the ground below, talking to the lichens on the rocks. These encrusted lichens send a message of color back to the owl, completing the circle. The tree in which the owl is observing is then revealed to be a piano keyboard, with all keys of the same wooden color, and a cryptic horse emerges from the eye of a tiger skull that was fossilized on top of a large glacier. This peculiar, emaciated horse is made of liquid plastic, and it embraces the tree in just the right way so that a harmonious chord is heard, releasing several colorful birds from hidden compartments in the lower trunk sections of the large tree. The owl doesn't flinch at this action, but only at the thunder, which still periodically occurs when an arc of blue lightning connects with the tiger skull on the glacier. The copper inside of the fossilized skull glows, heating the surrounding crusty air to a green hue, giving the illusion of green flames being emitted from the optic and nasal cavities, as well as the jawless mouth of the tiger.

The owl continues to flinch with every crack of thunder, and yet it knows that the time of feeding has arrived. The owl drops from the tree and then weaves in and around a few neighboring giants, ultimately disappearing into the darkness. The stars melt their images onto the branches of the home tree, creating an alchemy of pictures that etch their forms into the plastic, woody flesh of the plant.

This transfer of the night sky onto the tree was better than any soda pop Sunday, or any form of department store mannequin visitations, replete with telephone booths. Now with a solid-body, star tattoo, the home tree was able to make a polyphyly of its extensions, and grow fruits that resembled the funny green hammers found within pianos. Fortunately, these hammer fruits did not clack in the wind, which had now risen to a steady cold blast. Contorted, mauve octopods glided upon well-mowed lawns under the moonlight, harboring owls as well as small mammals of certain tasty compatibility. The octopods paid no heed and continued with their directionless gliding in the moonlight, free of fishing lures and other distracting watermelon seeds.

Once the scene unfolded, the octopods retracted their four out-stretched horn suction cups from their largest arms, and then retreated in a different direction in water that was spilling across very special, well-manicured lawns. After the odd parade of mauve octopods passed, the night forest carried on with its moonlight and owl-feeding. The owl returned from its feeding expedition, and nested within the night-tat-tooed home tree, noticing the change in feng shui polyphyly. It even realized the harmony of constellations that leave their own borders. A mole burrowed up from some loosely packed soil under the now-dry, well-maintained lawns. On its blind nose was a moistened postage stamp bearing the image of a fully diagrammed toaster/alarm clock in the archaic printing style of raised monochrome.

7

With the alphabet soup completely down the drain, the various pipes and other plumbing fixtures expanded and contracted, creating a subtle peristaltic motion, which ushered entire words to different, unexpected

destinations. This soup processing could have bamboozled any corpo-
rate soup executive who ever dared to sell pasteurized soup-concentrate
to those who demanded it, in the eternal importance of the soup.
Highways were built in honor of different soup-flavors, and so people
knew happiness for an hour or two. Suddenly the illusion of people
falling down diverse staircases was too noticeable, and service men and
women carrying nightsticks, flashlights and crab insignias on their uni-
form tunics appeared on the scene, in the same way the sun falls
beneath a table only to be observed rising above a pair of soaked feet.
After the wave of staircase vertigo had passed, the fallen people were
ushered up the stairs via adhesive tags. With the last of the people
dragged through trapdoors in a platonic ceiling, the staircases collapsed
into a soft cascade of yellow feathers with whom they had nothing but
gravity to discuss. The spinning feathers landed in various pots within
the inner garden of the soup-house.

Alligator coat-racks should be shellacked when they are brought
home from one of those do-it-yourself stores when the soul is feeling
daring. If the coat-rack is not allowed to have its protective resin, then it
will droop with boredom and indifference when the small kittens play
at its feet, with all limbs smeared in busted cans of infected soup-con-
centrate. After all pets are safely cleaned of all botulistic slime, the feline
juveniles are put to bed with their coloring books and iron shoes.
Sharks erupt from the paintings on the wall and lustfully regard the
well-crafted windows in a house that was built in another century.
Surrounding the sharks are companion globules of water that provide
them with air and a portable calendar.

After breaking through the sagging glass window, the sharks and
their traveling water landed on the lawn, and the side-winding sharks
awkwardly moved to a crop field of telephone poles, lurching all the way
through the dust, earthworms and discarded brunette wigs. Fruit bats
arrived to grab a few worms that they would manually insert into some
apples that they were storing in their cave, higher up on a neighboring

cliff-wall. This snatching motion closely resembles the brainy confusion of a few blindfolded raccoons as they shriek and make their way through with brute force and angry tails. This collective motion resembles only one movement, which in turn stimulates a rattlesnake telephone, alerting all who could hear that there was someone or something attempting to communicate by this exclusively sonic device. The rattlesnake phone continued to ring (or chatter), but there was no one to respond to the noise-making object, and loose branches from a palm tree were flung through the windows in a lovely invasion from the heavens, who happened to choose a visit at that particular moment, just when the soup business was rolling, and guitar boats were traversing the most majestic of rivers, singing to traveling souls the most peculiar of chord arrangements, yet which prompted the most restful, smurf-ful kind of sleep that was nourishing as it was sentimental, dangling loose accordions from tattered belts covering pairs of skeletons as they danced across a rattlesnake-strewn plateau with the caves of monkeys and other desert-life that lived in such a dry environment.

After striking a mouse, the rattlesnake had quite a lunch and soon after found a shady spot to doze. Even though it had no eyelids, the snake dreamed of a dark, pursuant circle with the power to make pens explode, as well as seduce roadside mailboxes to teeter and then fall over into a puddle of reddish, iron-rich mud that made a great breakfast cereal additive on weekends. This blood-red soil had been previously disinfected with fresh milk only minutes before, so the odd slurry was a storm wave within Jupiter's pregnant atmosphere and was able to get on with life even though its phone battery died. The rattlesnake twitched in its sleep as its unconscious mind regarded the premonition of the coming flow of red, iron-rich mud. Little did anyone know that the soil could have supported only the lushest of plant life (who treated this coming flood as an oasis), ultimately forcing all snake-life into balloons that would take them to caves where various sinisterly-occurring cliff walls were encrusted in different stages of weathered erosion.

Eventually the snake woke up and concentrated more and more on its surroundings, smelling for nearby things and also looking for heat. The soup factory closed down, and all of the large processing vats and other transfer equipment were shut off and allowed to collect dust and a few cat skeletons (and a even few dead dogs, too). Outside of the factory, the snakes and seagulls were able to coexist peacefully for many months at a stretch, and they traded sandwich recipes and other provincial trivia. This diversion was maintained as the weather permitted, and the now-red soil bore the marks of water run-off, alerting the snakes that the flood of water had passed and that they could return to their previous lives, forever in search of rodents and other tasty things. The red soil had a peculiar odor, but it didn't stop the herd of rattlesnakes from searching for blueberries and good places to sleep. In the end, all was well within the newly formed snake world, and the walls were rosy and the candles were strong. Their houses bore sweet dangling grapes, and their coin mints were prolific, making detectives scratch their heads. The streets were made of wood, and the firm night breeze was inescapable.

8

Self-effaced receptacles don their hockey masks and stride over a frozen sheet of silicon that was once a computer disk but is now an out-of-control smile bringing a sentimental rain-shower along with the piping reeds of flutes, converting the tears of water into the tempting icons of self-aware, overly-cognizant potatoes that might someday be used as a wrist-guard to translate one language into any other, in the usual way that smiles are contagious. Where are those puppy-dog, hanging, air-fresheners when they're really needed?

The smile of tomorrow is a metaphor that buzzes around neglected ears, and lineage playing cards are mischievously stacked against insurmountable odds that laugh in the same way a congested telephone is caressed by the animal model, the same model that stretched fossilized memories onto wet concrete in contorted forms that is just as much a musical poem as they are self-aware and free of all historical contagions. Disco bombing on the ninth tee. Laying bones not resurrected from jelly-doughnut future plans where rasping flowers shout the rhythmic shuffling of kneecaps. Rips in over-worn socks add augmenting bolts to secure the primal lifeboat firmly strapped against the mother-hull of a canoe that habitually floats past lychee fruit trees in the spring when they have their newest branches.

Precarious, uh, buildings are erected in the eternal reflex that is as much of a brain's memory as it is of that of the component cells' that twitch within their own totalitarian paradoxes. The, uh, buildings sway with the touching thunder that burns with the same intensity as the smile of an emotion, no matter how negative or positive the feeling might represent within the growing repertoire of hominid sentience. Impossible to blame companion stars who rely on industry instead of textbook inferiority. Once the mobilized swarm of butterflies is harvested from the underside of the buildings' leaves, it is channeled through the atomizer of an exquisite blend of perfume that could have been worn by any beloved visiting these local chemical bio-factories that reinvented the hand on every temporally-focused Tuesday within the linear passage of time, when some individuals concentrated on their wristwatches too much.

Can't see your own hands? A non-threatening, future key-chain is suspended within the ceramic heel of your left mountain boot, and once you eject this troubled boot-core, the internally suspended metal implements within the core are released, and then allowed to conduct their thorough examination, elucidating the lists that anyone can compose at the end of an old week and the beginning of the new one. This forward motion jettisoned the momentum within your wrists as they ineffectively hit the sand of a beach. The gray sand inverted your baby-words into the fingerprints of a universal hand that was especially out-worldly on the extremities of the second and third digits that were usually used to open laser doors that routinely housed nasal tissues and other mass-produced documents available for the taking. An arched rib-cage leans into the curve of a sharp twist of momentum, and a collision with a fruit-bat is narrowly avoided with a warning sound from the tail of a frightened sidewinder. This call from tomorrow is the same sound that the song of a loved one can evoke. Displaced path stones are the shuffled words that make the wristwatch of your lovely time-table that spells new promises that have never yet reached sentient ears and which follow oddly discordant time rhythms that nonetheless follow the daily, progressive emotive patterns of all players involved.

A striped bass falls over a water-worn rock and feels the ray of sunlight on its gill-flaps, creating an illusion of stream-fossils that is disturbing as it is shivery lukewarm with trilobite images. This demon straps its cornstalks by the ankles, and all collected data thereafter are the abacus of knuckles and other geographic dementia lavishly channeled to the listening antennae of a newly sentient crawfish covered with mud and other memories.

Golly, I love it when this information of knuckle knowledge is channeled into a trough to be ingested by the porcine neighbors who refuse to look up at the sky, even when the local warlock shoots several bottle-rockets towards the moon on clear nights when the surrounding castle architecture is protruding from your backyard like jagged teeth. This relationship is an oxide of sulfur collected in a sampling vial when certain nosey satellites are grazing the atmosphere of Jupiter. Once the sample vial is inserted into the analysis instrument, the spectrum of laughter is revealed in written form, and can then be digitally filed for later use at one of the breakfast parties that various siblings conduct when they are not overloaded with arm-lizards that crawl from elbow to elbow like fidgety jewelry that certain people hoard during their off-hours in crowded train stations.

9

A mirror full of subtleties wasn't enough to scare away the crows that gathered on the other side of the pane, with wide eyes affixed to the glass, staring at the flattened pomegranates suspended between the pages of obtuse, unabridged dictionaries that collected much dust over the years. An unwillingly descending plane loses altitude quickly as its aft engine leaks mucoid fibers of smoke and fiberglass debris. Once the plane has thoroughly collided with the nervous mirror, it returns for seconds, spilling gravy and splattering cranberry sauce in the direction of the raised eyebrows of the plastic crows whose flesh is drained of all blood and replaced with a viscous plastic polymer that is as disturbing to the touch as it is to the human palate that consumes the plastic bird flesh in a pre-civilized cave located above a beach cliff. The confused hominids don't have dental floss, so they abandon their plastic crow TV dinners, hurling them brutally upon the beach boulders. Then they resume their deceptive games of scrabble and family back-scratching until the waning light of the sun is no more, and they are forced to sleep on uncertain beds of seaweed stitched with a sinewy bark stripped from nearby trees on the beach hills.

The confusion surrounding this state of evolution forced all sentients within the vicinity to search their living quarters, all personal effects, and even each others', for signs of cracked glass within the threads of their routines. Yet the breakfast bell would ring on time the following morning, and the search might be resumed then. Nevertheless, the mystery of the plastic crows remained, and their shriveled, captured heads suggested a future nightmare comparable to a fractured hour glass that became a lost whisper within a beach whose sand-grains were too numerous to count. This frustration was immense and almost unsupportable, and yet the melted, shriveled heads of the birds became veritable beach-artifacts, available to whoever might have happened upon them, when the sun was temporarily irradiating each of them with a spotlight consisting of somber yet clear, green wavelengths.

The green scanning light had been extinguished, and the plastic skulls of the melted birds were left alone. Plastic-wrapped fossils of sea-urchins and other exoskeletal oddities were also seeping and crumbling from the cliff walls near the beach, and from time to time a fragment or two was sent careening down the steep walls, only to land next to the skulls, with a firm plop. Over time, as the plastic crow heads were buried with the gentle yet firmly persistent deposition of happy sand grains, this sluggish burial was supplemented with invertebrate fossils of the utmost sympathy, and so there was quite a dig-site in the making, leading certain felines with artificial glass eyes to twitch within the bleeding plastic cocoon of an immense library—the very same kind of library that would periodically rent its rooms for illiterate museum purposes and would throw certain individuals down the stairs in the exact same way mannequins sometimes fall down the complex rungs of fire escapes, or down the musical staircase of a jazz improv explosion.

A paralysis wedding is conducted upon the steps of the giant library, whose lower steps are occupied by sleeping elephants guarding the higher shelves of books with their sycophantile ivory architecture. This form of selling-out is jokingly wheezed over for a few moments, but then the gambling devices placed next to the rooftop gargoyles begin to writhe within their cement flak jackets. Electrical wires are used to communicate the entire list of obtainable certainties. Correspondingly, the next six hours are spent flowing between obsequious elephants and the alienated gargoyles that have managed to turn a healthy, polarized, uh, building into the most emotively twisted of pet fish that have created an algebra from the pulse of a relentless power filter that was really the traveling toothbrush of Jonah's whale, at least when it wasn't in need of a last-minute oil and brake-fluid change.

The communication was restored between the roof and ground levels of the upcoming fascist library, and each of the meticulously vacuumed floors was periodically flattened with the footsteps of paranoid people who were in a state of collective crisis over at least two things: 1) a vibrant argon gas plume threatening to storm the front door of the library facility, and 2) the upcoming slaughter caused by nazi-like invading personnel who had no faces and yet whose familiar gestures demonstrated the will to resist the psychological invasion afforded by the library, the staging grounds for the conflict. Fortunately, the girders and beams within the large, intimate space held tightly, and resisted the corrosive effects of the ionizing argon storm that had by all laws of nature passed right over the entirety of the library, even nastily teasing the fluorescent lights that irritated eyes reading from a treasury of technical manuals. While each nazi agent attempted to affix numbers and letters to each of the lost knowledge-custodians as they forever fled the circular, repeating hallways, the native personnel knew of the ancient pottery shards packed in straw within verminous crates (possibly also containing the nefarious, ancient bamboo jewel meat), and also of the insanity of the sculptures that would eventually turn the invading nazis into snippets of red ribbon to be fed to an epoxy glue-glutted grinder, someday creating some very interesting x-mas ornaments.

Inexplicably, the dream of the fascist library was far from complete, and the crab grass took its sweet time in erupting from between the stones in the front, garden portions of the library. Meanwhile, cowrie shells are thrown at the empty salt and pepper-shakers resting on the heads of the ivory-obsessed elephants who had been guarding the lower steps of the library. The tin shakers are easily dislodged from their resting places, and they mischievously clatter to the bottom, where the inquisitive felines are alighting the elephants with their naive, open eyes, only wondering what varieties of madness are currently unfolding with the circular halls of the library where one camp was viciously seeking to defenestrate another. Curious situation, with even more curious cats who had begun to ascend the stairs, ignoring the distracting crab grass and empty salt and pepper shaker tins. It was surely a busy day at the local knowledge depository!

When the intensity of the hurricane winds had had a chance to die down, the slaughter within the halls of the library commenced, leading to the flight of many librarians (or at least those nuclear few who had managed to escape). Despite this set back, the librarians who fled the scene of disaster managed to create new libraries of their own, nestled off within nearby, well-hidden places. Apparently the lesson learned was a reduction of endless front staircases, as well as the hoarding of elephant ivory and ivory-bearing elephants programmed to ineffectively guard the building upon the arrival of the worst of enemies, including nazis. After the libraries had become sightless geodes tucked away within the planet (always less than one meter from the surface), their limbs re-grew and became the arms of saxophones, jutting from man-eating plants that grew in a sinister side-garden that was but one trough on a devious salad bar hemisphere.

10

Your voice comes back to me in the form of a copper medallion that has not a trace of slag metal secretly hidden away in the core of the coin. Inside of the coin are two-dimensionalized branches of trees, but they are safely contained within the metal. Each flip of the coin is another body of communication, and its motion informs me that you will be attending your Thursday morning classes on the moon, where squid-birds are the local fauna and where disco songs from the 1970's spells the current fetish for the avian squids who avidly absorb the archaic waves of music. A drastic crossroads is approaching, and the spines bristling across your neck tell of the family line branching through the veins on your hand that grasps the newspaper from the lowest step of your front door. This ingenious bouquet is similar to an army medal that was once attached to a uniform but then removed and discarded like cyber-gold.

I've been watching your graceful tail swoop like a sluggish whip, and the voice that projects from your metallic fingers is dropping beneath a school of jelly fish. This motion circularly mimics an awkward chord on a self-conscious, horseshoe-shaped guitar. Once the gesture has been completed, mayors are elected into and out of office, and tomatoes are thrown into gaping fault lines, causing them to close. A chorus of birds' wings recedes, moving the theme from an A major to a D minor. This maneuver is as disturbing as the gaping mouths of sheep's head fish, and yet it releases a spinning top from the eyes of one of the birds. This ejection dons an archer's glove, sending a hot bolt down into the heart of a room filled with antique brass lamps.

Droplets of sweat are wiped from an avian skull, and lawn-chairs are consolidated into a corner. Gray locks of hair are thrown upon the old foundations of a severely weathered fountain from over four-hundred years ago, situated right next to the reposing vulture, who continuously mutters: "Old Spanish Fort, Old Spanish Fort," creating a futile beacon to attract the indifferent furtive glances of crustaceans eeking out a saprophytic living only a few feet below. Once this historical wreath has been gracefully ejected into the brackish water, your voice is still impaled within the softer parts of the coin—the ones found directly beneath the stamped date, as well as the place of its queasy mintage. After the coin has been successfully buried, it will rest easily as long as there are no metal detectors of small children to scour the mud for treasures, because, after all, the treasures are always out there. And as long as these treasures exist, there will be those who seek them.

The outwardly flowing tidewater (perceptible only to the long-running security camera) carries with it an abundance of crabs who don't mind spending a few hours in colder waters until they feel the need to nestle between the primacy of driftwood and confusing, strands of seaweed growing upon the steps to the depths, which will not be reached today due to a level four hurricane that was briefly mentioned in a weather report yet highly pertinent to the groups of animals involved who reside in the area. Yet the animals were thought to have abandoned their textbook ecological notions a long time ago, after the last major act of nature that caused all of the schools to close and the newspaper stands to collectively shave at an opportune moment.

Data, just data, dig? Suddenly, a collective of hands seizes another equal collective of spark plugs, and the task of activating a cobwebbed generator is accomplished with ease and a round of smiles. This activity calmly proceeds while people mirror the ease of a cerebral plan created by troublemaker pincushions visible within the simple confines of the furniture arrangements of the reflecting groups as they create the correct connections between car batteries and other interesting devices.

11

Yawn. The simple sigh of a vortex generator demonstrates the facile nature of modern technology as it kisses foreheads and bids small matchbox-sized vehicles a very pleasant evening. Above, on the aerobic ceiling, hang festive decorations: richly flowing garlands with small, ornamental icons of toothbrushes, irons, and oxygen tanks festively twirl in the soft, mountain breeze. This result enables chipmunks from both sides of a great mountain ridge to cheer and celebrate, searching the bottoms of goldfish bowls for buried pebble treasures—great chunks of agate and other troublesome minerals like staurolite, all highly reminiscent of the days of plastic commando beds and styrofoam lunchboxes that held paper-thin slices of under-processed deli meats and pickled vegetables that once spelt the alphabet of a kinky gourmet cuisine that held predominance long before the Mayan empire fell. This catabolic splinter was gently removed from someone's foot, and now all legs involved can walk again, without any pain or limping, creating the first sidewalk that was interconnected with wisps of concrete freshly mixed in that little traveling pail you used to take with you when you went from site to site, hanging garlands and tossing fossilized slices of bread from hundreds of years ago.

This sleepwalking fit of yours couldn't have lasted forever, could it? Your grandfather didn't seem to think so. When a baby falls into a bundle of blankets, the action necessitates a consultation of that special nine ball, revealing that the drop must be made again in order to determine the next appropriate chain of events. After the decision has been made like lice, a trip to the beach (complete with the heavy iron chains) is in order, and so the silhouettes of people are seen traveling across the country in a single-file fashion, pushing aside the great boulders of granite dropped a long time ago by a god who wanted to teach his followers a very important lesson. Needless to say, the lesson has been forgotten, but the granite remains, bearing carefully chiseled inscriptions illustrating cultural practices regarding the loading of dishwashers and other kitchen appliances. This anthropological method is devious as it is shriveled, thus the etched calligraphy is untouched by the abrasive wind as it foolishly attempts to drive little bits of charcoal into the crevices, but to no avail.

The line of silhouetted forms continues its march, deviously attached to the sky by finely crafted necklaces of beads carved from the choicest of minerals, including the dark granite boulders that had previously lain at their feet while they rested, howling at the moon occasionally whenever necessitated by other prowling night sounds that could melt the granite like butter. This night communication between shadow and sky is disruptive, in the way mixed paint can spontaneously un-mix itself in the darkest of floors of the most deserted of museums on days when solar eclipses pull some people away from their daily routines, traveling close to an old highway that was lined with trees bearing fruit within small glass bottles. Littering the side of this grove was a heap of glass shards, apparently left by certain pensive fruit goers. Someday the glass heaps would be in the solar museums also, but for now, they were to remain in their current form, safely beside the fruit grove. Within the museums, the dripping paintings eventually loose all of their paint to the floor (who always wins), and yet there is no real loss as the morning crews will eventually arrive to skillfully replace the images shed by the devious canvases.

The fallen paint remained in its corporeal form, effectively harvested and then bottled as a lean and stealthy house paint, almost like smart-paint, that could adhere to pre-selected targets in the most beautiful of ways, creating a new form of art that was viciously hoarded by a pack of man-eating snails (who especially liked munching on the frontal brain lobes). These snails slowly crawled over the subterranean tide-pool rocks worn smooth over the years by the old eyes of the inside of the earth.

Eventually one of the snails rose long enough from his lethargy to address his fellow countrymen and countrywomen:

"Lo, behold these fine pieces of regurgitated furniture that we absorbed from a curious, neighboring culture. Isn't this regurgitated furniture just the thing!? I am beside myself; what say you all?

The fellow carnivorous, man-eating snails dropped their own pieces of regurgitated paint furniture to profusely agree with attentive eye-stalks rising from necks that couldn't quite catch up.

"Oh Yes," piped up one of the snails, "we fully concur with your assessment, and would even add that we need some of that 'skoodley-be-bop' music purported to blend so well with the colors of the regurgitated furniture, you know, in a sort of mannequin-affirmative kind of way."

After this important communication of ideas between the carnivorous, man-eating snails, the previous tide-pool mulling activities resumed, at an appropriate snail's pace, ultimately keeping the animals very happy in their subterranean pools, that is, as long as no humans fell in during their off-hours within fields of finely-crafted sleep that was the spider-web of tasty dream fabrics, all of organic ancestry.

At the Threshold of Liquid Geology

1

The sunken ampoules of eyes are not far down, resting on a momentarily still bed of submerged sand. The hunted memories of easily rationed dream-segments are tattooed on the body armor of an annoyed centipede who has used toothpaste instead of cement when constructing an orange brick road that travels very far, once the laws of gravity have been defied. Angulated, bony fingers pluck at nosferatu guitar strings, and the road displayed sideways is used as a silicon information highway to replace a fertile bundle of pigmented ostrich eggs which the president dreams of when uncrossing his legs at an international summit. Virile cheerleaders bearing silicon cell-phones jump for joy when a life threatening to transform into a sickly commercial reverses its course and embraces the bulkheads of battle cruisers. The cheerleaders shriek at the ships that vow to stay in formation despite what the evil, saline weather might bring when a colorful umbrella is dressed up as a machine-gun.

Loose tracks merged with trailheads are frozen solid with the mortal scream of a large group of rabbits who have been herded into ozone-soaked corrals sent up to an oxygen-deprived elevation where trees are stunted. The coiled trees wear wristwatches around their larger limbs, yet the timepieces each tell a different time, only serving to evoke the perfumed foliage of magnolia flowers and the colorful, robust fossils of carrousels covered with sheets of a pink, gelatinous star-flesh constituted around the amusement-park bones. This all happened during a time of blind need, when coat-racks were empty and when lovers would not leave their beds (not even for work, nor for a grand prix of judgmental cattle when their odoriferous hooves broke the threshold of a celebrated coliseum whose fanfare could be heard into the nearest, closest town). Rattlesnake rings coil around fingers and toes, and the ornate breakfast meal is used as a bribe to comb the tangled hair of skeptical transients who have taken seats upon the pink gelatin carrousels.

The hooting and panting of curious, nocturnal mammals only serve to patronize the feverish efforts of travelers who have appeared out of the dark and who cherish the crystal surfaces of transitioning cattle cars delivering heaps of neatly stacked bovine cantaloupes. Laughing gas floods the marmoset keyhole of a door that was inserted on the side of the lead cattle car. This form of thoughtfulness enables the bovine cantaloupes to laugh at their own folly, in the same way villages of raised grass huts are erected on shores prone to flooding, with sheets of water that only a hurricane could bring, and when cascades of summer moths are released from the icon of tempestual fingers exquisitely etched onto the wooden door of the lead cattle car, or traveling-room #99.

"Bring it back, take it back, and satellite the planet with digital weather balloons of brilliant red and yellow markings," reads a road-sign advertisement built thirty years ago. The cattle cars eventually reach their final stop—six hundred kilometers from the northern terminus of a sentimental roadblock displaying the smile of a girlhood crush from a different chapter of a time-traveling cookbook. The pink, gelatin carrousels continue with their nervous rotations while the rattlesnakes eat the sand of the migrant desert, which houses this ancient, royal road. Sinister stoplights are placed at incomprehensible locations along the sandy road, and this obscene manifestation of motion-control creates various outbreaks of road-rage, consuming aerial forests of cascading hands reaching downwards, forever downwards.

2

A false smile beneath a question mark is no doubt as disturbing as a flat tire that loosely dangles from a rusted axle. Industrial life-ways stream aggressively like a row of garden lights whose queue is the alphabet in reverse. This life story of ceremonial elders is a tickertape flashlight wedged in-between two sheets of seawater that ultimately prescribes a great depth of water shouldering and disturbing the underwater houses. Wounded fish swim by with their leaking entrails, and the story made of water now is a vertical glass shoebox filled with protoplasmic debris spaced apart at close intervals. No tears for the obtuse corners of the vertical shoebox. Nice flowers are placed into the vertical shoebox so that they might absorb the nutrients as they bide their time in the sunlight, while unseen seconds speed across the face of a convenient foot-watch.

The foot-watch was correctly wound at every first hour of the new month, and this action enabled the watch to function as it spent much time with various feet. As if a plane had just made a crash-landing, the eye sockets of pet foxes released blasts of a very dark light, somehow causing many bees to career through the open spaces, slowly but surely chipping the plaster from walls and accentuating the pulse of the foot-watch. This beat of the footsy timepiece somehow encouraged the now-blind pet foxes, whose voluminous eye sockets were bleeding a peculiar variety of light that could only have been described as dark, in the same way a dreaded train pulls into a sinister dream station. Sparks of short-lived embers spew from a jealous firecracker, and this activity annoys the oddly flying bees, causing them to collide with the plaster with an even greater intensity. Screams are heard, yet the bees haven't even managed to release the cow skeletons that had been submerged in the plaster when it was still liquid. These maniacal screams came from the fast-paced forms of dogs who were rushing to the scene like a pack of determined white blood cells returning from the barber shop. The languid and furious approach of the dogs was a spray of teeth that would eventually augment the activities of the bees, causing the whitened bones to fall from the walls.

Even though the torpid canines had eaten rotten meat that very morning, the gristle and other connective tissues would be later regurgitated into a bloodstained mailbox. The bees were exhausted, but were more than thankful that they had not lost their stingers through this maneuver. The new freedom allowed them to seek out other reservoirs of plaster in the process of baking the skeletons of animals who merely reverted to the disorienting syntax of the overlapping life stories of monks. In their twilight feelings, these monks felt the urge to search for the Universal Shoe, a vessel of great fungal growths that would irridesce upon being shot with the beam of a forgotten flashlight. This light will not bend, and yet its bouquet can still seep through floorboards and other worn-out shoes, causing the retinas of the eyeless foxes to become soiled with information.

With the information swept into a corner, the burnt eye sockets of the pet foxes are gently stuffed with pink wall insulation, creating an optic cotton-candy dispenser revealing the same insidious side-markings of reptilian snake-hood which the dreaded train displayed as it reached the final stop. When all baggage and other personal items are collected, the train is turned inside out and hung over a thick branch to dry. Someday the tree will have an entire, inverted train-set adorning its numerous branches, but until then, happy ants crawl up and down the main trunk, singing songs about stir-fries and other culinary endeavors. This formic migration moves in a chainsaw-like fashion, and the tree growing in the attic rolls a marble towards the seated pet foxes who have their eye sockets stuffed with pink wall insulation, effectively trapping the dark light that had been previously emanating from them.

The screams of the dogs begin to disturb the mutual concentration of the pet foxes and the attic tree. Painted lotus root slices are tossed in their general direction, and later, a beaming woman enters the attic area through a door cleverly disguised as a night window. Celeste, the lotus root worshiper, appears to be alive and well, after having added perhaps twenty or so extra pounds to her strong frame that has traveled through so many wheat fields in search of miniature designer clothing and other sentimental trinkets. Celeste blesses the pet foxes and the attic tree (with its mutated train accessories), and she crosses the room to better renew her friendships with the momentarily paused entities. Celeste hears the screams of the dogs and peeks in the direction of the false window, searching for a moon that might re-liquefy the indigo night sky. She scans the deflated coats in the closet, wishing that they were filled with the animate creatures who were momentarily out of town, in the same way salmon sometimes have to breathe seawater. Rather than bearing crucifixes, heroic salmon are seen carrying live snakes in over-dramatic contortions. These family portraits of the salmon might have collected dust over the years, yet they are still Celeste's favorite, as she begins to reacquaint herself with the passage of the familial concept of time, in the manner one arbitrarily chooses to see his morning coffee in terms of molality over molarity (not to mention Christian morality). These large decisions were duly noted in Celeste-the-lotus-root-worshiper's note-book, which she sometimes took with her to her fourth grade class (which she visited every Monday), brightening the lives of many curious children who used her arrival as the perfect excuse to pause their tarantula dissections. And who said moths couldn't prove geometrical theorems in the dark? Ask the pet foxes.

After a cup of hot tea with milk, and a nap, Celeste, the lotus root worshiper, yawned and finished her inspection of the attic. Her knowing eyes burned through the walls in the same way a bobber suggests the presence of an unseen fishhook. The stalactites in the attic cave beg to be adorned with slices of colorful lotus root, and so Celeste sneezes and opens a gorilla-skull purse to liberate several generously pigmented lotus root slices, which are lovingly hung from walls, stalactites, as well as caved-in fireplaces that are no longer enjoyed.

Suddenly, the pack of languid dogs bursts through the fake night window that Celeste used as her point of entry. With the forceps of a loving night moon in an unnaturally azure night sky, the loose teeth of the dogs are removed, cleaned, and then replaced back into the sockets. Had something like this ever happened before? The dogs howled with their newly polished fangs, and they were very happy that the tooth batteries had not yet expired, effectively saving them lots of the local currency, which could have been used to make paper mache piñatas filled with moist amphibian eyeballs. The happy dogs continued with their joyous braying, not at all feeling any philosophical dichotomies between mind and body. This envious parade ended when an academic philosopher wearing a frayed, flannel nightcap entered, attempting to corral the dogs into one of the industrial playpens left behind by the last attic inhabitants. Celeste the lotus root worshipper sighed, and opened up a mystery paperback, having full confidence in the pack's ability to deal with this momentary menace. After the academic philosopher had been subdued with newspapers and a stalagmite easy-chair, the dogs resumed the celebration of their gleaming teeth, barely holding the fangs into the gums with a very effective bio-epoxy goo manufactured in a neighboring town.

To hell with those shadowy signposts at the meat ranch. The moon, reduced to a crescent, meets its upside-down image in a stagnant body of water currently breeding frogs and other leggedly moist things that eventually will migrate into the domain of the meat ranch. Celeste observes all of this through the night window in the tree attic. Ultimately Celeste the lotus root worshipper leaves the old attic for another two hundred years, and will only return once her geomorphic lotus roots have had a chance to replenish their stocks. Meanwhile, the living forms of squirming, mutated amphibians enter the meat ranch only to later reemerge eyeless and inanimate. This curious mystery tends to repel most casually wayward souls, but is continuously monitored by the more watchful types who truly enjoy buying stamps at the post office.

Black and white photographs are snapped of the eyeless amphibian corpses, and the images are sent back to the heart of the city, creating sensational journalistic explosions that only serve to vilify the jagged outline of the peculiar meat ranch.

3

Charred idols, gracefully set down upon a playing board, are no longer a threat once they have been categorized and stamped with the seal of familiarity. After their power has been reabsorbed by a grove of papaya trees, the ongoing threat is brought to a swift end. This stack of paper sits in mysterious offices where the paperclips have more value than the paper, leading to great misunderstandings between friends as well as umbrellas. A raccoon appears at the office threshold, sniffing under the door and listening for any telltale signs of life. Unfortunately, no animated signals are perceived, and so the raccoon concedes defeat, leaving the odd entranceway that is as nondescript as it is poorly publicized to the numerous inhabitants of plastic land-masses, which float across a turquoise sea of a lovely and completely refreshing shampoo.

The zest of this ocean is insignificant compared to the shower of fire-works created by the nocturnal intromissions of displaced sea-life, as the quest for perfection leads journalists to renounce their careers and become politicians. The comfort of the undersea carpet is no match for the oceanic shampoo, and therefore families pass their religion on to curious offspring who adolescently feel the need to emulate the powers of the Lord, playing games with bread and thorns, as well as sharing sardine fragments with less fortunate neighbors who don't believe in gODD but who cross their hearts when playing family games of grapenuts and dragonfly table-hopping. Once the grapefruit eyes of the large squid have been popped from the front walls of the house (the psychological complex of stability and cerebral security), strange watchers drive away in white vans containing only useless replicas of car batteries and other split devices that have been shorn of their hair and drenched with a sticky petroleum distillate. The application of these industrial agents upon car battery replicas and other split, shorn devices, facilitates an exciting influx of curious bees who end up chewing holes in the walls, and subsequently embedding themselves within the cocoon-like apertures.

The entrails of paper are removed with various gestures of feeble, kindly viciousness, and your carrousel mirrors the spiraling of inverted horses who left the foald after the detonation of a nuclear device within a confused and thoroughly stagnant potato-chip factory. This state of affairs refuses to call the mayor on the phone, and so shoe salesmen are contacted instead, initiating the raucous shouts of cheerleaders who scream and wave while observing a daring eighteen-wheeler crash through a field of lettuce crops.

Nervous toes tremble on the foot-saw, and this precipitates a swarming of frogs who enter befuddled banks in search of loans. The angry amphibian customers who are pushed out of line wring their hands while making the gestures of a pure grimace, otherwise known as the fine art of smeeking—something that sexually uptight people do when they are having inappropriate relationships with their barbecued stereo equipment. The sex light changes from yellow to red. The moist frogs pay no heed, and continue with the submission of their loan demands, effectively scaring the bank tellers greatly, forcing them to sweat profusely. Even though dog urine might not be sentient, it sure knows how to infiltrate the public transportation system. Ouch; a painful memory surfaces, spilling the piss all over the sidewalk, reactivating an old cycle with no other nebulous destination than the sewer system: that sweet place of ingenuity where mannequin factories are sometimes covertly situated.

The dog urine glides from sidewalk to subway entranceway, and proceeds to flow down to the tracks where the rodents and other throwaway items are hurled, ultimately adhering to the black, sticky diesel deposits. The urine avoids the tacky adhesiveness of the refuse, and its golden, yellow flow is unstoppable, streaming towards the tunnel where only mannequins enter but trains exit. Nevertheless, the dog urine is very happy to be underground, and it spends the remainder of its out-of-body existence coiled around pipelines like corkscrew icicles, serving to warn the passing blind dogs whose glowing eye sockets are mysteriously excreting fine steams of gleeked saliva, perhaps in anticipation of some far-off celebration.

The sun set just as soon as it rose, and the wayward freesias in the gardens (positioned outside of the city's core) quickly budded orange, whistling starfish that immediately dropped into the underbrush. The orange starfish quickly glided over the dark oak trees and resumed their migration across the gardens to some unknown place in the inner metropolis. Even though it was possible to observe orange, whistling starfish moving along the brick edifices, most of the people did not bat an eyelash, and continued with their usual, routine activities. When the starfish decided to cease their whistled rendition of the Mary Poppins theme song, they rested their suction cups for a moment, allowing them to slide down bricks and panes of glass. Eventually the orange starfish began a cheery round of something by Tony Bennett, and they resumed their merry way, oblivious to street-signs as well as the French hotdog carts.

At one point, one of the orange starfish was run over by a taxi, forcing the helpless echinoderm to secrete a far-reaching stream of fluid through the tip of the compressed arm, with the fresh, visceral ejaculate coming to rest with a firm splat on a neglected mailbox with more than a few dents. Even though the starfish left the scene in order to heal its damaged arm, its ejected echinodermatic innards, left to rot upon the side of the seasoned mailbox, continued to emit sound waves that carried the notes of Tony Bennett with pure fidelity. The inner core of the city was at least one degree hotter for the next few days, due to the unexpected starfish disruption.

4

Released fingers liberate chains of iron. Tropical sweat from the tennis elbow covered with car rust. The motion of the wind that could push aside the garden leaves. To reveal a new language of names that creates a flood of ancestral knowledge from the side of a palm tree. Or perhaps the fond memory of lotus roots as they are periodically worshipped by fanatical root advocates who travel from town to town, searching for other kindred root advocates, discussing ancestral soil details, as well as photosynthetic banter when the time permits.

This virtual mop of fertility wags its long eyelashes in a nocturnal fashion sometimes used by those night-dwelling marsupial camels that always manage to have an extra hump of fat allowing them to go extra miles in extra long, dark deserts under the hollowed hills of Mars where old books sleep amid eye-sucking lovelies that lurk at the bottoms of spiral-ish descending staircases, where ordinary folk shouldn't go. This dark drop in the human neighborhood of finely crafted love ballads innervates the alien mountain ranges, seething with a hot blood of cerebral stomach bile that could digest the first rays of an alien morning where the sheets of moist rock were more than active.

The bile carves out cavern systems similar to the workings of moles, and these interconnecting tunnels eventually will be used to ferry massive supplies of carefully grown pumpkins arranged on beds of Spanish moss for the midnight delivery timetable that the Mountain Martians are so fond of observing. With all of the pumpkins safely delivered to various dead-end caves, the local inhabitants become able to provide the interior areas with a light system, created from lots of wires and small light bulbs, all made deep within the planet by heat and high pressures. Every so often, differently sized umbrellas are handed out to various individuals on an as-needed basis, giving all citizens a chance to exercise their free umbrella rights on days when rain appears unavoidable.

5

Tracheal shifting behind a wall of snail shells. Soiled carpets thrown from twenty-story windows. Graduate departments having midnight cookie sales after an enthralling seminar given by an enthralling visiting professor. Ruptured tins of pork and beans, smeared with eye-shadow and tied with brass band ribbons cut in vacuous places by the mayor of the town, after the chicken bones have been removed from his latex shower shoes. A brief appearance by Wonder Woman disrupts the ugly cycle, and the resulting chaos is channeled into a steam engine that comes to life.

Wonder Woman skips away, jumping from the hood of a dilapidated truck and into the clouds where a peanut-butter helicopter is waiting, with peculiar men inside. Wonder Woman greets the peculiar travelers, tipping her worn-out top hat, resulting in an uncontrollable spray of flowers from the brim of the hat. This response melts the blue sky into a glass picnic basket, such that the woven, wicker fibers assume an existence very similar to that of a lonely desert piece of obsidian without any predilection for trees. The short-circuit of the trees is liberating, and so the obsidian picnic basket falls into the poorly-made nest of a pelican that has strangely erected its new residence at the top of a very tall eucalyptus tree whose slender leaves exhale the blood of cirrus clouds. Once the obsidian picnic basket has landed in the pelican's nest, the bird hiccups and then coughs up a tantalizing bass guitar that is to ultimately threaten the safety of the early morning, as it might arrive several hours hence.

The pelican did not know how to play the bass guitar, and so the instrument was carelessly deposited within a cocoon of spider webs, left to hang from the most spider-infested bough, leading to the ultimate pleasures of the pelican's home-tree.

The simplicity of the next minute was truly a leaking glass of cold water, half-hearted and half-filled like a gutted pumpkin around the early spring in Venezuela, when the condor sunfish would systematically contract their irises in order to better view the moon in the cold morning breakfast virus. Other kinds of tropical fish brought along hair barrettes and saddle soap in order to better care for the horse-life that had erupted from the geometrical uncertainties of cheese. Once the horse-life had been sequestered within the intimate shadows of cold stone castles, tear-jerking piano music happened to tinkle its way into the basalt rooms. This was a nebulous manifestation of an emotion that had run loose from a hot desert of rock-kicking boots. It was also enough to send a gale of hot wind that flushed the already ruddy faces of the confused who had peopled the thick leaves of an armchair family album from over a millennium ago, when their photo-developing skills weren't as keen as they are in the grinding present—the geology of hands.

The dark uncertainties of time were the forms of captured people who were transformed clock hands, forever circling a blonde wig-encrusted municipal timepiece, centrally located in a dying metropolis. This face of the clock (with its imprisoned hands) eventually convened with a tongue spider who had emerged from a pocket of dense rain safely stowed in a thermos bottle with marshmallows, waiting in anticipation for the approaching moment when an encroaching mathematical reality will be leveled with zeros.

The density of the planter's fingers is irrelevant, and the bulbs were deftly removed without disturbing the soil, now making the planter a digger. The digging creature continued with the fruitful bulb extraction, releasing the embryonic plants into buckets of mineral-rich water, which the bulbs then drank. The digger then became a planter again, and proceeded to put the saturated bulbs to bed, almost like a pair of filled socks. The bulbs were really the doorknobs to underlying caskets of penguin skeletons. When the flowers erupted in rosy plumes of scorching flame, it could be said that the doorbell to the underground octopods had been pressed. Minutes later, the response took the form of a cat's cry mixed with cinnamon, and all of it dropped onto a dangerously festive sombrero that was thrown down upon the unsettled world of the flowery door-bulbs, measuring the minutes into the next world.

The eruption of the flowers appeared from a lost skateboard, and the sunset coincided with the rich hues of the penguin death bouquet. The opened flowers emitted the fragrance of a freshly mutilated pineapple (complete with toothpicks), and the lovely fruit odors were complimented by a carefully placed squirt of molasses on the front windshield of a priest who had broken the speed limit. The colorful flowers were grasped by the wind and driven away towards another continent, while the penguin cemetery was brimming with healthy plant ovaries, almost ready to burst and then spill the seeds upon the dead penguin soil.

After the seeds had been dispersed, they immediately began sprouting and then drove their roots into the ribs of the penguin remains, consequently increasing in size at a phenomenal rate. After the growth of the plants, the spying cats were able to count the stars on the tips of their eyelashes, reducing entire galaxies to pocket-sized watches that were noontime lozenges of the awkward cherry variety. These lozenge clocks stopped their ticking, and so many destructive bomb blasts were conveniently avoided as the rain-clouds drew a large shadow over the penguin cemetery, promising to bring a rainfall to the new cohort of sunset plants.

The clouds moved abruptly, creating uncertainties about their true dimensions, while heavy sheets of rain deluged the cemetery. The soil was carried away, leaving the now-unearthed bird skeletons with twisted sunset flowers jutting from their stacked ribcages, with the occasional worm here and there. Suddenly the odor of a dark octopus-vulture crossed the exposed graveyard, greatly agitating the flowers, who crouched within the hidden eye sockets of reptiles and other snake creatures that might have flown kites around power lines and any other available electrical appliances. Memories of that tomb flooded through the scent glands of the animals, drinking from an electrical river moving across a woman's ring as she adds wood to a fireplace.

As if her arm were a continent, the woman with the river ring makes a sweeping motion apparently attracting the attention of the dark octopus creatures who had been asleep for so long (at least on the cosmic time scale). The motion of the lightning water conforms to the limbs as it softens the hands. The strange weather that has fastened itself to the corner of an unknown room was glistening with a dangerous fireplace.

On the outside of the building grew some curious vines that were alive as they were in debt to a nickel-plated screwdriver used all by itself in the erection of a palace or perhaps, uh, building that was to house the growth of six-wheeled automobiles with televisions above every seat. Such a rise in praiseworthy technology led to the creation of musical disk libraries with efficiently categorized songs to be sung with snap beans and garbage-can mallets. When the snap beans are harvested and the garbage-can mallets acquired, the symphony of raucous hammer collisions and treble-range bean-snaps takes its full prominence as a baby's tooth sluggishly implanted within the electrical river ring of the woman who managed the fireplace room, recently wallpapered with the curious eyes of raccoons.

The woman crossed the room with the fireplace, picking up a nickel-plated screwdriver that had been jovially seated next to a generously sized beaker of perchloric acid. With the tool, the woman with the electric river ring took apart an already loosened ventilation grating in order to notice that the air system to the house had been glutted with rubber insects. Over the next hour, the woman laboriously removed the insects and replaced them with clear marbles that were gray as they were clear. The woman with the ring then proceeded to adhere the marbles to the ventilation shaft with a tacky spray-substance that would still allow them to catch the light of fluorescent gray moths as they marched through the entire network of air passages of an upper Mesopotamian igloo. Yet the inner inhabitants of the fire igloo were toasty-warm. The nickel-plated screwdriver is then diligently thrown at the magazine rack.

The ghost of the woman's fingers and the electrical river ring became a wallet-sized x-ray exposure of a liberated hand with the fourth finger wrapped with a band of silver with flowing river encryptions. The x-ray image supported a fleet of teeth with the uncanny ability of spontaneously arriving at any maritime destination within seconds of departing, suggesting some kind of crazy clonal infrastructure within the fleet of teeth that were the fossilized letters of an ancestral basalt megalith.

A dove with paled feathers sits on a frozen ledge, admiring the far-away stone, with its circular sea of teeth caught within the currents of modern forms of diversion as well as arachnid procreation. The rock has its fractures, but its circular, watery nature compensates for these carvings. The rest is cared for by the alphabetized fleet of infant teeth encircling the movement in a timeless embrace. The minimalistic traveling time is reduced to the limping crawl of a six-wheeled sports car as it rolls onto the cold forehead of the dove while the fractured rays of the sun push shards of glass ineffectively into the letters on the ancestral megalith.

A frozen rain begins to pour, and nearby villagers open up their transparent plastic umbrellas that bear the image of an x-ray of a giant's hand. The droplets of frozen rain bounce from the umbrellas, and so the villagers are left in peace to procrastinate in their corn flakes. The frozen rain continues, however, annoying even the UFOs that while away their hours in an extremely languid manner during their espionage events of humans. So far, the UFOs have decided that basketball shoes and cake-mixers are their favorites, but alas… Nevertheless, the world still turns, sometimes perturbed by the tidal fluctuations from a lopsided moon, yet always passing in and out of the light.

The crystal skyscraper couldn't have been shinier, as a swarm of birds suddenly blew from the rooftops. The birdsong was a culling shriek that bounced over the tails of fish and across the water of the natural ponds, which mired the, uh, buildings within their crystal seclusion, constantly guarded by patrols of man-eating hippopotami who used toothbrushes at night. The suitcases of the man-eating hippopotami were filled with bowling paraphernalia, and their authoritative gait spoke of a vigilant nature so profound, as if every second in the passage of time were being carefully measured and monitored in order to make the most of their ephemeral states of entropy, in order to measure unknown footsteps with calipers and magnets. Each hippopotamus had an extremely useful lunch-box, and within each lunch-box was a chorus-line skid row of mutated orange groves (that were really the birthing places of plastic fish which could melt into a bush of fire), periodically washing up on glass beaches made from the erosion of the crystalline skyscrapers.

The hippopotamus sentinels considered opening their lunch-boxes, but they decided not to. Instead, they took a five-minute nap, relaxing their man-eating limbs and dental extremities. Upon waking, they resumed their vigilant, circular march, with a pronounced spring in their step and a twinkle in their carnivorous eyes, as they scanned the landscape for both invading and escaping targets.

Suddenly a dark octopus screamed at having its family picnic, complete with the red and white-checkered tablecloth, so rudely interrupted by such apparently heathenly feeding frenzies. The sentinel man-eating hippopotami gingerly sidestepped the screaming sub-earthly octopod family, and continued with their hunting efforts. Later that day, the local authorities found smashed lawn chairs next to baskets of healthy salmon, neatly packed in ice for a safe and steady transport to someone's cargo freezer on a ship sailing through many icebergs.

6

A melting iceberg sloughed off several cliff-sized walls of ice into a viscous sea that was clear and had many eyes looking upwards from depths not far beneath the surface. Surly fantails lazily push aside boulders of invisible water, making all umbrellas seem like anachronistic toothpicks to be discarded behind television dumpsters wearing the stripes of dixie like a leather athletic band that some gentlemen wear through their noses.

Hooks on chains are pierced through cheeks, and the ancient Assyrians lead a long queue of prisoners who specifically requested a game of pin-the-tail-on-the-donkey. After the apples have been bobbed for, a kinetic collision of fingerprints on microscope slides creates a family masterpiece. The chains, made of wax, generates a human candle that melts on its way to a backyard concert of caterpillars, with all of that good, clean garden mood-lighting next to the tomatoes and the wormholes in the cedar fence. So many details and yet so little time to correspond with Uncle Jim and Aunt Gertrude.

A sentimental meteor falls between the grid of paper that is a transparent obstruction, and only serves to confuse the dolphins with large noses protruding from their fins. Why do dolphins have to be so goddamned cute?

Up in the sky, a lunar eclipse is beheld, with fresh plumes of raw soap. The soap helpfully removes the clutter of nuts and bolts that restrained the clouds for so many years, and a noxious string on a lamp breaks, creating discordant winks from the left eye of an elephant whose front torso is really a doorway to a famous sports stadium. Illiterate eyebrows find Alaskan crabs lurking in the shadows of concrete stairways, and this development signals a rise in financial insanity, especially when someone's grandparents are found accidentally within an old ice-cave in the Antarctic continent. Once the ice-suite, now the perfect tomb, is discovered, the grave-robbers are kept at bay while improper authorities brandish metal spikes and other dangerous, one-haired implements in order to keep the curious out of the main circus arena.

Meanwhile, young girls play with ice-cream machines, throwing the salt everywhere, in an act of utter confusion and superstitious neediness.

A runaway church bell is allowed to ring out upon a deserted valley where school buses were swallowed by unpredictable plate tectonics and where the underlying lava seethes with dark emotions when the clothes-pins are removed from an ailing pine tree that had refused all grafts prior to the mischief caused through the mishandling of the sunlit ice cream machine. The old sea salt crystallizes everywhere, sending shooting headaches through the iron plumbing, which forces logistical remedies to a splendid medical supply warehouse in which plastic mannequins are seen posing with musical instruments in the display windows littered with dust and other frayed refuse.

These future memories are encrypted with dust fingerprints allow-ing the maw of a large-mouth bass to easily fit over a permissive door-knob, now blocking the exit-way to a hieroglyphic museum, where dutifully inscribed icons of house-wares and automobiles appear on fragile clay tablets made by children when they are time-traveling between lunch and recess. A suckered, vegetarian mouth cleans the parking lot of all troublesome algae, effectively releasing the wolves to eat the last grouping of cars parked there. Abandoned, emotional salad material rots in Styrofoam jackets next to the parking meter, and this chain of events is worth little more than a starship massage, especially when it is performed correctly with sparkplugs and a propellered dis-tributor cap.

Sheets of Madonna ice might try to immortalize an automobile con-sumed by shark teeth, but the windshield does not break. The resulting confusion from such a dental paint-job is debilitating, yet it does absolutely nothing to mar the instructional spots of a poisonous tree frog that happened to take a nap on excessively dusty crossroads where the old stone signs have weathered while still keeping all travelers informed of their own whereabouts. As if an insecure Australian Arawana couldn't find smaller feeder-fish with which to cram its expandable gullet.

Merchants cut their own words with ice, decimating the lovely igloo boxes that used to hang from trees in the way birdhouses did. A plaster dressing of cinnamon heals a broken leg, and a dictionary uses a free visit to a gynecological doctor for a readjustment of its faceplate as well as of its iconographical kidney stones. Once the concerned mothers care for their broken-legged children, carrots are peeled and then allowed to soak in a briny swimming pool housing many of the brilliantly jeweled manta rays accidentally captured during backyard logging ceremonies, which eventually leads to some very befuddled cats.

The muscle is unfurled and then extended, dazzling the patio-side manta rays who continue to remain perplexed by the unknown logging ceremonies. The manta rays admire their sparkling chest-gems, which had originally appeared as a subcutaneous eruption, but now is a full-fledged protrusion of skin and fiber that leaves shards of crushed opals for dark cowboys to find when they arrive lost from the heart of an unbearable Texas desert. The seeds of desert plants and trees are the only mathematical objects available for the taking after old horse races have been allowed to run their course, as a desirable young woman plucks the right chord from a soft lap-guitar, reverberating through her lost gypsy wagon like the unpatented trademark of eggplant-colored weather balloons sometimes used to measure underarm humidity and other important ambient changes. The echoing parallels the fish-ghosts who are deposited on automatic mornings when the bumpers of cars have been polished with ear-wax and the eyelashes of fruitbats visiting from the next town over where sand leeches have excavated a fossilized traffic signal spurting a fine, wholesome stream of goat's milk from the red-light casing.

The young woman with the limp, lap-guitar smiles and examines a pile of letters that she had stowed in a slot on the back of the soft musical instrument. The letters are all useless to her now, and this confusion sparks a granite outcropping of cauliflower earage that painfully bleeds through the soil at her feet. Nevertheless, the letters remain confusing, and they are reinserted into the slot of the deflatable guitar. The rubber wood is the angry representation of tea-sharks who collect antique, ornate porcelain teacups and hoard them within the confines of their display furniture. The woman then carves a pumpkin, installing a green light within the hallowed fruit, and rechecking the mail obsessively every twenty minutes, due to a shortage of pool cues, which used to litter the cluttered kitchen table. The green-lit pumpkin will eventually melt, but only after the woman takes a sensuous bath in the cold springs of northern Vermont, where the cheese is good and where pine forests are sometimes adorned with sea urchin and starfish remains, evoking nostalgia for older days when the then-quiet earth looked more like a picnic basket than a gold-plated bowling ball wrapped in a pastel sweater (to boast of fashion and also to derive warmth).

A flock of fruit bats appears, and each of them kisses the woman with the deflated guitar. After each of the fruit bats pays its romantic homage to the soft-guitar lady, the woman emits a supersonic note, thanking the bats for their admiration. The bats depart, and the woman resumes her obsessive task of checking the mail, probably for the forty-ninth time that day. The unruly bleach is thrown into the Queen's toilet of a far-away country, causing purple wavelengths to be emitted, revealing the presence of at least once fluorescent compound. What has that Queen been doing with her spare time?

Meanwhile, after the mail is perused, the old grandfather clock in the attic chirps with fossilized bones of prehistoric birds, creating a splendid collection of curious artifacts, recreating a sacred moment from over eighty years ago. The nuisance of the cargo flares erects a fragile lattice of tumbleweed sculptures that have annoyingly agglutinated around the now informalized clock. The happy march of seagull/crow hybrids down a familiar boulevard is distracted by their own fourth digits, and this plurality of trees (constituting the smallest measurable unit of time, at least in some circles) helps regulate the congested, road-raging traffic, where all vehicles bear the signature, namesake teeth of wild dogs. At the moment where the bird hybrids are happily sauntering down a highly familiar boulevard, the Queen of the faraway country makes the terse decision to flush the royal toilet. As if on cue, her Prime Minister contacts her via cell-phone to inquire why she must waste so much water during a very important cabinet meeting.

The Queen of the other country has no answer to give, and thoughtfully initiates a discussion regarding quantum mechanics as it applies to physical sports like volleyball and barnyard golf. The Prime Minister has no choice but to agree with her assertions and declarations, else his severed head would become her prized bowling ball during her undersea voyage in the hibiscus submarine. The Queen has nothing more to do before her paradise cruise other than flush the royal toilet again and then pack all of the royal luggage—all six-hundred pieces, as determined from the last check.

The piranhas finish their cow's leg for dinner, and retire to several safe and informative learning games that most fish tend to enjoy during their off-hours, like when they are not mating or foraging. Once the learning games are initiated, a memory card of an antique warplane drops from the side of the game contraption, revealing an entire deck of cards clumsily packed into the inside of the archaic memory card. The learning box has a crank on the side, and once fresh machine oil is used to douse the internal gears, the learning game box of the fish is used to generate a new game every day. On some days, beads of glass served as playing tokens, while on another, a hefty ostrich wishbone collection is used to execute glacial lodestones with the deadliest of cutting motions, similar to the family lawnmower currently being pressed with the slacks, completing an ancestral wardrobe that had uncomfortably remained incomplete for many years.

The marching crow and seagull hybrids precipitously halt their march of happiness down a familiar boulevard, feeling a sense of fulfillment at the collective realization that their post-Christian morality has gone through a state of reformation, causing them to avoid TV dinners and to wear only knitted socks on Thursdays. When the crow/seagull hybrids have found their fish-song nirvana, they don their bathing suits, preferring to acquaint themselves with electric coconut trees tended by Coconut Man himself, whenever he so happens to visit on Sundays bearing entirely full wheelbarrows of freshly shorn coconuts, and the mysteriously lost episodes of "The Little Rascals," conveniently electro-engraved on a shiny wafer-disc. "The electric coconut trees appear in rare form today," decided the seagull/crow hybrids in their bathing suits perched in these beach trees. The incoming tide brings fresh saline air, and the smell of the ocean caresses the senses of the hybrids.

The seagull/crow hybrids made one last collective coconut wish, and then disappeared into a current of air that joyously pulled them to the outer ocean, where the sunlight was a cherished food. The ocean sunlight food was accidentally spilled onto the bottom of a reticulated hourglass, spraying out new fronds of gem-like icicles that frightened many small children yet which promised a full bushel of religious seafood very well groomed and carefully packaged behind a velvet curtain of sea kelp obtained from the backpack of a postal killer whale.

The whale was traveling along its various delivery paths, providing valuable reconnaissance services for the underlying Feds who were currently spending their free hours in disreputable movie theaters where the floors are sticky and where there's no real privacy in the bathrooms, next to the prophylactic vending machines and the customer piñatas frugally assembled with low-quality art supplies obtained from the backyard of a penguin retirement home. With such inferior art supplies, the sea urchin pediatric empire would be threatened, and those infantile sea urchins with multiple spine-cowlicks would be isolated from the rest and then tickled with the primitive knowledge of priceless archaeopteryx feathers (provided by a recently opened time capsule from that period). The time capsule also contained equipment that would support a carbon-dating fetish. Even though this type of dating service inspired much loneliness, fresh jasmine tea was poured down tennis shirts, and the fragrance from this tea caused flowers to jump from Hawaiian shirts. This confusing dating behavior was not only radioactive, but it was hotter than the feeblest napalm event from the twenty-third century when nose-cracked pimiento fragrances were the ear canal of a toxic organic spill on an ocean. Also where the ugly ducklings ruled over the seagulls and the crows, and where toothpaste invisibly leaked from eyelids on most practical days. This volley of leaking eyeballs led to some rather clean teeth, and the disappointment of a purified Mexican radio station was enough to scare gambling husbands to throw their money at disconnected slot machines with loud sound systems.

With the frivolous distractions locked within a glass canister, the beach tree woman (with the vanilla bean parachutes) throws a scaffolding of colored sparks over the gambling establishments. This action returns lost husbands to their wives and makes the airfare rates drop in perfect harmony with the love of mountain tops and winking eclipses that burn through the thickest of mountain-glaciers, giving exciting core samples as well as snow sculptures that resemble a race of humans with deer-like biological qualities. These sculptures are smoothed with warm water, revealing the odd facial characteristics that show unkempt beards of primitive tribal chants. The horns jutting from the skulls were the result of tree growth in the upper hills of the continent. After the language is transferred from natural stone tablets held in the sculpted ice hands, the liquid glass from an iron cauldron is pumped into a mold bearing the shape of the malformed, subterranean octopus. If the superstitious icon is released from the mold, it is shifted to lean fingers that place it into various states of volatile media. This sexual shiver sends a colossal shudder through a neuron of snakes deep into the heart of a snail factory, where genetically modified snail cells are used to secrete a shell-like polymer to effectively encase the memory of any given moment in a formalized jacket that could be worn to dinner as well as to bed.

This assemblage of memories constructed within the modest confines of the snail factory caused the nearby landscape to become stained with variously seeping hues, ranging from orange to purple. These veins of color emanating from the factory comprised a matrix of territorial markings that could only come directly from an establishment specializing in the secretive activity of snails.

7

After the Easter bunny had decided that it was utterly too late to go out to the store for more egg dye, it sat upon the floor of its perfect house, rolling hard eggs into the holes in the wall occupied by mice. Each mouse had a frayed, flannel tail, suggestive of polished neurons artificially grown around metal and plastic. With the frayed neuron mouse-tails wrapped around a scarce supply of festively decorated eggs, it was apparent that no fertility goddess would be visiting that week. Life was a veritable mess of confusing identities crammed within a busy train-tube.

The weakness of the eggs contradicted their bright colors, leading all limping, sentient life to decry the unfairness of the brittle eggs, as their colors chipped in the same way nail polish flakes from a decorated broom handle, with only the finest army medals hanging from the punctured wood. There wasn't even enough time for the monkey-bears to finish their odd, twilight meal of cabbage and broccoli (raw, of course). The eggs were greedily stuffed into a padlocked briefcase, and taken through many x-ray scans in the airport. As there was nothing infectious or in any way hazardous within the suitcase, the cargo of brilliant but delicate eggs was allowed to pass without further inquiry.

Meanwhile, an old cow sits on a couch watching television and doing nothing much else, leading airport investigators to incessantly worry about the peculiar movement of time, due to the erratic ticking of dys-functional clocks and watches tending to chime the hour at inappropri-ate times, in the way a traffic signal switches from green to red and ultimately, to purple. Ianesco's kitchen clock used to do that, too, once upon a time.

Eventually the kittens return from the broccoli patch, and they find that their fur has been shaved, especially around the back of the head. The remaining fur on their heads contrasts very sharply with their hair-less, shorn bodies, giving them the appearance of having a nifty human hairstyle. These shaved young cats are entered into feline beauty con-tests, where their front and hind claws are painted with pink nail polish. This action pleases the cats as well as their owners, who have paid lots of hard-earned money for the shaving and nail-painting activities.

Although these young feline lovelies, with their human-style hair-cuts, will not be entering any beauty contests next month, they still treasure their hairstyling and manicure memories. What irks them still, however, is the mystery regarding their successive births, which ulti-mately led to their formation of a family unit, as well as a season of free tickets allowing them to witness burly firefighters extinguish raging fires, which sometimes engulf neighborhood houses.

On one special Friday evening, the kitten family decides to attend one of the special conflagrations exclusively promised to be quenched by the powerful water of the firemen. After the kittens have taken their fireside seats, the firemen get to work, dousing the flames with water, creating bizarre memories from before the womb, possibly from before the moment the young felines were initially conceived. With jaws dropped wide-open, the kitties ravenously observe the drenching of the wild flames. Their whiskers twitch when they contemplate the averted damage, and they celebrate the uncontrolled thoughts of the firefighters that now permeate the charred concrete. The cat brain suggests the ele-mental avocado of a phone-call that went sour, of a lemon tree whose flowers must eject a fine spray of laughter that cannot break the sound barrier, which will give the local congressmen and congresswomen pause, forcing new laws of facial hygiene to be enacted before the general public. Not that public opinion will support this development, but the congress-people still try, creating two-dimensional playing cards from legislative buckets that hold drooling rainwater. The bifurcating driblets represent the flow of blood from the vampire-attacked nipples of unwary men and women who chose to attend a local school instead of washing their parents' ears for them during only the most unearthly of midnight hours. As if pool cues couldn't hold back the flow of semi-coagulated blood that penultimately stains busy passports and then moves onto white-cotton cooking socks worn only when the family meatloaf is being broiled during repressive and fake spiritual journeys advertised by a cartoon television network.

So much for a lazy horse, yet its toothy shoes malinger in the Himalayan mountains next to a rusted, abandoned well burnt by marauding Spaniards many, many years prior to a virgin, avian snowstorm that deposited many oblong coat-racks bearing healthy red fruits grown by the local Himalayan farmers. The joys of agriculture couldn't measure up to the feline entertainment-conflagrations that begot them.

As quickly as one fire is obliterated, two more arise as replacements. The resources of the firefighters become saturated with an overpowering sense of duty that leaves them feeling helpless, at least until a skateboard arrives, carrying a collection of yellow heirloom tomatoes that were once the pride and joy of a Midwestern family but have now moved onto bigger and better things, like certain metropolitan fertility banks where frozen sperm and eggs are mixed, creating some of the most interesting things. This state of affairs may carry on for a month or two, but such fertility activities do nothing to silence the flames of the charred, uh, buildings.

When a springtime forest remembers the ancestral fires, the bark on each tree cringes, like crawling skin peeled away from the skull of a vigilant water moccasin that tends to bite the fingers of small children, but not their feet. What a joy to prepare dinner for legions of young, pulsating feet that will someday blossom into hiking floral arrangements, which rangers and wayward fire chiefs could worship when they aren't doing important ecological things, like protecting the outer environment, all away from the dismal, grimy cities that erupt on the land like concrete zits.

Despite the challenges of forest life, the hiking floral arrangements make dates and then break them—they shovel pails of sand only to douse them with gasoline and lit matches, creating glass. They even touch the sensitive ears of owls with the stiff whiskers of large Bengal tigers who have somehow managed to infect the limbs of trees with glorious amber stripes of furry brilliance, turning trunks into bones and leaves into sporty Hawaiian beach apparel. All of this just to make sure the environment is protected from sources of pollution, like smog, rust and treacherous spider webs that sometimes get caught up in one's hair. A tremendous sacrifice of ducks and other apparitions of purity that have hyperactively set up residence on a dark, galaxial rim of outlying gas giants. Forever out of the orbital reach of Tom Thumb's long, gangrenous fingers soon after a cascade of blinking eyelashes can survey the stellar surroundings from a rather comfortable tin can.

The kittens lick their fur, removing ticks and other parasitic life, which threatens their immunological sanctuary, especially when attractive bombshells play with cell-phones and habitually forget to rake the colorful leaves of autumn from neglected summer homes. Every now and then, one of the kittens discovers a wound on one of its legs—a gaping sore caused by a certain praying mantis who steals teeth in the middle of the night yet who refuses to leave payment under the pillowcase. This form of dental treachery scares the young cats into leaping from inexperienced footbridges into cool, bromylated water, and the tender felines rise to the surface of the orange water, completely covered with starfish.

Even though starfish might be highly attracted to the legs of land-dwelling mammals, unfortunately there are no forms of bleach that could remove the color from ugly tennis jackets. With the color removed, the tennis jackets are thoroughly scorned by the greedy starfish, and the sea creatures capitulate to a life filled with well-tended legs somewhere out in the dizzying heat of Arkansas, where the citizens there have developed a forehead fetish.

If only the sad olive trees could be immortal. The reflections of a plastic death marry the gasoline fumes from an overturned car ominously fixing to explode in the most southern of peach-tree, hair care accessories that some women like to collect on their pre-pornographic walks through a molybdenum clothing store, where nice men like to peek in through the windows during religious holidays when lima bean soup is more effective against insomnia than sleeping pills.

A fisherman from the Caribbean plays with his long hair while singing intimate lullabies having to do with the obsessive pursuit of raw mackerel. The raw mackerel is of course important, but not more important than clothes, money and other superficial items of utter pettiness. If the legs of the cat had no holes in them, then there would be no exit for leg-mackerel, and they would remain comfortably trapped within these agile, furry limbs for most of eternity, leading to the unhappy precipitation of mashed pomegranate seeds. The fish seeds release their final breath, and the felines resume a game of panty-billiards that had been initiated four hundred years ago, when people were still afraid of tomatoes, and when the stock market was nothing but a cruel and scary fantasy.

But upon the arrival of great hordes of the highly paranoid fruit bats, the pomegranate seeds were reintegrated within the folds of smashed skin, and reconstructed fruits were delightfully soaked in a mild brine to create a nutritious bat soup, which these fruit bats would consume before a great journey to a new set of caves on another continent. This faraway continent was the very same one where other fruit bats resided and played the cello during idle moments when the seagulls became the horns on a sweaty forehead during a steep hike up frozen mountains. The skeletal architecture of the fruit bats was an x-ray bath towel that once was on sale during an anthropologically important religious festival involving the throwing of horseshoes at furniture. Once the moisture-soup was absorbed, each paranoid fruit-bat became a red maple leaf that was carried away by the wind, erasing grimaces with the sunset of red maple trees, and using laser surgery to attach fresh eyeballs to sightless coconuts.

0-595-24021-6

Printed in the United States
62447LVS00003B/94-102

9 780595 240210